PREPOSTEROUS. TALES

"Enthralling and candid. Once I started reading it, I didn't want to put it down."

   - *Roddy MacLeod MBE, Principal, The National Piping Centre*

"It's filled with gossip, insight, history, laughter, tragedy and a little bit of payback — all packaged within Bill's delightful gift for language."

   - *Jim McGillivray*

"Written with wit and humour. To hear the stories from the horse's mouth was fascinating."

   - *P/M Richard Parkes MBE, Field Marshal Montgomery Pipe Band*

"I found it fascinating...I couldn't put it down."

   - *P/M Stuart Liddell, Inveraray & District Pipe Band*

"A real eye-opener and entirely relatable...I see myself in him."

   - *L/D Stephen Creighton, St Laurence O'Toole Pipe Band*

"Revealing...There's much more to the person than the pipe band persona."

   - *P/M Ryan Canning, Shotts & Dykehead Caledonia Pipe Band*

"Bill's writing style engages you and keeps you fixated...A read of some magnitude."

   - *Ken Eller*

"Unabashedly candid...Very easy to read, like someone telling you a story."

   - *Ann Gray*

Preposterous

Tales to Follow

Bill Livingstone

 FriesenPress

Suite 300 - 990 Fort St
Victoria, BC, V8V 3K2
Canada

www.friesenpress.com

Copyright © 2017 by Bill Livingstone
First Edition — 2017

All rights reserved.

Cover photography courtesy Stuart Lowe Photography, Tornto

No part of this publication may be reproduced in any form, or by any means, electronic or mechanical, including photocopying, recording, or any information browsing, storage, or retrieval system, without permission in writing from FriesenPress.

ISBN
978-1-4602-9285-3 (Hardcover)
978-1-4602-9286-0 (Paperback)
978-1-4602-9287-7 (eBook)

1. BIOGRAPHY & AUTOBIOGRAPHY, PERSONAL MEMOIRS

Distributed to the trade by The Ingram Book Company

"You may ask yourself, well how did I get here?"

—David Byrne and Talking Heads

Preposterous

Bill Livingstone

Table of Contents

Foreword		x
Acknowledgements:		xi
PART 1		1
1.	The Northern Meeting: Inverness, 1974	3
2.	Copper Cliff	18
3.	Family	29
4.	Learning	39
5.	To Toronto and Child Services Be Damned	42
6.	Changes	46
7.	The Coppertones	51
8.	Lily	57
9.	The Law School Years	63
10.	Mother and Father	69
11.	Look at Me Now	77
PART 2		101
12.	Teachers and Tutors	103
13.	Piping Guys I Have Known	116
14.	The 78th Fraser Highlanders Pipe Band	144
15.	The Northern Ireland Adventure	164
16.	Bagpipe Follies: A Potpourri of Funny Incidents	176
17.	Loyalty and Otherwise in Pipe Bands	207
18.	Whither the World Pipe Band Championship?	220
19.	The Art and Mystery of Composition for the Bagpipe	229
20.	Half Full or Half Empty?	237
EPILOGUE		
Live in Ireland—in Scotland		242
GLOSSARY		249
APPENDIX		
Some Adventures in Medical Malpractice Litigation		251

Foreword

PREPOSTEROUS: "contrary to reason or common sense, utterly absurd or ridiculous"

At the urging of Mike Grey and Andrew Berthoff, I undertook the writing of a memoir. The process started in Barbados in January 2011, and was finished in July 2016. Lily and I are in love with Italy, as is Mike Grey. When we had returned from a trip to that lovely place, and this project was underway, Mike emailed me and asked how the holiday was. I replied, "Preposterous, tales to follow." Mike said, "There's the title for your memoir."

Gore Vidal wrote in *Palimpsest: A Memoir*, that "a memoir is how one remembers one's life, while an autobiography is history, requiring research, dates and facts double checked."

David Sedaris has said, "A memoir is the last place you'd expect to find the truth."

What I have written in these pages is very much how I remember my life. It is not an autobiography. I have, however, tried to be historically accurate, and where I could find sources to confirm facts, I have used them. Where I have been unable to locate confirmation, my best recollection will have to suffice. The art and business of piping and pipe bands is not as well documented as some other areas of human endeavor.

David Sedaris is a favorite satirist of mine, and his slightly snarky comment about truth resonates with me. Undoubtedly a few folks (please let it be only a few) who were present at the events described in this memoir will have different recollections of them. But my description of them is my best effort to record my truth about them.

Acknowledgements:

Thanks to Andrew Berthoff who provided an initial copy edit of the manuscript, and gave me many valuable suggestions on content and style. Thanks also to Mike Grey who reviewed the (nearly) final version and steered me in the right direction on many points concerning the history, and the role of various players in the tale. Despite my many trips to Scotland in connection with all things piping and pipe bands (numbering 60 to 70 I'd guess) it's likely clear that I failed to get a lot of names and titles correct. If you concede however, that Scotland is a country that decides to name a place Auchtermuchty, I may be forgiven for the odd lapse. Any mistakes that remain are entirely my fault and I absolve these men from any responsibility for them.

PART 1

1

The Northern Meeting: Inverness, 1974

The Great Glen in Scotland is a rift valley that bisects Scotland in a north-easterly direction. This geologic fault, which is millions of years old, runs straight from the Black Isle at its north end to the head of Loch Linnhe at the south end. Some sixty-two miles long, it has within its boundaries some of the most beautiful scenery in Scotland, and links a series of lochs and waterways: Loch Linnhe, Loch Lochy, Loch Oich, Loch Ness and finally the river Ness. As Loch Ness becomes the River Ness, and the river enters the precincts of Inverness itself, a series of lovely tumbling rapids and islands break up the flow, and salmon fishers can be seen fly casting in their waders. The river gradually settles into a serene wide flow of peaty-colored but clear water, with the Ness Walk and its many glorious gardens providing a fine border on either side. It finally passes what was once the Caledonian Hotel, with its grand view of the river as it flows towards the Moray Firth, only a short distance away.

This story starts (but doesn't have its true beginning) at the Caledonian Hotel, because in 1974 the Caley, as it's called, was the home of the Northern Meeting Piping Competitions.

In the year 1788, thirteen Highland gentlemen met and drew up resolutions for an annual meeting "for the purpose of promotion of a social intercourse, and to liven up life in the highlands with activities for the Pleasure and Innocent Amusement of the members." The original seventy-nine members consisted principally of landowners in the area, but also public officials and assorted lawyers, doctors and other gentry. Over time the various activities have changed, and the Northern Meeting no longer organizes the Highland Games at Inverness, although dress balls, cocktail parties, luncheons and the like still take place. The group's activities eventually evolved to become the Northern Meeting Piping Competitions, still thriving two hundred and twenty-eight years later. Winning a prize at these contests is the absolute pinnacle of success for pipers from around the world.

So here I found myself at the Northern Meeting, held as always at Inverness over two days — in this particular year, on Thursday and Friday, September 12 and 13, 1974. This was my third trip to this storied event; I had only come back to piping in 1969, after a ten-year absence.

On the Thursday the competitions for the Highland Society of London's Gold Medal for Piobaireachd were held. The Gold Medal was judged by Seumas MacNeill, Capt. John MacLellan and Maj. Gen. Frank Richardson. I was awarded second prize, behind Jimmy MacGregor, who at last had his Gold Medal, finally knocking it off in his 50s.

The March competition was held on the same day, and, playing "Bonnie Ann" for a bench composed of David Murray, John MacFadyen and Ian Cameron, I was awarded first prize.

What an amazing day for me, a Canadian piper, the son of a coal miner from Ayrshire. Not much remains of my memories of that evening, but for certain there was some cheer enjoyed by my wife Lillian, and my dad, Bill senior, in the local pubs of Inverness. My mother, Mildred, had died in 1972 and sadly missed the piping roller coaster that I had climbed aboard.

In 1974, the piping events were divided between the Caledonian Hotel ballroom and the Doctor Black Memorial Halls. The Caley ballroom was a fairly cavernous place, with rows of folding metal chairs designed to test the padding of the most capacious posterior. The Doctor Black Hall was much smaller and more intimate, so much so that the audience always seemed to encroach on the piper's private, or at least performing, space. So it seemed to this piper, who has always been something of a tense performer. The Doctor Black Hall also featured a grand piano, that had a most disconcerting habit of resonating a discordant hum of overtones from one or more of its strings when the powerhouse notes of the chanter—Low G, B, and D—were sounded.

Awakening on Friday, September 13, I felt energized, confident and strode purposefully to the Caley for the Strathspey & Reel event. The bizarre events I am about to describe took place as I entered the ballroom from the back. I was about to make my way up to the stage when I was confronted by Maj. Gen. Frank Richardson, who said in his English public school accent that he'd "like a word with me". I have learned over time that when someone from the United Kingdom uses that expression, what usually follows is less than pleasant. It can be one of the more ominous phrases in the English language.

So, take a picture of this: I am paused in my already fraught march to the stage to have General Frank upbraid me with, "Now, Livingstone, you went to bed last night thinking you had foxed the judges, and we can't have it."

I had no idea what the hell he was talking about and I told him so in those very words.

Imagine, if you will, fellow pipers mingling around, audience members eavesdropping on this performance, and General Frank in his stentorian voice and plummy officer's accent, bellowing this news to the world. You see, Frank was profoundly deaf, and that always led to reasonable concerns regarding his ability to properly hear a musical competition, let alone judge it, and about that, other worries abounded too.

So with the baffling self-confidence of the nearly deaf (think of trying to talk to someone who is listening to loud music on headphones), General Frank told me, and the many others assembled nearby, that it had been reported by an audience member that I had made an error in my tune. As luck would have it (whose luck, one wonders?), it appeared Capt. John MacLellan had made a recording on a cassette tape recorder, kept under the blanket that draped the judges' table. While it was done secretly (I suppose there's no other word), Capt. John had made the recording for his own purposes and private enjoyment.

Whatever the thinking, they had felt they should listen to the tape, and the three judges had repaired to a hotel room to do just that. On doing so, indeed they discovered that I had made a note mistake and decided on the repair work they should undertake. This "fix" was to remove me from the prize list, and advance those below me one place.

Now, I'm not awfully good at hearing a not-so-veiled suggestion that I had cheated the judges. Nor am I easy with class condescension. And to be candid, I have never much yielded to authority, particularly of the military variety, and will readily respond with what might be termed insubordination, if in fact I were subordinate in the first place. Sometimes this could be seen as downright insolent. So I slipped into my most North American vernacular and appropriately accented English and said something like, "Well, if that's what you want to do, there's not a goddam thing I can do about it. But if you do go ahead with this crazy scheme, you'll create more problems than you solve." In the result, as we say in the law, I persuaded him not at all, and the strange events proceeded apace.

So with this exchange with the General finished, I walked to the stage, both bemused and thoroughly pissed off, and rattled off "The Piper's Bonnet" and "The Smith of Chilliechassie" for first prize in the Strathspey & Reel.

Later on the same day, the Jig competition was held and as reported to me (I don't recall), there was a short leet, and all pipers in the leet, including me were requested to play "Alan McPherson of Moss Park," a fine composition by Pipe-Major Angus MacDonald of the Scots Guards. It appears that we all had this tune in our lists. I accept this intelligence on faith; I knew nothing about it at the time since I was closeted in a tuning room before playing, and left the competition area immediately after playing, the usual routine for me. In the result, I was first in the Jig as well, and ahead even of P/M Angus, whose tune it seems was the set piece for the event.

So the result of all of this nutty carry-on is that folk remember only that in 1974 I had the Gold Medal taken back (and even that was not so, only second place), and the singular achievement of first in the March, and in the Strathspey & Reel, and in the Jig were lost in the controversy. I believe that only Donald MacLeod has achieved a similar set of three first placings at the Northern Meeting, but I must concede that his was accomplished at the very highest level: first in each of the Clasp, Former Winner's March, Strathspey & Reel, and Jig.

I have often wondered what the decision would have been had the mistake been made by someone else. I raise this, because rumours were rife that Jim McGregor's tune also had a note error — again I personally have no evidence of this, but it seems that the source of the report to the judges of my own error was also the source of the rumor that Jim's tune was flawed.

The papers made hay with the story. Here's an excerpt from the report of the events in the Aberdeen *Press & Journal*:

> TOP PIPERS SLAM "TAPE SCANDAL"
> *The very foundations of world piping were racked by a 'bugging scandal' at Inverness yesterday. For on Day Two of the Northern Meeting the man who was announced as second in the Gold Medal piobaireachd competition was disqualified after the judges had listened to a taped playback of the man's tune.*
>
> *The "secret" playback was made, it is believed, after a complaint about a serious error in the tune of Mr. William Livingstone—all the way from Whitby, Ontario—and top Pipers yesterday were scandalized especially since the prominent notices outside the competition halls read "no cameras or tape recorders."*
>
> *Now all competitors will move up one place in the gold competition. Said Mr. Livingstone: "I am very*

disappointed but accept the judges' decision. I will be back next year."

But other competitors, although shy about giving their names, were not as merciful towards the judges, General F.M. Richardson, Capt. John MacLellan and Mr. Seumas McNeill. *"It is an absolute scandal"* said one prizewinner. *"We had no idea there were tapes being used. It leaves a bitter taste and even tarnishes the Gold Medal. What would happen if the winner was found to have made a mistake on a taped playback? The judges' decision should be final as stated on our entry form."*

One competitor, Mr. Andrew Wright from Paisley, went as far as trying to raise a petition to have the judges' decision quashed—but few would put their names on the list, though heartily agreeing with him.

One of the judges, General Richardson said:*" It came to the judges' notice that the player to whom we had given second prize had made an error in the course of what all would agree was a well-played tune.*

"We happened to have had the tape recorder under the judges table so the tune was checked and we found we had indeed overlooked a substantial mistake—of an unusual nature."

"In the circumstances we never even considered covering up our own error. There can be no Watergate at the Northern Meeting. Pipers do not lie to one another—whatever politicians may do. I am happy to say that the piper concerned who had himself felt uneasy about his tune, accepted our decision most manfully and without

bitterness. He can certainly return to Canada happy in the knowledge that his playing had given genuine pleasure to the judges and to the audience."

General Richardson said he himself did not know a recorder was being used. "I am very sad we have had to do this--but think it is better to have faced up to the fact that we made a mistake and corrected it."

General Richardson who judged his first northern meeting 40 years ago said the judges had heard a marathon of 39 entrants in the piobaireachd section, although he was not putting that forward as an excuse for having missed what he described as a "serious error".

The piper who originally came third and is now officially second, Mr. Arthur Gillies from Taynuilt Argyle, said: "I would have been happier to see things left as they were. Third to second means nothing to me—I have been second in this competition three years. But if it had been knocking me from first to second that would've been different. I feel sorry for Mr. Livingstone."

So back to the three great prizes I was (and am) so proud of—it's sobering to note the prize money: ten pounds for the March, the same for the Strathspey & Reel and five pounds for the Jig. Set against the cost of perhaps $3000 for the trip, it's clear I was not doing this for the money.

Knowing the tone of my comments to Gen. Richardson, it's a delicious irony to hear him speak in the newspaper report of the "sporting way" in which I took the news. Still, I did manage to keep my head down during the entire imbroglio and for this I thank John MacFadyen, my tutor at the time, who called me aside that morning and gave me succinct advice: "Keep your bloody mouth shut." I did. How right he was. The event soon blossomed into a full-blown scandal. Andrew Wright and James McIntosh set about trying to organize a petition with the pipers, demanding the restoration of the original prize list. As mentioned above, the Aberdeen *Press & Journal* (fondly called the P and J in northeast Scotland) thundered "tape scandal rocks the Northern Meeting," with Gen. Richardson promising there would be no tape scandal at the Northern Meeting, which was barking nonsense as in fact they had already created that very dreaded thing.

This reference to a tape scandal had a particular resonance at the time. Richard Nixon was being hounded from the White House, due to his combination of villainy and stupidity in authorizing a break-in at the Democratic national headquarters in the Watergate Hotel. The depth of his ignominy was revealed when this fellow, leader of the free world, was found to have secretly tape-recorded all conversations that took place in the Oval Office of the White House.

When the House Judiciary Committee finally demanded and got production of the tapes, they revealed that Nixon knew of the planned break-in, authorized it, and ordered the FBI to drop its investigation of the affair. This came to be known as the "smoking gun tape," and confirmed the cover-up that had been so broadly suspected. Impeachment was a heartbeat away.

Nixon resigned in disgrace on August 8, 1974, and President Gerald Ford granted him a full unconditional pardon on September 9, 1974, three days before the Northern Meeting in Inverness. The pardon in no way diminished the ignominy that Nixon suffered.

These were momentous events with world-shaking implications. It may safely be called hyperbolic for General Frank Richardson to have drawn upon them to describe a piping fiasco, but there you have it. By the way, I only know the word ignominy because of a remark in court from a highly pompous local judge,—and former thespian—who said to a lout in his courtroom: "I have never seen such ignominy, calumny, and perfidy in all my days. Be gone from my sight." The ruffian looked around and said, "Wha'd he say?"

I had to look it up... ignominy, that is.

To return to the events under discussion: I would have given a great deal to have been in that room when the three judges were discussing what to do. I can't imagine who led the way, but I can describe my knowledge of the three of them. Capt. John MacLellan was indeed a very great piper, with a bold, direct and incisive playing style and a mind to suit. He was a man who exuded great integrity. I was, and still am a great admirer of his, and learned some years later that he regretted the whole affair.

Seumas MacNeill was a successful piper, with a Gold Medal to his credit, who once made a somewhat plaintive remark that were it not for Donald MacLeod, he, Seumas, would have possessed the greatest record of all in the former winners March, Strathspey & Reel. (Clearly this was a time pre-Alasdair Gillies.) What he possessed in abundance however, was an acid tongue that he unleashed with relish.

Gen. Frank Richardson was a distinguished army surgeon, a soldier first and foremost, and the winner of a Distinguished Service Order for taking up his pipes and inspiring and leading a flagging Scottish battalion to overcome enemy resistance during the Eritrean campaign of 1941. "Clearly a man of some character and bravery," concluded *The Independent* in his obituary, September 10, 1990.

Another obituary, by Gen. Sir Michael Gow in the Glasgow *Herald*, described him as "co-author of the definitive work on the pibroch, of which, incidentally, he was twice world champion performer." Some pretty serious military hyperbole here. Typically pipers don't refer to world champion performers, but it's generally held that winning the Gold Medal or, better yet, the Clasp, is symbolic of being at "the top of the piping tree." This, Gen. Richardson was not. A close friend of mine, and a great piper in his own right, having himself reached the top of the piping tree, has heard the general play and describes it as "truly awful."

So what's to be said of the general and his piping knowledge? I know that he had tuition from John MacDonald of Inverness, and he made notes of these sessions. Some samples of these appear in the museum or archives of the College of Piping in Glasgow.

All well and good I suppose, but I guess anyone can make notes from a master musician about tunes: "In bar two of the ground, treat the C as a long themal note, and pass smartly to the following D," etc. etc.

Where is all this leading, you might ask. Let us first recognize that the general was a member of the Royal Scottish Pipers Society. This organization, tagged affectionately, or one suspects somewhat sarcastically, as "The Jolly Boys," is based in Edinburgh and comprises "gentlemen" pipers of professional standing, usually members of Britain's aristocracy, occupying an amateur position, that is, never having competed for prize money. This venerable body in 2008 upheld the one-hundred-year-plus tradition of excluding women from its ranks.

So let us return to the scene of the judges huddled around the tape recorder, listening with stunned disbelief to the truth that all three of them had missed the mistake. It's delightful, to me at least, and maybe not overly speculative to consider the dynamics at play in the room.

We have the acid-tongued Seumas, never one to avoid controversy, especially if he can be a moving force in it. He is at the time of these events, likely writing *Piobaireachd and its Interpretation* with General Frank. He has already written a volume simply called *Piobaireachd* and has asked General Frank to write the introduction. In the law we discuss conflicts of interest, not so much in terms of genuine conflicts between duty and self-interest, but more in terms of the potential for that to happen, or even the appearance of the possibility—one recuses himself if that is a possibility. Maybe it never dawned on Seumas that it might be a problem.

And then there is Capt. John, Principal of the Army School of Piping, soldier to the core, sitting with a Maj. Gen. determining this issue.

And finally, General Frank, awful piper, hero of the realm, the very model of a model major-general—lots of notes from "Old Johnnie MacDonald" and deeply into the Jolly Boys' mentality, that being that they were perfectly entitled, never having played in competition, to judge those pipers who do.

I speculate that Gen. Frank took the lead, if for no other reason than that he was willing to break the news to me, openly, publicly and with a certain edge of smug pride that he had "caught me out."

I love to imagine the conversation:

> GENERAL FRANK: Who was that bloody woman who made this complaint?
>
> SEUMAS: She's from North America, a piper, and she was following the score.
>
> GENERAL FRANK: Well I wish she'd kept her mouth shut. Now what do we do?
>
> CAPT. JOHN: Gentlemen, I recorded some of the players for my own listening pleasure and I think I have Bill's tune on the tape. We could check the tape and find out if it's true or just mischief making. . We may not have to do anything, but at least we'll know and can deal with it...something like "we're aware of it, but the tune had sufficient merit... blah blah"
>
> GENERAL FRANK: You recorded them?! Where was the tape recorder?
>
> CAPT. JOHN: Under the table.
>
> SEUMAS: Literally or figuratively?
>
> CAPT. JOHN: No really, it was there and I taped some tunes.
>
> GENERAL FRANK: Do you have it?

CAPT. JOHN: Yes it's right here in my briefcase.

GENERAL FRANK: Well let's get to the hotel and have a listen.

CAPT. JOHN: Do we all think that's a good idea? I mean if she's right, we have egg on our faces, and then we would have to deal with the fallout.

SEUMAS AND GENERAL FRANK: Let's at least listen to it.

(The scene: the three wise men in an Inverness hotel room, huddled over a tape recorder, listening to the tune)

ALL THREE VARIOUSLY: My God she's right... Jesus Murphy... how in hell did we miss it... dear, dear... what a mess!

SEUMAS: What, if anything, should we do about this?

CAPT. JOHN: I say leave it alone; pipers make mistakes all the time. Why can't judges?

GENERAL FRANK: But, really, gentleman, this young man scoffed away with the prize, knowing he'd made a mistake and hoping to bamboozle us and all of piping.

CAPTAIN JOHN: I'm not so sure of that, General. Most pipers I know will stop if they are aware of note errors. I know Bill, and I'd say he would have stopped if he knew he'd gone wrong. Pipers often make mistakes and are not aware of it. Anyway it's the piper's job to play and ours is to adjudicate. We did, if imperfectly.

SEUMAS: And what about the clear rules set out in the entry form and in the program: "The judges' decisions are final." And even more troubling, what about the notices prohibiting tape recorders?

GENERAL FRANK: Ah yes, but exceptions prove the rule. Here we have clear evidence that this tune was unworthy of the prize, because of a significant mistake.

CAPTAIN JOHN: Really? We all enjoyed it enough to have missed that fact, and placed him second.

GENERAL FRANK: Still it's not right, and I really must insist that we fix it.

SEUMAS: I have an idea—why not draw straws, and the one with the short straw will decide the outcome... Oh dear, General, it looks like you have to make the call."

My imagined conversation amongst these three gives me a chuckle as I wonder how they could have thought this bizarre outcome would pass without, at the very least, controversy.

And so it came to pass. In a perverse way, it gave me a notoriety that could not have been bought with the help of Hill and Knowlton (the PR folks who helped to bring us the first Gulf War). I was the subject of talk everywhere in the piping world and I still get asked about it to this day. It reminds me of Robert Burns and his take on folk discussing him even in derogatory terms.

My dad and my grandfather both loved Burns, and often quoted him in these words: "The country tongues may clash and clatter / The mair they talk a'hm kent the better." (The actual quote is a little different: "An tease my name in Kintry Clatter / The mair they talk I'm kent the better / E'en let them clash." It appears in a poem by Burns, never published by him, to his little daughter born of love, as his poetical response to gossip reviling him as a fornicator.) Perhaps we can see this as an 18th century recognition of the notion that there is no such thing as bad publicity.

So to the moral, the nugget of truth at the heart of this charade. Pipers demand, and are entitled to expect, judges with full street cred. If you haven't done it you have no earthly hope of understanding the business of competitive piping. There are plenty of literary critics who opine on the works of others, and the good critics are those who have toiled in the same vineyards—Anthony Burgess, Christopher Hitchens, John Updike, Ian McEwan and the like. Their critical posture is informed by an intimate understanding of the form and the work. It is not enough for a piping judge to have learned a bunch of tunes and even to have a working knowledge of how they should go. Competitive piping is a game like no other, and pipers want to be judged by people who can play, who have proved that fact on the boards, and who bring an empathetic if not sympathetic mentality to the process. They should have undergone the same baptism by fire as the performers.

Now that I am judging I'm constantly flooded by anxiety and concern for the players, because I know how nearly impossible this game is. What we do on the bench is so much easier than what is done on the other side of it, because it's not just great playing that they have to pull off, it's competing with the stress levels at the highest peak. I once trod the stage at the Eden Court playing in the Clasp, and my pulse pounded so frantically in my neck, I was sure a stroke was on its way.

So the presence of the Royal Scottish Pipers Society on judging benches for the top competitions—or any competitions—was never welcomed by the competitors, and did nothing whatever to enhance the credibility of the results. Indeed, if folk were willing to talk about this more openly, there would be some very shocked reactions. This is not to say that these are bad people—they are not. In fact I have known many of them and find them bright, charming, funny and engaging.

The universal example offered of a great judge with no competing history is James Campbell, the son of Archibald Campbell of Kilberry.

That's true I think, but my feelings and those of most pipers I know, will always favor the one who has done it. The crucible of high-level competition cannot be duplicated in any other format.

With all of this said, it must be admitted that all three of them signed off on this course of action, and I may indeed be completely out to lunch on my speculations. But if the third member of the bench had been, say, Bob Hardie or Robert Brown and not the General, the fallout may well have been somewhat different. This affair brought into acute focus the rule at all Northern Meeting competitions prohibiting tape recorders in any of the venues. In these current days of recording devices the size of a chocolate wafer, it is likely that the rule is unenforceable—unless audience members (and judges too, let's not forget) submit to the same kind of full search as an air traveller suffers, up to and including removal of ghillie brogues, sporrans with metal parts, and full body scans designed to disclose devices hidden amongst the naughty bits of piping enthusiasts. That's never going to happen. So it looks like we will have to rely on common sense from here on out.

I feel a little sheepish for opening this series of recollections with something as lame as a piping competition. Sorry that, unlike Keith Richards in his memoir, I cannot start with something akin to his recounting of his arrest in Fordyce, Arkansas, the heart of redneck country, along with his pals, in a car filled to overflowing with dope of every kind available in 1975. The Northern Meeting fiasco only cost me a prize, and in the long run not even that as I eventually won the Gold Medal. And what notoriety came with it. The whole schmozzle was known only to those few thousand people worldwide who know or care much about piping. Keith, however, went on to incredible fame and fortune. My experience at the 1974 Northern Meeting and Keith Richards's crossing that dreaded line in Arkansas, were incidents close in terms of the time of the two events—but there the similarity ends. This illustrates one, only one, of the many differences between rock stars and pipers.

2

Copper Cliff

Neil Young raises his high reedy voice, and sings plaintively:

There is a town in North Ontario
With dream comfort, memory to spare
And in my mind, I still need a place to go
All my changes were there
Blue, blue windows behind the stars
Yellow moon on the rise
Big birds flying across the sky
Throwing shadows on our eyes
Leave us
Helpless, helpless, helpless...

My story begins in a town in North Ontario, but not the one of Neil's magical imagery. It's called Copper Cliff and it and its 3,000 souls sit perched on the Canadian Shield. This is a geological feature of some considerable enormity. It's roughly circular and extends across Ontario and beyond, from the Great Lakes, all the way around Hudson's Bay and Labrador up to Greenland. It is very old, being a mantle of pre-Cambrian rock, and during its prehistoric period mighty peaks (up to 39,000 feet) have been eroded by glaciers and other forces of nature, leaving a rolling, undulating landscape of hard rock barely covered with soil. What trees and vegetation survive here have to be made of tough stuff, and so, too, with the people who live there.

I was born on March 20, 1942. It was a Friday. Here are some other things that happened that day: U.S Gen. Douglas MacArthur famously addressed journalists in Australia, after having been driven from Bataan by the Japanese: "I came out of Bataan and I shall return." And he did, some two years and thousands of lives later. There is no suggestion that my birth on that day had any role to play in those events.

On March 20, 1942, in Zgievz, Poland, one hundred Poles were taken from a labor camp and shot by the Germans.

On March 20, 1942, in Rohaytn Ukraine, the German SS murdered three thousand Jews, including six hundred children, annihilating seventy percent of that city's Jewish ghetto. Elsewhere in the German leadership of the time, we can read the following excerpt from Joseph Goebbels' diaries:

> *March 20/42: finally we talked about the Jewish question. Here the Fuehrer is as uncompromising as ever. The Jews must be got out of Europe, if necessary by the applying of the most brutal methods.*

While not exactly on my birthday, Goebbels is seen writing in his diary the following bit of ghastly information a week later:

> *March 27/42: beginning with Lublin, the Jews in the general government (i.e. German occupied Poland) are now being evacuated eastward. The procedure is a pretty barbaric one, and not to be described here more definitely. Not much will remain of the Jews. On the whole, it can be said that about 60% of them will have to be liquidated, whereas only about 40% can be used for forced labor... A judgment that is being visited upon the Jews that while barbaric, is fully deserved by them.*

So, as I entered the world, jaundiced (as in yellow colored, not cynical—that was yet to come) with my head sporting dents and wounds from the surgical tools used to haul me out, this terrible stuff was going on in the world. My taking up of the bagpipe a few years later had then, and has now, no discernible impact on the "real" issues around the globe. I dare say that, outside of those few pipers who served in the military in various ways, the same can be said of almost all of us pipers.

And now, to return to the regularly scheduled program already in progress...

My hometown, Copper Cliff, is what was called and still is, I think, a mining town or a company town. Actually it may be more like a mill town, processing and refining the minerals mined throughout the Sudbury basin, a place full of evidence of a meteorite collision. The Canadian Shield is rich in minerals and ore, and many years ago, mining interests discovered the riches to be found in nickel, silver, copper and further north, gold.

Copper Cliff was a company town in the classic sense. I doubt these things even exist anymore, but in that time it meant that the company (in this case Inco—the International Nickel Company) owned everything, as in every damn thing. They owned the houses that they rented to certain Inco workers, and they owned the public elementary school, the high school, the buildings, and the teachers who taught there. They owned the police force, and my uncle John was a member of it. They ran the hospital and paid the doctors, all of whom worked out of the hospital (no private practice doctors here). The streets were arranged in a clear and well-understood pattern. If you lived on Orford Street, as I did, you, and everyone else in town, knew what your father did at Inco and how much he earned. (Here read in my dad's case: a sweating, gas mask-wearing workie in the smelter, and about that scene, you'll hear more later). If you lived on Nickel Street, your dad was most likely employed in "the Office," a kind of rubric for white shirt, tie and superior intelligence, or so we were conditioned to believe.

Power Street denoted an even higher placing in the social structure, while Park Street was reserved for what clearly were the elite.

"The elite." I once did a paper in a sociology course where I described the social structure of a company town—my company town. I recall discovering that of the fourteen or fifteen top dogs, all but one were Freemasons. The lone holdout was both Catholic and Italian. The Inco brass killed two birds with that guy.

God help you if you lived on Poland Street or Finland Street. These streets seemed reserved for places that exuded, twenty-four hours a day, the heavenly aroma of coffee and cinnamon buns and doubled as boarding houses for workers in the Copper Cliff smelter. It was a shame that they were so disrespected; these places were wonderful and warm.

Perhaps even lower on the ladder was the territory known as "Up the Hill." There on Venice Street, Milan Street, Genoa Street, etc. the Italians were consigned, or confined. Their homes, modest as most homes were in town though even more primitive, sat right next to the roaring smelters and the belching sulphur gas. When I say "right next to," I mean in terms of feet. The inhabitants were universally immigrants from Italy, there for work in the smelter, and all sentenced to this bleak place. They sent their kids with names like Corelli, Del Vecchio, and Montesi to school (the only school in town, remember) where they attended with kids with names like O'Connor, or O'Riordan, Hobden, and, yes, Livingstone. I don't know how they felt about this, but somehow I think they were perversely proud. They were good athletes, tough, resilient kids, but likely feeling their place. I know I sure as hell did, and I didn't have their difficulties.

Yet for all of that they created a pretty vibrant community up the hill. They made their own wine, and to the delight of us youngsters, they bootlegged cases of beer. This was the time in Ontario when in order to buy alcohol, you had to have a liquor permit. It came in the form of a little book in which every purchase of booze was carefully recorded. So it wasn't just a matter of being of age, you had to submit to the intrusion of Big Brother into your swilling habits. And we worry today about a loss of privacy!

They also had their own community centre, called the Italian Club, referred to by us "mungycakes" as the Wop Hall. Every Friday night the hall showed movies for kids, and everyone from the "regular" part of town trooped up the hill and sat on the floor of the auditorium/dance hall, engaging in non-stop screaming and near-riots, while food, bags of chips, and assorted other objects flew through the air. When the place was completely out of control, the lights came on, the projector stopped, and a voice of doom warned over the loud speakers that they would they would shut down the movie completely and not return our ten-cent admission fee unless order was restored.

The Italians had their own grocery stores, Falcioni's and Pianosi's, that specialized in Italian foods. They also had Toppazini's Bakery, maker of incredible bread, most especially their fabulous coronet bread. Every special dinner at our home required a trip on foot about two miles up the hill (almost no one had a car) to buy the coronet, fresh hot and smelling swooningly gorgeous. The Toppazini family donated two hockey players, Zelio and Jerry, to the NHL. Jerry carries on business as the owner of Toppers Pizza chain throughout southern Ontario, whose ads brag of their "authentic Italian bread recipe." A rare treat was the occasional chicken and spaghetti supper in the basement of the Italian club—irresistible stuff and to this day amongst the finest simple pasta dishes I have ever eaten.

The first home I remember in Copper Cliff was 11 Evans Road, a tiny place: kitchen, bathroom off of that, a "front room" or parlor with two bedrooms squeezed onto the side. It was here, at the kitchen table, that I had my first lessons on the bagpipe.

My dad was teaching my brother Ranald, who, at the time was eleven, and I was four. The two of them would sit at the kitchen table, music book opened, sounding away on the practice chanters. Family lore has it that I was a most annoying kid at these times, wanting to get in on the strange but enticing action. Apparently as a result of being repeatedly rebuffed or ignored, I would crawl under the table and from this ideally placed launching pad, would deliver a "lower punch," as it came to be known, to the delicate regions of dad and brother. This finally led to their capitulation and I was allowed to join them at the table. I was ultimately outfitted with a very small child's practice chanter, a family heirloom passed down through dad's sister Betty, a piper herself who had died many years before in childbirth.

We moved from 11 Evans Road when I was seven or eight, so I don't remember much more from that house, except for two incidents. My dad had been able to create a tiny practice goose, with a specially made bag, to use with the aforesaid child's practice chanter. My method of playing this thing involved walking around the house and yard, honking horribly away without much in the way of stopping. There was a crew of workers doing waterline repairs in the road in front of the house. I considered it my chosen mission to play the goose for them for the best part of the day, until one of them led me by the hand into the house and pleaded with my mother, in heavily accented English, "Lady, please make him stop." This was my first experience with what all pipers learn will be a lifelong pattern of insult and rejection.

The other incident I recall came about as I tried to grab the crêpe paper streamers off of a passing wedding parade of cars, and nearly got crunched in the process. My dad spotted this and dragged me into the house, where he delivered several mighty openhanded blows to my backside. I realized later, of course, that I had scared the hell out of him, and he was simply trying to impart a lesson, but that did not stop me then from howling like a beaten dog. I was not hurt physically in the slightest. It was the first and only time that my dad ever struck me.

Back to Copper Cliff: on the eastern limit of the town, really not a defined edge, the town ended, and a few feet later the smelter—the the heart of Inco's operations in the Sudbury area—rose up. Huge buildings humming and whining, acre after acre of industrial devastation, hot metal and slag cars to-ing and fro-ing. Row upon row of blast furnaces, molten metal being carried in giant ladles the size of small submarines by overhead moving cranes, with bits of white-hot crap falling out of them, and the mind-numbing hiss of mighty industrial production, punctuated by warning horns, and all viewed through a smog of sulphur dioxide so potent that it would sting your eyes, nose and throat to the point of tears.

Workers wore "gas masks" that were little more than cloth nose and mouth covers, dipped in some solution intended to neutralize the paralyzing acidity of sulphur dioxide. They did not work. My dad worked here, and when he later became a shift boss in the Orford building and I was a summer student at Inco, he showed me through this inferno (not Dante's; that's only in fiction). This was the real deal and the guys who worked there pretty much all succumbed to some form of lung disease—emphysema, cancer, COPD, you name it—anything you can get from inhaling eight hours a day, five days a week, concentrated SO_2 and SO_3, not to mention the particulate crap that filled the air.

Most men went nearly deaf. Did I mention that it was about 2000°C in there? Except of course in winter, when the open ends of the building allowed the wind and cold to freeze one side of your body while the fluid bed roasters cooked the other side. The people of Copper Cliff were the beneficiaries of other wonders brought by Inco. When the wind came from the east, the SO_2 that was spewed from the three iconic stacks turned around and fell upon the town. You could watch the stunted grass and few brave garden plants shrivel and die before your very eyes. Later on, Inco built the tallest stack in the world, and it had the advantage, at least for the denizens of Copper Cliff, of carrying the poison all the way to Scandinavia.

But there was so much worse. One of the by-products of the mining and smelting process was a never-ending supply of a slurry made up of water and minuscule sand and metal particles. This gunk was passed through an enormous network of pipes about twelve inches in diameter, raised on trestles, and the stuff was dumped over an area of hundreds of acres. Eventually the water evaporated, leaving metallic dust as fine as talcum. We kids played on the "sand" dunes left as a result, and rolled around in God knows what stuff was there. These tailings dunes were to the west of town, so when the wind blew from the west (of course the prevailing wind direction in continental North America), sandstorms that would have made Lawrence of Arabia homesick, would rise up, turn the sky dusky, and land on and in every nook and cranny of habitable space in the town. My mother was a clean freak and when the tailings blew, every door and window was hermetically sealed. It did no good. The stuff penetrated everything, leaving grit and film on every surface, even I think the vertical ones.

And there's more. Inco built an iron ore recovery plant directly southwest of our house. When winds were favorable, the dense orange smoke, smelling of elephant farts (a more refined scribe might say rotten eggs, but it doesn't do the aroma full justice), assaulted the senses. The creeks in Copper Cliff ran, and still do, an alarming orange-red color, and their banks crack off and away like the rust off the fender of a '54 Ford.

Mrs. Sharko, the Polish neighbor across the street, went to the Office (remember that institution?) to speak, I believe, to Ralph Parker who was the head honcho at Inco. She complained about all of the conditions I'm describing and wanted something done for herself and her husband, an Inco man called Mike. "Does he want a job or not?" came the empathetic reply.

The result of all of this assault on the land, was that there was barely a tree to be seen, no vegetation, and huge outcroppings of bare black rock. The thin layer of soil washed away with the loss of grass, green cover and roots, exposing the Canadian Shield in all its raw state. Where once there might have been hills with some form of life on them, there were acres and acres of slag dumps. The molten waste was taken by electric cars, that were essentially huge submarine-shaped things with openings on top, and the stuff was emptied and dumped down long artificially created cliffs. At night this produced spectacular shows reminiscent of movies of lava flows in Hawaii. There was an upside though—watching the slag being dumped was a favorite activity of the randy young folk of Copper Cliff and Sudbury, and led to many a serious romance, and unfortunately to some unwanted population increase as well.

The town sits at a latitude of 46.49° north. This is almost exactly the latitude of Bern, Switzerland, which is at 46.57° north. This is not likely to be a helpful observation. Bern is where Albert Einstein worked, where Toblerone chocolate bars are made, and where elemental cheese (commonly known as Swiss cheese) marched outward to world fame. It's true that Einstein's theory that nothing can exceed the speed of light has recently undergone challenge because of the discovery of some very speedy neutrinos, and that eating the Alps-shaped chunks of Toblerone is downright hazardous to your mouth and teeth, and that the flavor (the term here is used loosely) of the holes and the actual cheese in the Swiss cheese are difficult to distinguish—still, these things all resonate around the world.

Berne boasts (why do they always say that) of a climate that sees the daytime temperature from January to April reach a maximum average daily high of about 8°C. A better, that is to say, more accurate comparison for Copper Cliff would have us look to Fargo, North Dakota, in the American Plains, sitting at a nearly identical latitude of 46.52° north. In case you don't know much about Fargo, watch the movie of the same name. It's a terrific Coen brothers yarn, but more importantly for our purposes, illustrates the bleak, freezing (average temperature January to April -10°C) snow-covered wind-blown landscape, with human breath misting, if not freezing, on exhalation.

Fargo is pretty much Copper Cliff without its scourged landscapes and Godawful industrial crap everywhere in the air, water and land.

My dad left Scotland for Canada at about age twenty-one, seeking to escape the fate of the pits (coal mines for non-Scots) into which he was inducted at age fourteen. He horrified me with stories of the young boys being sent into the narrowest places, perhaps eighteen inches high, because their slight frames allowed them to slip through. You can imagine, not a lot of serious education took place for him—no formal schooling after fourteen years of age—but he was a very smart and intuitive guy. He was a serious reader, and dragged me regularly with him to the aforementioned Copper Cliff library. I was too young to see the details, but I know he read a lot of history, Scottish and otherwise, and Robert Burns, Walter Scott and the like. He was the first of the family to come to Canada, and he must surely have planted a seed in the rest of them because before too long, his parents and all of his siblings (save one) immigrated, too.

His parents, my paternal grandparents, came over: Grandpa John, known to his wife as "Speedy," and the said wife, my Goagie. I expect this may be some mutilation of a Gaelic word for grandma, although when I check with Gaelic speakers I know, none of them seem to recognize it. Also landing by boat (I hesitate to imagine the ship or the trip) were his brother John, his sister Winnie, and his sister Betty. Everyone, for a reason that likely would merit a study of the collective family brain wattage, ended up in and around Sudbury—except for Betty, who perversely married Jim MacLennan, a police officer in Timmins, a place even farther north and more inhospitable than the Sudbury area.

Never mind. I'll admit to a sense of bafflement about these decisions, but I am left with no alternative other than to accept them since the choices they made determined my fate. But, really, if you make it all the way from Scotland to Ontario, what muddled thinking would have prevented continuing the journey to Vancouver... Lotus Land, mountains, the Pacific, zoned-out people, but all of them outdoorsy hikers and joggers. Vancouver had its share of ex-pat Scots, and pipers too, and more than one with great pedigrees and a history of having studied with the masters in Scotland before immigrating to Canada. One of these was the great Jimmy MacMillan, who undertook the teaching of the brothers Lee--Jack and Terry, both of whom went on to spectacular careers in piping. So it was that Vancouver became the ultimate birthplace of the Simon Fraser University Pipe Band, now known only by its initials (SFU), and sometimes pronounced sfoo—although doing so might cause a small but still unwelcome oral spray.

And so Copper Cliff it was, complete with wooden sidewalks, and horse-drawn milk delivery— by carts in summer, by sleighs in winter— delivered by the Copper Cliff Dairy, known for its fine products, with bottles left on the door step in accordance with the order left by the lady of the house. These horses were kept in stables at the far end of the field close to our house. They were large and uniformly bad-tempered, and instilled in me a lifelong fear of the beasts. They did, however, produce great quantities of manure that was diligently mined by my dad and the aforementioned Polish neighbor, Mr. Sharko. They trooped over the field pushing large wooden wheelbarrows, and shoveled the stuff into them, tracking it all back for application to the vegetable gardens. It was a peasant method of adding much-needed compost to the thin layer of poor soil, and it worked. We got potatoes, onions, radishes, tomatoes, chard, peas and beans and a hardy kind of blackcurrant. True, the weeds were vicious, given that the stuff was full of seeds for them, but my dad kept up a tireless war against them and usually prevailed.

He even mixed the manure in a barrel with water, leaving it to brew and ripen, and this "liquid TNT" was reserved for plants that were struggling. They usually leapt out of the ground with one or two applications. That was likely a result of shock. My mother chastised my dad more than once for placing this awful (offal) brew under the kitchen window.

3

Family

Let's start with my mother's family. My mother, Mildred, was the middle child of John and Marion Glover. The old historical stuff gets a bit murky. My Grampa Glover (so named to create ease of distinction from Grampa John, the rogue from Ayrshire) was a Barnardo child. These children were mostly orphans from the UK and in the custody of Barnardo Homes, an enlightened institution that imagined that shipping them off to homes in Canada would give them a better chance in life, rather like getting rid of a litter of unwanted kittens. History does however ascribe an honourable nature to John Barnardo, but things often went wrong. Many of these children suffered as unpaid child labourers for farmers, and often much worse.

Grampa Glover never talked about it, so I don't really know how it went for him. But if nothing else, he was tough and smart. A small guy, maybe 5'5", with sandy blond hair and a wry, docile disposition. He died in his mid-nineties and outlived all of his children. He became some kind of accounting/office wizard at the Canadian Pacific Railway. Always quiet, gentle, in the background and always referring to "Mother."

"Mother" was Gramma Glover. A fiercely intelligent and neurotic woman, she had jet black wavy hair till the day she died, that when it was let down reached her waist. Dark brown eyes, black threatening eyebrows, and a laugh that when it made its rare appearances sounded more like a howling roar of the word, "HOW!"

Gramma Glover was from a family of United Empire loyalists. These were the folks who, during the American War of Independence, declared their loyalty to the Crown by voting with their feet, hightailing it to Canada. She apparently grew up in the Kingston/Ganonoque area of Ontario (I only have old family recollections to support this), and how she met Grampa Glover is a lost mystery.

Looking back on her, with the hindsight that a lifetime gives, it's pretty clear that she was a bit nutty. She showed I now see, all of the signs of fairly profound depression, with an unrelenting sad countenance and a very negative and down view of anything going on around her or her family, including her grandchildren. This could flip in a heartbeat to raucous laughter and fun, and a flurry of baking pies and bread that no one in his right mind could resist. Perhaps the diagnosis in today's world would have been bipolar disorder.

These were the days of no medical insurance and no money. So when teeth went bad, out they came, to be replaced with ill-fitting, painful falsies. Grandma Glover lost her uppers, and one half of her lowers to the mid-point at the front of her mouth. Either because she didn't care or they were too painful, she usually left her false teeth in places other than in her mouth. This tended to give her the look of a very sad, but somehow tormented and threatening terrier. My cousin Margie, Winnie's daughter, was scared stiff of her. (Winnie was my aunt, my dad's sister.)

Gramma Glover's maiden name was Filtz, a fact that has always intrigued me. Her coloring was dramatically Mediterranean, bordering on Middle Eastern. Her three children, my mother, my uncle Jack and my uncle Stuart, are all of the same hue. It appears that this familial trait passed down to me. Was Filtz a Jewish name, or the name of a German Jew? I wonder. I have been taken for an Italian, a Greek and an Arab, and many of my law school friends were Jewish. Maybe they thought I was one of them and not goyish after all.

I first attended a summer piping school in about 1972. It was run by John MacFadyen and held in mid-July of a truly sizzling Ontario summer, and my skin had been toasted to the color of a brown loafer.

John and I at this time hardly knew one another at all. This school was held at Mac Campbell's farm in the most southerly part of Ontario, in fact of Canada—hot as hell, and all held outdoors. I was off some distance, blowing my pipes, and as it was later reported to me, MacFadyen asked someone, "Who is that fucking Ay-Rab playing bagpipes?"

So to the extent that it matters, my guess used to be that I'm of Scottish descent to the point of one half Scottish (my dad), a mix of English and who-knows-exactly-what from my mom's side. I have actually had some DNA testing done, only to discover that my genetic background is indeed primarily Irish and "Northern European." Disappointing really—not the Irish part, that's fine, but rather the absence of something a bit more exotic.

My mother's family had some peculiar ways. Gramma and Grampa Glover owned a sizable piece of land on what was then MacLeod Road in Sudbury, about four or five acres. They had quite a nice house on one part of it, with a kitchen, living room and bedrooms and bathrooms. For some reason they gave that home to my uncle Stuart and moved into a house that was not much more than a shack on the same property. The home given to Stuart was sufficient to provide a home for him, his wife Helen and their five children. Stuart was a conductor on The Canadian, the flagship coast-to-coast passenger train of the Canadian Pacific Railway—all tricked out with fancy glassed-in double decker observation cars. Helen, as was the norm in those days, did not work outside the home. But next door, on the same parcel of land, Grampa and Gramma Glover built, and lived in, a preposterous little structure consisting of a kitchen and a second room that was a sitting room during the day, and a bedroom at night with foldout beds. It had no running water, but rather a pump in the kitchen that drew water straight from a well. No toilet. No bath. Outhouse in the back. Inexplicable, really.

The children, my mother Mildred, Uncle Stuart and Uncle Jack were all very bright and neurotic in differing degrees. My mother, known by all as "Momma Mill," was a profound worrier, especially when it came to her boys. She had suffered a bad bout of postpartum crazies after I was born, and had to put all the knives, scissors and sharp objects in cold water for fear that she'd awake and come to kill me. That later morphed into a form of fierce overprotectiveness, that I often used to tease her about, by calling it Smother Love. Jack, the youngest, had been in the merchant Marines in World War II and had been torpedoed. He suffered a head injury and carried a metal plate in his skull that tortured him with unremitting pain all of his life. He married Marcia, a French-Canadian nurse, and they produced a brood of four girls. No one ever said it blatantly, but the marrying of a French Catholic pretty much sealed Jack's fate. He was the youngest and might reasonably have been favored, but this fouling of the Anglo-Protestant nest was too much for his parents. For the last several years of his life, Jack couldn't work because of the pain. He received some kind of veteran's pension, but Marcia worked full-time as a nurse and kept the family afloat. Jack had endless treatments at Sunnybrook Hospital in Toronto, at that time the place where veterans were sent, including, finally, severing the nerves that were thought to be the cause of his pain. He ultimately took his own life with a shotgun to the head on the back porch, where the girls found him as they came home from school. He obviously intended that they would find him along with several pathetic notes scattered about the house describing what bills were due and how to pay them.

Stuart played snare drum and bass drum. I think he must have picked the idea up from my dad, who of course had married Stuart's sister and who was involved in what pipe band activity there was in Sudbury. Uncle Stu, a really smart guy who could recite *Omar Khayyam* front to back, had a wicked and often caustic wit, and was fond of me. I was very close to him and I tried to emulate his repartee, a trait that annoyed both my dad—because that was not a strength of his— and my mom, who felt Stuart and I were excluding dad. I believe this was all true and I wish now it had been different.

Anyhow, the upshot was my dad and Uncle Stuart enlisted during World War II, became a part of the Royal Canadian Air Force and were stationed in Glace Bay, Nova Scotia, where my dad became the pipe-major of the first RCAF pipe band in Canada. Since I was born in 1942, one may conclude that a furlough from military duty provided the opportunity to bring me onto the scene. I don't know much about the "activities" in Nova Scotia but I do know my uncle was colorfully and perhaps enviously referred to as the "Station Goat."

So there I was, with, on one side, my mother's family: depressed Gramma Glover, milquetoasty Grampa Glover, their three very bright and in varying degrees neurotic offspring-—Mom, Uncle Stuart and Uncle Jack. And on the other side, my Dad's family—the rather louche Grampa John, Goagie, my other Gramma, Dad and Uncle John Livingstone, the Copper Cliff cop. All of them were migrants from Scotland, making their fairly successful way in Copper Cliff.

When I was about seven, Goagie took the short walk from 18 Orford Street, where she and Grampa John lived together with my cousin Donald MacLennan, for an evening visit with me, my brother Ranald and my mom at 11 Evans Road. She was a very large woman, and on that night tears—actually not so much tears as great fountains of water—fell from her eyes. She eventually got up to leave and walk the five minutes home to 18 Orford Street. She was dead in the morning, and I have a cloudy recollection of her playing with me that last night.

This set off a chain of events that would change us all forever. First, Grampa John and Goagie had somehow parlayed their unique Scottish identities into a special status in the town. Goagie was a Gaelic speaker from the Isle of Mull, and Grampa John was a brazen and shameless "professional Scot". He wore the kilt on any occasion which could conceivably justify it, and always wore a Balmoral on his head, whether in the kilt or in civilian clothes. By some social alchemy this led to Grampa John and Goagie acquiring one of the rare privately owned homes in Copper Cliff. Remember that Inco owned everything, including the houses, yet here were Grampa John and Goagie with their own privately owned dwelling. The land was still admittedly owned by Inco, but the house itself was theirs. In later life this arrangement has me thinking it was so like the "chattel houses" that are such a feature of life in Barbados. Chattels, in the same sense that a chest of drawers or a bed is chattel, that is, movable property, and unlike land that is immovable property. At the same time, however, these chattel houses operate as houses or, more fundamentally, homes.

In any event I cannot guess how this happened, but I do know that 18 Orford Street was a house cobbled together from two of the small, simple "kitchen, living room and two-bedroom" tiny houses, and 18 Orford looked a bit odd. You could see the join where the two former houses met. Still, here was a house with a large kitchen, dining room, huge living room, fireplace no less, three bedrooms and an add-on "sun porch." The sun porch featured full glass wooden framed windows facing south.

There was a wood/coal burning Findlay stove in the kitchen for heat and cooking, and oil burners throughout the place to deal with the wicked cold winters. It seemed luxurious to us then, but truth be told, it was long johns draped over the oil burners in the winter mornings, waiting for the one-piece garment, buttons down the front and a "trap door" at the back, to be tolerable to human skin, and as soon as they were pulled on, a scramble back to bed. Bank the coal fire in the kitchen every night and remove the clinkers in the morning (clinkers were chunks that wouldn't burn), head out to the coal shed, load the coal scuttle to refresh the fire, and bring it into the house dragging coal dust with it, and carry cans of kerosene into the house to refill the oil burners. You know that smell of jet fuel in modern airports? That's kerosene. And pour that indoors into an oil burner and see how nice it all smells, especially when you inadvertently splash around the funnel: pour in raw kerosene, light the fire and behold in your own home the exhaust from a 767. This situation led to a simple routine: arise to a house at about 5 to 10°C, heat it to about 20°C in no time, and fill the air with bad-for-you crap. But so what? It was like that everywhere in that part of the world. You'd try to keep some moisture in the air with pots of water on all of these furiously burning heat sources, and stifle the nosebleeds at night and off to bed. Repeat.

Sounds ghastly, doesn't it? It was not. We didn't even sense we were poor. We had food to die for. The cupboard, thanks to Mildred's amazing prowess, was filled always with at least two pies, pumpkin, apple, cherry. Cookies, date squares, raisin squares, homemade bread. And this is not even to mention the frequent appearance of steak and kidney pie (O Jesus, golden flaked pastry crust broken open to allow the fabulous liquid of the filling to escape and go candied and crunchy on the top!) or even simple mincemeat pie—not the North American "raisins/currant" dessert pie, but more like a cross between the Scots meat pie and a Québecois tortiere. And, oh my God, potato scones— tattie scones, pan fried in triangular shapes, slathered while hot with butter, rolled and eaten with strong cheese, the melted butter squishing out the ends.

So now with Goagie gone, here was the new living arrangement. Grampa John had us come to live with him at 18 Orford Street. His domain became the aforementioned sun porch. Ranald and I shared the adjacent room, a small bedroom, with bunk beds still intact from Evans Road. My parents occupied the middle bedroom and my cousin, Donald MacLennan, was in the third bedroom. Donald you may recall was the son of Jim MacLennan and my dad's sister Betty, who died giving birth to him. Needing a mother and proper home, Goagie and Grampa John took him in and raised him.

A fair struggle, you might imagine, with six people contending for the one bathroom in the house, not to mention the frayed nerves and contentions over small bones that can, and will with perfect predictability, erupt when Mom and Dad and their two sons live under the roof of Dad's father, with a cousin thrown in just for good measure.

I don't know what the quid pro quo was. I do know that the rent paid to Inco for the privilege of occupying this scrap of real estate was very modest. The rent was for the land only – recall that all they owned was the house itself. So I imagine that my parents paid the rent to Inco and covered the cost of heating, electricity and so on, and Grampa John was fed and watered by my mother. In return we got a bigger and better house, some kind of cachet (remember the professional Scot, John Livingstone) and Grampa John had his needs looked after now that Goagie was gone.

Grampa John was an amazing piece of work: crafty, smart, devious, charming, eloquent and mean to the bone.

This man taught himself to read. He was able to discern the difference between consonants and vowels and went on from there to discover the secret of written English. He became the janitor and caretaker of the Copper Cliff high school and toiled at that job for many years. He brought home supplies of those coarse beige paper towels, soap and other toilet-friendly articles. I didn't twig at the time, but fairly clearly he must have been purloining these items from the school.

After Goagie died, he launched into a relationship with one Miss Lottie Snaith. Could Dickens have come up with a more intriguing, even threatening name? His routine settled into ritualistic and obsessive ablutions on Thursday mornings with bathing, shaving, applications of cologne, and then into the double-breasted grey wool suit. He took the noon hour bus to Sudbury, where he went to Miss Snaith's home, not returning until late Sunday evening. We were never entirely sure of what happened on these extended weekends, but as often as not he returned to Orford Street in a belligerent state of high intoxication.

On more than one of these horrific occasions he baited my father to come out and have "two minutes in the snow and will see who's the better man around here." He would even smack my dad, who always resisted the surely overwhelming temptation to drop the mean little bastard in his tracks. And my dad was not normally a shrinking violet if pugilism was in the air.

When he could not excoriate my dad anymore, he would stand on the step at the threshold of the kitchen where the junction with the dining room was located. I so clearly recall him torturing my mother into near insensibility standing on that step, and pronouncing that "the Glover family motto is emblazoned over every one of their doors: Greed and Avarice Live Here." He once topped this with the taunt that she should "take your fat greasy weans and disappear." This was almost more than she could take, fierce and proud mama bear that she was, and she lifted a pot of boiling water from the stove and focused her now white-faced black-eyed mad gaze on him, her arm back and prepared to let him wear it in the face.

The crafty old bastard never blinked, and instead jutted out his jaw and said quietly to her, "Bow wow." This was a universal insult of his, a remark of complete disdain and disrespect meaning, "You're all bark and no bite." She, trembling, put the pot down. He knew she would. I thought she'd let him have it. If she had, she'd surely have gone to jail. I was scared witless.

Grampa John's trip from Copper Cliff to Lottie Snaith's home each weekend was a four mile trip to the bus terminal in Sudbury. He'd trudge from Orford Street to the stop near the Copper Cliff Dairy, and return home the same way. The trip involved travelling a stretch of Highway 17.

Highway 17, the TransCanada Highway, runs between Sudbury and Copper Cliff. There is a bleak stretch, about two miles long, without habitation or lights. The only light that comes there happens when the slag is poured on the northeast side of the road, and some red-colored brimstone tumbles down the cliffs. The exception to this blackness was the De Luxe Drive-In, home of the best burgers and hot dogs in the entire universe. It was only a small drive-in joint but it cast enough light to startle and waken a drunken bus passenger, boozed out after four days in the company of the mysterious Lottie Snaith.

As the Sudbury to Copper Cliff bus passed the Deluxe, Grampa John thought he was home and demanded to be let off. Sadly there were still some two miles of dark highway before the bus would reach Copper Cliff. Grampa John began to cross the highway, murkily thinking he was at the dairy at the intersection of Balsam Street and Evans Road, his usual stop. He was smacked by a west-bound car hightailing it to Espanola, Sault Ste. Marie, or perhaps the unfortunately named, but quite close by, village of Sinnottville. Grampa was well and truly crunched, with broken ribs, internal injuries and cuts, scrapes and bruises.

Now in these days the ambulance service was run by the Jackson and Barnard Funeral Home in Sudbury. The emergency vehicle was duly dispatched to the scene of the carnage, and Grandpa opened his eyes to see the gaunt and sepulchral face of Ray Barnard, funeral director, hovering over him. With the healing power of a yellow card in soccer, that funereal face jumpstarted Grampa into action with a firm command to poor Ray: "Keep your hawns off me, you bloody ghoul!"

It's an enriching and illuminating experience to grow up surrounded by such a cast of neurasthenic and fairly mad people. Eventually we, Mom, Dad, Ranald and I, settled into a "fairly normal" family routine. Throughout my primary school years, nothing was terribly amiss in my own life, until puberty hit, about which, more later. My Dad worked at Inco, became a shift boss, and gradually was able to get off shift work, surely the most soul-destroying and enervating routine imaginable. "Steady Days" was the term to describe the new schedule, and it deserves to be capitalized, for the change it brought about in my father and the rest of the family was pronounced. He worked five days a week from eight a.m. to five p.m., was home at a regular hour, and actually spent much more time with us. We ate dinner as a family and no longer had any need to tip toe around the house all day, while Dad tried to sleep so he could work the midnight shift. The poor bugger would frequently roar out from the bedroom, "Less noise!" even though the house was as quiet as the tombs of the Pharaohs. Circadian rhythms completely destroyed by waking and sleeping at all the wrong times, made the act of sleep impossible, from being too tired to fall asleep to then, after finally drifting off, being jolted awake by a dream, a muscle twitch or some imagined noise.

Mom prepared meals for everyone, although Grampa John rarely ate with the four of us. My mother would plate his breakfast, lunch and dinner and take it his room, which was formerly the sun porch. I think in retrospect that this was done by agreement amongst the adults, and was intended to preserve some semblance of normalcy for my family even though we were living in Grampa's house.

4

Learning

The actual business of learning the bagpipe happened almost entirely at 18 Orford Street.

There is so much I can't remember and so much that I wish I could. I do recall many sessions with my dad at the dining room table, practice chanters in hand, and going through the Willie Ross collection, with all five volumes pretty much covered over the years. I just can't call up the details. My dad taught me to sight read, and while I was okay at it I was still one of those from that era who wanted to have the thing played over first, and then the sight reading followed.

My dad was taught piping in Ayrshire by a man named Davy Hendrie. He was not merely a good piper, but was said to have had a degree as a Master of Music. Gordon Walker is one of the greatest pipers of the past few decades, hands turning out technique like machine gun bullets. If you've never seen him in action, he's a true showman, a dandy on the boards with a sartorial style equal to that of the great John D. Burgess, and has a celebrated wit and sense of great fun. He's also a native of Kilmarnock in Ayrshire, my dad's home country. Gordon and I share more than just a connection to Ayrshire and Kilmarnock. It turns out that his teacher, David Kay, was also taught by Davy Hendrie. Anyhow, during these early years I think that I actually took to piping quite naturally and readily, and I do know that I liked it a lot.

In northern Ontario, there were few opportunities for piping competition, which is of course the primary impetus for most pipers to get better. If I have this right, I believe I had only four competitions up to the age of seventeen. The first was at the Sudbury Indoor Games, where I won some prizes in the appropriate age categories as the system was then structured. My parents also took me to southern Ontario, where I competed at Fergus and Maxville and won prizes in the under-18 light music. My mother was so chuffed at my first prize in the Strathspey & Reel at Fergus that she tore headlong down the grassy tree-lined slope of the games park, hooting and cheering, when my name was announced.

But the real game changer came at the Sault Ste. Marie Highland Games. "The Soo," as it still called, is a twin city straddling the border between the U.S. and Canada across the St. Mary's River. It is called Sault Ste. Marie on both sides of the border. My father was the Pipe Major of the Copper Cliff Highlanders Pipe Band. It was associated with the Cadet Corps of the same name, and Dad taught many, if not most, of the pipers in the band, including of course me and my brother Ranald. He produced several very good young pipers in this band, only to have it later stolen away from him, a story I set out in more detail later on. My uncle Stuart was the leading drummer.

My dad had arranged for the band to travel to the Soo by train to compete at the games. (Maybe Uncle Stuart and Grampa Glover had something to do with that by reason of their CPR connections.) I was a piper in the band, and this train trip was an amazing adventure for a kid of thirteen or so, especially with the Georgetown Ladies Pipe Band on board. They were also headed to the games at the Soo, and their band was filled with girls more or less the same age as many of us boys in the Copper Cliff Highlanders. It was a splendid opportunity for some pretty sappy teenaged flirting and romance, the kids completing the scene with all the dreadful pubescent baggage of that time of life. This train carried a corpse in a coffin loaded into the baggage car, headed to its final destination somewhere in Northwest Ontario. The coffin served as a drinks table and a resting place for the bottoms of the grievously disrespectful band members. But the real payoff for me in terms of becoming a good piper was competing for John Wilson, Edinburgh, who was judging almost everything at the Soo games.

John Wilson was the famous piper who had become extremely good as a young boy, but who at age thirteen or fourteen blew some fingers off while playing with an unexploded blasting cap. This happened in 1918, while World War I dragged on year after year, and during that period he had collected some bits of stuff and ordnance from Arthur's Seat in Edinburgh, where troops had been training in the use of grenades. He held one of these things over the open fire in the kitchen range and a terrific explosion tore through the house. He lost the index and middle fingers of his left hand down to the second knuckle, and his left thumb down to the first knuckle. He recovered. He persevered. He became one of the greatest bagpipe technicians I have ever heard, with the ring finger (the E finger) of his left hand, still intact, draped over the chanter along with the pinkie and the remaining three stumps fingering F, High G and High A. And not just a great technician, but one of the most successful pipers of the 1920s and 30s, winning virtually every prize there is while competing against the likes of Robert Reid, Malcolm McPherson, G. S. MacLennan, J. B. Robertson, the Bobs of Balmoral, and other historic luminaries.

After the games were over, as always seems to happen following a piping event, a ceilidh in the Sergeants' Mess in the Armoury broke out. The adults were drinking, there was the usual banter and songs, a few tunes on the pipes, and then I was corralled to play. Like any thirteen-year-old kid, I had no fear of playing in front of anyone, so I simply got up and rattled off, like kids today still do, a bunch of jigs and fast stuff—modern hornpipes didn't then exist. I can still see John Wilson sitting at a table with friends, a beer in hand, watching me with a smile on his face. What I later learned was that John then approached my dad and told him he could "make something out of me."

5

To Toronto and Child Services Be Damned

There followed some very interesting and clandestine planning in which I had no involvement. On my dad's part, I'd guess there was some scheming, since the object was to get me to Toronto, 240 miles from home, and away from a frantically neurotic and overprotective mother, where I could be taught bagpipes by the great John Wilson, living for all intents and purposes on my own. My mother came by her neurotic temperament honestly, and likely through her own mother. She was frightened for me in any and all situations. Home from school late, I'd meet her on the road looking for me. Any illness, injury or even a slight cold caused a fearful reaction in her, which was identifiable by her rapid blinking, and my immediate trip to a doctor in her company. I can still recall her face in these moments. No wonder I blossomed into a fully blown hypochondriac in my own right.

My dad had an old pal, Peter Finlayson, who was a piper and who had played with the RCAF pipe band during the war many years before in Nova Scotia. He was a Scot, and by my dad's lights one of the finest march players he had ever heard. I was very young, but I remember thinking when I heard him play that dad's assessment was right—he was damn good.

Peter led the way for me. He lived in Toronto and was a member of the Earlscourt Legion Pipe Band. He arranged for me to live with a couple, fossils to me at the time, but likely younger than my current age, called George and Lizzie Blye.

Lizzie Blye—another name worthy of Dickens. George hung around the Earlscourt band, but not as a player. His interest lay in setting up and maintaining bagpipes. He was clever that way, and did away with all of the hemping of joints by lining the tuning pins within layers of cork, which he artfully applied with glue. These joints remained usable for years.

My routine became to practice with Earlscourt one night a week, and then practice with the 48th Highlanders Pipe Band another night a week. I have no idea how I got sent to the 48th or who arranged it, but I know that the great Canadian piper Reay Mackay was there, and the pipe-major was the preternaturally crabby Archie Dewar. This was the classic regimental pipe band, with a massive repertoire of two parted marches, which would be played in a big room, while marching in a circle around the drummers. It made for a god-awful cacophony, and to me, even at that age, represented something antediluvian.

Saturdays were devoted to lessons with John Wilson. These were group lessons, and I see now that this was the most efficient way for John to add a boost the income he earned as a commissionaire at a bank in downtown Toronto. One hour with six pupils was more rewarding than six hours one at a time. But it was okay. I was a pretty good sponge, and in the short time I was with him then I learned "Sir James MacDonald of the Isles' Lament" and "The Bells of Perth," and got started on "The Big Spree" before the long arm of my mother dragged me home.

It's really an amazing story when you consider it. Here was a fourteen-year-old boy just out of grade school, who had hardly ever been away from home, entering his first year of high school and shipped off to live in the largest city in the country, with people his parents didn't know. In today's world of do-gooder-ism and state intervention, I likely would have been apprehended by the Children's Aid Society and placed in foster care, while some twenty-five-year-old recent graduate with no life experience poked around our family members to determine if I could be safely returned home.

I know much about these green and hopeless social workers. I was one of them. I had a job for a while at the Children's Aid Society in Sudbury as a "protection worker." I was assigned to arbitrate on the ability of parents to provide care for their children. Some of these parents were younger or hardly any older than I was, and some were very much older. Either way it was horrible. All of twenty-two, with no kids of my own, a BA in psychology, and no real-life experience, I was meddling in the lives of people, most of whom seemed generally to me to be mired in poverty and hopelessness. So as a protection worker I'd visit the home of some hapless family, usually as a result of a complaint made by a neighbour to an intake worker, report my findings to my supervisor, a gay man—and while today that would likely mean nothing, recall this was some fifty years ago when the closet doors remained firmly shut. So a kid with no children and no life experience gets together with an older gay man with no children or even experience of them, and grabs the kid or kids from the home. Then off to court to give evidence to a judge who would rule on the propriety of the actions taken. I can't recall losing such an application.

Back to my Toronto adventure. George and Lizzie Blye lived at 1520 Dupont Street, a neighborhood of two-story brown brick homes. It's in the central west area of downtown Toronto. I was enrolled in Western Tech and Commerce, which required me to take the Annette Street streetcar. I have no recollection of the instructions I was given in order to get on the streetcar, where to get off, and how to get to the school after that. All I remember clearly is a sick feeling of fear in my gut every time I took that car and went to that school.

It was, and I gather still is, a tough school. Consider if you will: one of my classmates was a boy called Geekie. He was a good-looking kid. However his special trick was to spit on the back of the teacher's suit jacket as he walked up and down between the rows of desks. Nice. And he was not the worst. Not even close.

I had arrived in Toronto near the end of August to get settled in my new living arrangements, get enrolled in school, join the 48th Highlanders Pipe Band and get started with John Wilson's group piping classes at the University Avenue Armouries. It all came to a halt late that fall. My parents had come down to visit and obviously to check on me in the surroundings of the Blye home, and observe the tender ministrations of Lizzie. Mrs. Blye was preparing dinner for all of us, and it seems she found her way rather fulsomely into the cooking sherry. She had a gas stove and oven, and she was preparing to put the final touches on the culinary masterpiece. She seems to have turned on the gas for the oven, and seeing that she had been a little slow to light it, she grabbed some newspaper, lit it aflame, and approached the oven with wobbly care, flaming newspaper extended, and the oven lit with a heart-stopping WOMPH. I was back in Copper Cliff in days.

And thus ended the second stage of my learning the pipes. My dad had been my only teacher until John Wilson, and I had then only two to three months with him. But I was lucky, because I had started so young and played so much that the skills were laid down on the hard drive, which was to be my salvation later.

6

Changes

Now I'm fourteen and puberty is upon me—and with a vengeance. Until this time, I was a pretty regular and unexceptional kid, apart from the bagpipes thing and that indeed set me somewhat apart. But this change in me was unbearable. Apart from the usual urges and yearnings that testosterone brings, I was at this point besieged by anxiety, fear, depression, sadness, feelings of hopelessness, and profound and debilitating hypochondria. I died repeatedly of brain tumors, leukemia, throat cancer, bowel cancer, tuberculosis, heart disorders, and any disease mentioned on radio or TV.

I found myself frequently weeping uncontrollably for my lost young life, and was overcome with self-pity. I was a frequent visitor to the Copper Cliff Hospital, the only one in town, where I was checked out and assessed for these myriad non-existent illnesses. I soon had a profile there, and to give them their due they were pretty sympathetic, because this was not remotely normal behavior, and I was obviously troubled. But all patience can and in this case did finally run out.

And while I'm confessing, I might as well make a clean breast of it. I believe that the illness, as I later learned to accept it, was triggered at the time of, or perhaps even by, puberty. Not only were my hormones a torment, but my brain chemistry went off the rails. This crazy disorder finally led me into the hands of a wonderful doctor, a psychiatrist, whose patient I became at about age twenty-four and who treated me for upwards of thirty years. He used classical talk therapy, Freudian and Jungian principles, and relaxation therapy. This last involved lying in a darkened room with the gentle recorded voice of a therapist trying to persuade me to start with my toes and work north, willing each successive body part to become too heavy to support, and imagining it becoming so heavy one could feel it falling through the gurney.

This of course was doomed to failure for a couple of reasons. One—and this alone would have cinched it—place a raging hypochondriac in a darkened quiet room, and within minutes this subject will focus on his heartbeat. The shrinks call this pathological heart consciousness, and I have to hand it them—they're right. The single-minded attention to your heartbeat can, and usually does, lead to escalating anxiety, fear and certainty of an impending heart attack, with the real and actual heart rate rocketing into the mid-120 bpm range. Not much hope of relaxing in that situation.

But add to that the fact that the therapist spoke in an exaggerated Peter Sellers Indian accent, so that when I wasn't dying of a racing heart I was giggling at the accent that Sellers so brutally and funnily mocked, leaving an indelible imprint on my mind and memory. (Younger readers may not get this reference—it's from a great movie called *The Party*. For those folks I refer you to Russell Peters' brutal imitation of his own Indian dad's voice: "Somebody gonna get a-hurt real bad."

I survived on every anxiolytic know to medicine at the time: Valium, Librium, Xanax, Ativan, sublingual Ativan, clonazepam and chloral hydrate. I'd guess that I didn't sleep properly for upwards of twenty or so years. But then medicine changed or caught up, and what I had suffered with for years now came with a diagnosis and treatment, whereas until that time, the general feeling and theory—one that I myself shared—had been, "What the hell's wrong with you? You've got everything—you're a lawyer, you have a beautiful and wonderful wife, you have this hobby—no this avocation, well really this parallel career in piping—and you're sad?" Damn right—and ask anyone who has suffered with it. You can't reason yourself around this, or pull yourself up by your own bootstraps, or just get out there and conquer this thing.

When you spend many hours curled into the fetal position, no amount of self-motivation will do the trick.

So ultimately I was diagnosed by my shrink with clinical depression, or mood disorder, or affective disorder. All the same thing. It's caused by an imbalance in the brain, the culprit being a substance called serotonin. When you lose the right supply of the stuff, the bits in your brain that are supposed to talk to each other stop doing so, or do so ineffectively. Presto—the shit hits the fan.

Once the diagnosis was made, then the process of finding the right medication started. In my case I was started on Sinequan. The effect was to clobber me into stupefaction—yes, I slept for the first time in weeks, but I could barely focus during the day. This is often a problem for depression sufferers. There can be a long and frustrating search for the right medicine for each patient. These drugs are called serotonin reuptake inhibitors—SSRIs—kind of a self-explanatory term. They prevent the brain from gobbling up the stuff, and help it to either produce more of it, or leave what's there alone, with an improved patient as the result.

The problem is exacerbated by the fact that the full effect of the various drugs is not obvious for sometimes weeks. Meanwhile, as the experimentation with the different drugs goes on, one can vibrate like a tuning fork, shake like a Parkinson's patient, suffer diarrhea like a victim of some E. coli infected water, or on the contrary get as bunged up as someone who lives on cheese alone.

One may well ask, how did you get out of law school, keep a job as a practicing lawyer, or keep this bagpipe thing going? There are likely a couple of answers. First, it is not particularly unusual for one who suffers depression to be a high-functioning person. The default defensive position of a depressive is to put on a happy front: nothing wrong with me, just have a look. But most importantly, this battle is not just mine. This is also Lily's—my incredible, beautiful, smart, supportive and intuitive wife of forty-nine years, at this writing. Loves me without reservation, helps me at every turn, won't tolerate bullshit, supports and actually pushes me into all that I do. I am truly blessed (here is an atheist mouthing the overtones of religiosity, but indulge me here). It reminds me of some wag's wisecrack that behind every successful man stands a surprised-looking woman.

The plain truth is that it's hard to find a simple answer. There are plenty of examples of high-functioning depressives, but I was not always one of those. Dysfunctional would best describe my general performance in many aspects of my life. I practiced in a small firm where my partners were incredible—when I couldn't carry my weight they carried it for me. Had I worked in a big firm in Toronto I wouldn't have lasted two months. To bring this topic to full circle—since I have been diagnosed and appropriately treated with the correct medications, my life has changed. That awful torment, fear, self-pity, anxiety and hypochondria is so much better. I have no embarrassment about this. I have never concealed this aspect of my life, but neither have I taken out billboard ads to trumpet my situation.

I'm glad that by some combination of luck and serendipity, I got better. Maybe there is someone reading this who will see that there is a way out. Trust me, to live like that is God-awful. I say, if drugs make me better, and they do, then bring them on.

It takes many depressives years to realize that they are victims of chemicals at war, and not just lazy-ass wimps unable to get on with it.

None of this is to say that finding the drug, the magic bullet, was the whole story. That was preceded by years of psychotherapy or psychoanalysis, most of it going on while I was trying to complete law school, the bar admission course, finding and keeping an articling position with a law firm and striking out on my own with my law school classmate as a partner, in the hope of making a living as a lawyer. This process is not for everyone, and judging by my experience, not for most people. It requires an individual who has come face-to-face with a debilitating, nearly crippling mental or emotional condition. It's hard, tedious, emotionally painful, and very slow indeed and in my case my resistance was pretty dramatic. The process was I talk, and talk and talk, and he listens. And sometimes the talk is so embarrassingly narcissistic that listening to yourself is just too much. And then there are periods of freeze-ups—no words can come, and you withdraw into your protective carapace and say nothing for a long time—20 minutes, half an hour—and the longer it lasts the more difficult it is to break it. And meanwhile your shrink sits silent and patient, staring at you, and waiting you out. And often it seems meaningless. Who cares about all of my secret phobias, torments, needs and peccadilloes?

The resistance takes other forms, too: showing up repeatedly late with the periods of lateness gradually getting worse. Finally the threat to bill me, not the government health plan, for the time dedicated to my appointment but not actually used. Over time I begin to get this guy. I talk. He listens. "Anything you'd like to tell you about that?" How did you feel about that?" "What did you do about that?" "How do you feel about that now?" "What do you think you were trying to say with that behaviour?"

My shrink finally revealed himself to be of Eastern European Jewish descent, with a raucous and bawdy sense of humor, and with warmth and compassion coming from him in obvious waves. He became my friend and will be so forever. After I no longer needed him I still saw him all the time, because we made each other laugh, shared our personal stories of financial adventure, pets, families, movies, politics. He knows more about me than anyone and, as hard as it all was, he saved my life.

This long and I hope not-too-lugubrious digression started as a description of the wheels coming off in my teens. And as if all of that chaos wasn't enough, I fell in love with rock and roll.

7

The Coppertones

Eighteen Orford Street was a hive of music, much of it Scottish music. Besides the pipes in the house, my parents had a wide circle of friends who played, sang and danced. There was a lady by the name of Della LeCouer who played a thumping East Coast down-home style of piano. With her was her "close friend," Alec Penner, a barber in Sudbury who played fiddle. We had Robin and Bonnie Swain, she a local TV "celebrity" for her cooking show. She sported a powerful soprano, singing romantic poignant songs from the Burns repertoire, accompanied by my mother on piano, playing from sheet music in a rather refined style, so unlike the powerful rhythmic thumping given the keys by the above-noted Della LeCouer. Bonnie and my brother Ranald, with his booming, quasi-operatic voice, would sing duets and occasionally Sam Laderoute, bad piper and saboteur of my dad's leadership of the Copper Cliff Highlanders Pipe Band, would engage in Ottawa Valley style step-dancing. We also had a man named Tom Graham who'd descend from the frozen tundra near Timmins, Ontario, and play a quite sophisticated violin.

And these gatherings happened frequently. They were of course true ceilidhs, and I have often thought of them as I ponder the interesting business of how people who have left their homeland seem to cherish their culture more than many who remain home.

All of this musical carry-on demanded a piano in the house. One arrived, and it must have been a serious financial step for my dad. But there it was. From the moment it arrived I couldn't leave it alone. First thing early in the morning, I'd sneak into the piano room, close the door and start tinkling away as quietly as I could. Mom decided lessons were in order, so I was sent to Mrs. Beatty. This mental giant sent me home after a few months, complaining that I was unteachable. Seems her objection was that I wouldn't play the pieces in the right key. I'd learn them by ear and then transpose them, unwittingly, to whatever key struck me, a sign apparently of a serious lack of talent. Right. So it fell to me to teach myself. As I felt my way around the keys, getting an intuitive understanding of harmony in my own unorthodox and crazy fingering of the keyboard, a dim possibility of making music on this device appeared.

Soon we had a record player in the house. By today's measure, with electronic devices of every kind abounding, this was the equivalent of a steam-driven machine for listening to recorded music. It played only vinyl records about the diameter of a small round pizza and the thickness of a millimeter or so, rather like a black plastic platter, and that was the word by which they were known. This record player was encased in an elegant mahogany wooden box, and it was built to play records at 78 RPM. One song at a time, and one song per side—the A side the hoped-for hit, and the B side a kind of throwaway, but which often surprised the record execs by eclipsing the A side.

My self-education on the piano began in about 1955, when I got hold of records by the amazing Little Richard singing "Tutti-Frutti" and "Long Tall Sally." Little Richard was a wonderful madman— heavily made up, he was the first flamboyant gay performer (which in those days no one said aloud), a bluesy rock 'n roll piano man, right leg draped over the keys while pounding out the most compelling, barbaric rhythm imaginable, with his powerful voice which could lapse into falsetto or scream with equal vigor. The titillating suggestiveness of the lyrics made for wonderful fun for me, but earned a very sour Presbyterian scowl from my mother.

Long Tall Sally she
Built for speed she got

Ev'a thing that Uncle John need
Oh baby, yeah-a-ah baby
Yeah-a-ah baby
Gonna have some fun tonight
Saw Uncle John with
Long Tall Sally
He saw Aunt Mary comin'
And he ducked back in the alley
Oh baby, etc.

This amazing allusion to heated heterosexual goings on, all coming from a guy who was both a preacher and a gay man, in 1955—it was too delicious.

He followed with "Lucille" and "Jenny Jenny," pounding the chords out in hammer blows of 16th notes. I was hooked.

My tastes, while never straying too far from rock, did finally metamorphose when I first heard Ray Charles on the radio in Ottawa one summer afternoon. I was playing in that city with the Campbell Pipe Band, whose pipe-major was my brother Ranald, then living in Ottawa . That song was released in 1959, so I would have been 17. What I heard rocked me to the core: Ray Charles's incredible electric piano playing—jazz-infused, but still down home bluesy and rocking—his phenomenal voice and phrasing, and the startling "call and answer" effect of the traded "hey-hey-hey" between Ray and the Raelettes.

I went in search of an electric piano and found one in Sudbury, no less, with exactly the same tone as Ray's—it was produced by keys striking on little vibrating forks, something like what is found in some harmonicas. As time and my rock 'n roll dreams progressed, I began to travel with my Sudbury friends by car to Toronto to hear the incredible music scene in and around the downtown bars. At Le Coq D'or on Yonge Street, a regular feature was Ronnie Hawkins, at best a second-rate rocker guy from Fayetteville, Arkansas, but, oh my, his band! Then called the Hawks, they would later take the world by storm as The Band. Four brilliant Canadians: Robbie Robertson on guitar, Garth Hudso, on organ and piano, Richard Manuel, piano and vocals, Rick

Danko, bass and vocals, plus the incredible Levon Helm on drums, he from Arkansas.

Some of the best stuff was played at the Saturday afternoon jam sessions. The Hawks would jam with other musicians in and around the Toronto scene, and there were some amazing moments: take a picture of David Clayton Thomas, later of Blood, Sweat and Tears, belting out blues with his incredible horn of a voice, sounding like Jimmy Rushing from a bygone area.

And Richard Manuel channeling the voice and styles of Bobby Blue Bland and Ray Charles, with the band backing him so beautifully.

I was sold and gobsmacked and wanted desperately to play this stuff—all of it. I didn't cotton onto the Beatles as a style I could even approach. I especially was not taken by the Rolling Stones, who didn't seem much better than my own band. It was blues, rock and rockabilly for me, but not as the Stones cribbed it. I tried to get to the source stuff and be true to that.

In my teens I had a group. You often hear the expression he "formed" a group, but I don't recall any such deliberate planning. I just met and played with various musicians in town. The group went through several iterations but eventually settled into Gene Dubreuil on guitar, Claude Demers on bass, me on keys and vocals, and the improbably named Vicki Vairo on drums. We played high school dances—"hops"— and later bars and clubs around Sudbury, and a young person's dance every Sunday night at the Caruso Club. Because the group started out in Copper Cliff, we were called The Coppertones. Silly sounding now, but not in those times when bands were called anything—the Aces, the Spades, the Diamonds, the Ascots, the Rhythm Kings, the Capers and so on.

We played and played. We practiced, we rehearsed constantly and we got first comfortable on our instruments and then good. Everyone knows the aphorism that posits that in order to truly master a skill it takes 10,000 hours of practice. The Coppertones didn't reach that level, but we played a hell of a lot—likely an hour a day three days a week, gigs Friday and Saturday at three hours each, all of which led to some thousands of hours of practice.

So, as I have said, the Coppertones practiced and played a lot—but nowhere near the hours that I devoted to the bagpipe. And my relative skills on the pipe and the piano reflect that, but what the hell, what a time we had. I began writing songs and we played them. These were not the greatest, but not the worst either. They had the feel of stuff like "Hang On Sloopy" and Little Richard's pounding. So violent was my playing that I often had the hammers flying right out of the upright pianos I usually had to play at these various venues. The front panel of the sound box would be removed, to permit a microphone to be dropped in or a contact mic attached to the sounding board, and more than once a hammer flew by my ear. Somehow a local radio station got wind of us, and they began to record us in their studio and play us on air.

Remember my first record player. As I played along with the records of my heroes, I of course duplicated the keys they played in—or more accurately, that I *perceived* they played in. It turned out, however, that the turntable did not turn at exactly 78 RPM—rather just a bit less, with the result that the pitch of the recording was slightly flat, so that E, A and D were in fact E-flat, A-flat and D-flat on my piano. I learned to play in E-flat, D-flat (or C-sharp), B-flat and all of the black keys, which I later discovered were the harder ones. It was not until later that I learned to play in F, C and G, and I never did get comfortable in E and A.

The graduation to other keys came about as I started to try to mimic other piano players, now using a much better record player, and now tackling more challenging stuff, like "Stormy Monday Blues," the classic slow blues tune, and, even crazier, Dave Brubeck's "Blue Rondo à la Turk." It was through this process that I came also to understand the basic wonderful structure of the 12-bar blues—the most versatile, predictable and yet fresh form for hanging a musical story on.

By this stage, the band was getting pretty slick, and we were playing the more sophisticated watering holes around Sudbury, if it's not too much of a stretch to use the adjective sophisticated here. We closed every set with the piano piece, "Cast Your Fate to the Wind," and played a polyglot selection of blues, hard rock, Bo Diddley, Misty, Stardust, funky arrangements of "Hound Dog," more akin to big Mama Thornton's gritty original then Elvis's wimpy rip-off from her, as well as the Beatles' "She Was Just 17," Bobby Bland's "It's an Ill Wind (Share Your Love)" and Gene DuBreuil with the odd country rock vocal.

The US Marines have a motto—"There is no life like it." All I can say is they should try playing bars, clubs and dances in those times, because that experience truly captures the incredible joy and rush of "no life like it." In fact a few months after Lily and I were married and I was just starting law school, Lil and I were in Yorkville, a hotspot for all music in Toronto, when I ran into a sax player I'd met while his band was doing a gig in Sudbury. I had sat in with them and they wanted to fire their piano player right there on the spot. He asked me to go on the road with them. Lil could see my wheels turning and it was obvious that she'd have none of it. And quite right. So goodbye to rock 'n roll and let me be a lawyer instead.

Still, while it lasted it was one of the great fun periods in my life. University during the day and, in the best years, playing in bars five nights a week, with all the fun that could be had doing that, and to my everlasting gratitude, the Caruso Club on Sunday nights.

8

Lily

One Sunday night at the Caruso Club in midsummer 1964, there appeared an incredible girl—long hair to her mid-back, bleached gold by the sun (I later learned) after a month In California visiting her sister. Tiny delicate figure, face to break your heart, and wearing a white-with-blue-polka dots dress encircling her frame with exquisite care, and stopping at a modest mid-knee length.

The band had finished a set and before leaving the stage, I turned to the wonderfully named Vicky Vairo. Now imagine, if you will, a deeply Italian man, swarthy in complexion, no more than 5'5" in height, sporting a voice and accent you'd swear was from New Jersey or Boston despite his northern Ontario roots. Don't ask me how that happens; I think this way of speaking is driven by the DNA in the double helix of the Italian male.

BILL: "Vicky, do you know that girl?"

VICKY: "Yeah, I know dat brawd."

BILL: "Who is she?"

VICKY: "Lillian Chillak—why, you wanna meet 'er?"

BILL: "I have to meet her, man... I'm gonna marry her."

True story.

He introduced us. She shrank from me as if were a snake in the act of moulting. She had seen me in the clubs around town. Didn't like me at all. "What a creep," she thought. "Wise beyond his years, told off-color jokes and a generally horrible guy." These were pretty much the words she used, in answer to the question put to her about how we met by the host of CBC television's *The Fifth Estate*, which did a feature on me called "Pipe Major". Incidentally I garnered some fair notoriety from that show. The Host, Hannah Gartner, was interviewing me at historic Fort York near the lake front in Toronto. We were sitting together on a concrete platfom supporting a cannon, or some such thing, with me holding the pipes. She asked if could play a tune, and I said "Of course" and with that I stood up. She asked, "Do you have to stand up to play it?" Says I "Yes. This not a guitar woman." These were not so much the days of political correctness. Lily's discomfort arose out of some pretty harmless stuff. While running the band on stage I also had to act as a sort of MC, pulling stupid one liners like, "Hey Doc, I haven't been feeling myself lately... Hmm, that's good!"

This is what you had to do in Sudbury if you wanted to work as a band, and did we ever want that.

To add to her image of me as a bit of a slime ball, I was driving a metallic blue Austin Healey convertible with a twin straight pipe exhaust system. It made what I thought was a cool and manly rumbling noise and added to my slick image of myself. Dear God, the follies that can come with being a young man. As we were leaving the Caruso, Vicky picked her up (she was a featherweight) and deposited her in the passenger seat of the Healey, and off we went to the Edelweiss Restaurant, a favorite late-night eatery. It went badly. I was not deterred.

It was only a few days later when we saw each other again. There was a rock show at the Sudbury Arena, a place that seated maybe 3500 people, and Vicki arranged for us to go. Lillian thought it was sort of a "group date" with several of the group attending. She was manifestly disappointed to discover that this was a real date, involving three or four couples, of which Lily and I were to be one. Despite the music of Roy Orbison, the Everley brothers, and a young guy from Ontario with a couple of hits, the atmosphere was frosty.

After the show, we all headed to a local "hotspot," The Silver Beach Inn, located on the shores of Long Lake, and an establishment that offered great chicken and spaghetti (the Italians again), served alcohol, and had a dance floor. As the evening turned chilly, I draped my jacket over Lil's shoulders. This simple gesture opened the door. She suddenly saw me as not such a bad fellow, and we were off.

Lil (as she was then called) was still living at home with her parents and in training as an x-ray technician. She prefers that I say as a little as possible about the trouble with her parents that overtook her, so I will offer only the most condensed and edited version. Her parents took a hellish dislike to me, either because I was neither a Ukrainian nor Catholic, or for some other reason that crazed them; I was never told. They insisted she give me up, and she refused. So she was banished from her home, and continued as an outcast from her family for seven full years. I will never forget her courage and determination as she spent the first few nights away from home, holed up in a room at the Nickel Range Hotel where my band was playing. (For trivia lovers, the Nickel Range was managed by Alex Trebeck's father—he of *Jeopardy!* fame.)

Lil and a friend, also training for x-ray, shared an apartment in Sudbury, and lived a very difficult and poverty-stricken year in that setting. Despite her awful circumstances, she stuck with me, and we conducted the most wonderful romance imaginable.

When I had graduated with my BA from Laurentian University, I had applied both to Osgoode Hall Law School in Toronto, and to Berkeley in California for postgraduate studies in psychology. I was accepted at both but did nothing about it—having too much fun with the band, I guess.

Here are some thoughts about Laurentian in those days. It was a brand-new university, operating on the principle of a Federated School, similar to the University of Toronto, with distinct universities/colleges associated with various religions. I was enrolled in Huntington, which was the United Church-affiliated college. The Anglicans had Thornloe, and the Roman Catholics the University of Sudbury. When Laurentian came into existence in 1960, there was a scramble to find vacant buildings or even small spaces in downtown Sudbury where classes could be conducted. Huntington's home was the building formerly occupied by the Jackson and Barnard funeral home. (Remember Ray Barnard and my busted up grandfather on the side of the road?) The funeral home had moved to elegant quarters elsewhere, and their old building became available.

Lectures were held in what was clearly the chapel where funeral services used to be conducted, and small seminar groups occupied what were once grimly called "viewing rooms." Our combined students' lounge and lunchroom was the former embalming chamber, with marble slabs for the prepping of the deceased, tile floors, and channels in the floor for, we surmised, the draining away of blood and other fluids too revolting to contemplate.

Laurentian now boasts one of the most beautiful campuses of any university in the country— magnificent buildings, 750 acres of lakes and Northern Ontario outdoorsiness, a medical school, a major cancer centre next door, Science North and the largest underground neutrino observatory in the world (which, by the way, is where the fault in Einstein's theory about the speed of light was discovered).

Our courtship proceeded apace for the best part of the year. I had taken a year off from school, mostly playing in the bars and clubs, while Lily finished up her training in x-ray. Somewhere along this path, it became obvious that something had to break. I simply had to marry her, and it seemed that she felt the same way. So one day, we were sitting at the kitchen table at 18 Orford Street, and I recalled my applications of the previous year to Osgoode and Berkeley. With just about this much forethought, that is to say little or none at all, I said to Lily, "Why don't we get married and I go to law school?" I got on the phone to the law school, told them that I had applied for admission the previous year but was unable to attend, and asked if they would still offer me the chance to attend that fabled school. In no time (in fact right during that phone call) Osgoode confirmed that my application and acceptance were still good and so it was that this crazy scheme got underway.

My first classes at Osgoode started at the beginning of September, and I came back to Sudbury for our wedding on October 9, 1965. This was a wedding of considerable difficulty, yet incredibly joyful too. Lil was still completely estranged from her parents, and she was having great trouble with this. We had approached them for their blessing and participation, but were coldly rebuffed. Again, respecting Lily's wishes, the less detail here the better.

So it fell to my parents to help with the wedding. No one could afford a hall, or a band, or a fancy, or even not so fancy, dinner for guests. A beautiful dress was made for the bride (not the usual monster with train, veil and so on) and we were married in St. Mary's Ukrainian Catholic church by Father Zimbalist, referred to archly by my mother as Father Bucolic. Bright as she was, she was also a superb satirist.

This beautiful little church was a lovely place to say our vows for life, especially since all of the rich traditions of the Ukrainian Catholic church came into play. The ceremony is conducted with ornately embroidered towels or shawls, which are interlaced with many colored threads, symbolizing all of the threads of human life. The bride and groom stand on the towel, and it is looped around their wrists. Each of them holds a candle throughout, and crowns are placed on their heads, symbolizing love, purity and fertility (although in our case the third was amiss—but two out of three has worked for us for a lifetime).

Finally, the bride and groom drink from a common cup, expressing a wish for a life of harmony.

All of this beats the pants off of the typical modern wedding, with homemade hand-knitted vows, and kills dead the usual desiccated Protestant liturgy, with not the slightest magic or mystery in it. Anyway, I loved it, and it seemed to work for us, as I sit here writing this on the very day of our 47th anniversary. (Now 50th as of this revision) Talk about a guy blessed.

And then following the wedding, it was back to 18 Orford where a repast was laid out typical of Mildred's feasts. Of course steak and kidney pie (snake and pygmy if one was being irreverent), turkey, ham, whisky, wine, home-made bread, and pies for desert.

This was followed up with one of the famous ceilidhs, and then the bride and groom set off to the Sorrento Hotel in Sudbury for the honeymoon—just one night. The next morning cousin Joe drove us to Toronto to our own little basement apartment in someone's home, and there the real work began.

9

The Law School Years

Now the really tough times set in. Lil could not get work as an x-ray technician, and ended up taking a job at Eaton's, a huge department store in Toronto, ultimately working as a keypunch operator. Older readers will remember these cards—rectangular holes were punched into stiff paperboard in a pattern that machines could read in order to process orders, payments and the like. Kind of like a player piano roll.

Even her job keypunching did not come easily for her. Eaton's was hiring for the Christmas rush, so sometime in October, she applied and got a job sorting catalogue and Christmas orders by hand. When that ended, they offered to send her to keypunch training school. Of course she went and then landed the job as a keypunch operator.

Long hours. Back-breaking work. Poor pay. And she needed to take every minute of overtime that was available to fund our living costs. And to top it off, this was the beginning of my most terrible trouble with depression. It was very hard to function. I was anxious, hypochondriacal, and frightened all of the time—absolutely no help to Lil in any way. Whatever overtime was offered to her, she took, and then came home to my dysfunctional self, and had to shop, prepare food, do laundry, iron shirts, and all on a slender frame that was getting smaller and smaller.

After more than a year of this, a serendipitous thing happened. On her way home on the transit system, a lady dropped something on the platform. Lil picked it up for her, and that caught the eye of one Carita

Cooney, an x-ray technician from Sudbury who, though a bit senior to Lil, had worked with her back in Sudbury. She immediately offered Lily a job at the Addiction Research Foundation as an x-ray technician, and despite her lousy hours and bad working conditions at Eaton's, Lil had to tell her that she couldn't take it unless she could be paid as much she was getting as a keypunch operator. Carita pulled it off (I'm sure Carita sang her praises to the bosses) and Lil went to Addiction Research, and settled into a more sensible life and schedule. She still worked hard and remained the sole provider, but it was much better for her. I continued to be useless and lost in my own troubled world. She was still stuck with that.

Law school itself was quite horrible. The first day there, the Dean, Alan Leal, known as "Buck", told our first year-class of some 150 souls to look around and identify a few of the people in the group because "by Christmas, one-third of you will be gone."

Jesus Christ.

And he was right.

The work was hard, the reading burden unbelievable, the competition brutal. Folks would razor out the case books and law reports, the legal cases we were to read, with the sole purpose of screwing—i.e. outright sabotaging—their classmates. Digital printing now makes this impossible. This competition was unrelenting for three years. I cannot imagine how I ever did it, but I passed all courses and by third year was doing pretty well—that is to say, I manage to maintain a "gentleman's B." But looking back, I was never more dysfunctional with my illness than I was during those years.

And Lil was carrying the full financial burden, apart from some meagre income from my various summer jobs. There was a period during second year, when we were living in a drab brown brick three- or four-story apartment building at Bathurst and St. Clair in Toronto. This may have been the worst of it. The walls were whitewashed with some kind of crap that rubbed off on your clothes. There was an alley behind the row of apartment buildings that was a haunt for peeping toms. We would shut the apartment down into darkness and peer out the windows, peeping on the peepers as the voyeurs would climb the trees to get an even more detailed view into the windows at all levels of these buildings, but the fools would give themselves away by lighting up cigarettes. It was plain that these guys could not be hovering in mid-air—they had taken up static positions. Frequently, there were quite a few of them angling for the best viewing locations, and traffic in the alley could become pretty busy.

Often, as Lil and I left for work and school in the morning, a couple of the working girls in the building would be coming home to sleep and rest up for another night of trolling.

In the apartment below us there lived a madman who would, despite the fact that we were totally silent, frequently explode and begin pounding on his ceiling, our floor, with a broom handle or shovel, screaming that he intended to "come up there and break both your fucking legs."

We had a TV that flickered a pathetic pale blue picture, the images on which could only be seen if the apartment was plunged into total darkness.

We had perfected the dismal art of collecting pop bottles (soda bottles in the U.S.) for the deposit returns, which could add up to enough to buy a large bottle of ginger ale and some hot dogs for a real treat on a Saturday night while watching the Toronto Maple Leafs—who were, at that time, still a real hockey team.

The aforementioned Vicki Vairo and other old friends from Sudbury dropped in once for a visit. Vicki couldn't stand it. After only a few minutes it was, "Man how can you live in this shit hole? I gotta get outta heah!" And he did, never to return to the place again.

Much of my time at Osgoode Hall was spent in ducking classes and playing cards with some other slackers in the cafeteria. I often had to borrow class notes from friends, as my absence from lectures was that pronounced. And through all of it, one could not escape the obvious fact that I was a coal miner's son, first in the family to go to university let alone law school, surrounded by classmates whose parents were doctors and lawyers, professional people of all stripes, including even a Justice of the Supreme Court of Canada. Fish out of water doesn't come close to describing the feeling. So I reverted to a fairly typical model for me: defiant non-conformity. Otherwise I doubt that I ever would have made it.

We have all heard the old saw about how hardship and poverty builds character. If I may say, that is pretty much a load of crap. Poverty grinds you down, steals your will, shames you, and robs you of every shred of self-esteem and pride, and it took a long time to recover from that. Looking back on those times, it's striking how much Lily, and also piping, helped me up and out of all of that.

To become a lawyer in Ontario at this time required at least a BA which takes three years, three years of law school itself, one year of articles (i.e. a hands-on apprenticeship with a practicing lawyer or a law firm), followed by the Bar Admission course, which was based on the notion that if one was admitted to the bar in Ontario one would have skills in civil procedure, criminal procedure, basic accounting, contracts, tort law and so on. This torture ran in consecutive two- to three-week intensive courses, followed by an exam at the end of every segment.

Terrific reading loads, and personal pressure. Here I am, seven years into the process and I'm terrified I might fail the Bar Admission Course and never get to be a lawyer. On top of that there was a desperate scramble and contest to find a placement with an established firm.

I ended up serving my articles in a large firm in downtown Toronto, and it was very clear to me that once I was called to the bar I could never function in that environment. God knows it's even worse now—young associates are given a target of so many billable hours per year. If it's say, 2200, that's about forty-two hours a week over a fifty-two week period. The problem, however, is that if you work for eight hours a day, you'll be lucky to create four to six billable hours out of that. So the result is that at the factory firms, with hundreds of lawyers and associates, you are expected to work evenings and every weekend. It's a murderous way to live.

And more to the point in many ways, was the awful notion of working in downtown Toronto, where even in those days, congestion and getting around was a daily hurdle. And as I learned in my brief tenure downtown, many of the lawyers would eat their young rather than deal fairly with one another.

So for me the only choice was to strike out on my own. I had decided I could never return to Sudbury to practice even though my relative notoriety in the area would have made building a practice fairly easy. I simply could not go back to that place which, for me, had taken on a sad aura. Instead, I joined with my classmate, Peter Magda, and together we opened an office in Oshawa, Ontario, about 30 miles east of Toronto on the shores of Lake Ontario. Peter was a local guy, and very powerfully connected through his father-in-law, a major business and social figure in the city.

While these plans were taking shape in August of 1968, before I started my articles, Lily and I went to the Canadian National Exhibition, later to be the site of the hugely successful world Scottish Festival and Tattoo. The CNE is an annual fair on a grand scale, which signals the end of summer in Toronto. It features exhibits, auto shows, festivals, major entertainments, a gigantic midway, roller coaster, agricultural stuff and so on. There was and still is, as I recently learned driving by the place, an open-air stage, shaped like a scallop shell, and performing in it was the 48th Highlanders Pipe Band. I was inexorably drawn to this. I felt smitten— I've often compared it to someone who suffers from malaria. Years can go by without any symptoms, and suddenly there is a relapse. That's what happened to me on this day. I was transported back ten years to my last real experience with the pipes. It seemed I didn't even have to think about what to do. I looked up John Wilson, who was still alive and well and living in Toronto, called him and asked if he remembered me. He said that he remembered me very well. I arranged to begin lessons with him right away. I bought a practice chanter, and soon we were at it once a week in his basement at 122 Johnson in Toronto. Our first tune was "MacCrimmon's Sweetheart." We hammered this tune without mercy, and I entered the "open" piping at the Toronto Indoor games, intending to play in the March, the Strathspey & Reel, and the Piobaireachd.

I was very lucky that in those days you could play what you wanted; there was no requirement that competitors had to submit a list of several tunes. So I played the only one that I could: "MacCrimmon's Sweetheart." The results were, for me, astonishing. I won the March, Barry Ewen won the Strathspey & Reel and I tied for first in the Piobaireachd with Jim Thompson, who was enraged at John Wilson the judge, and the teacher of each of us, who could tie me playing "McCrimmon's Sweetheart," a lighter tune, with Thompson and his "Lament for the Children." What a debut—no one had ever heard of me, heard me play, or even actually met me. John Wilson put it quite succinctly, alluding to my black hair, declaring me the dark horse of the day.

10

Mother and Father

By the time we'd been about a year at 18 Orford, life had settled into what I now think of as a semblance of "normal" family life. My parents did what all other parents in our town did. Mom was a stay-at-home mother (there really was no other kind in these days), Ranald and I went to school, and we both learned and played the pipes. I was good enough in school, and I thought Ranny was too. He was a boisterous, outgoing guy, who had discovered a flair for becoming the centre of attention and being something of a comic. He and his pal, Wayne Nute, created comedy routines that they staged in figure-skating shows and swimming-pool shows. I thought he was the greatest: smart, funny, a good athlete and good piper. I hero-worshipped him. He won what then were called "Oratorical Contests." Students would compete within their own schools and then at higher, district levels, delivering speeches or essays that they had composed using a list of subjects from which they could choose. They were judged by English teachers and the prizes were highly valued. My family all got to go and watch Ranald orate and it was something terrific. Later on, I too entered these contests and I also did very well. But please be kind in your judgment of the opening sentences from one of my own prize-winning essays and speeches, which I recall delivering in as ominous and stentorian a voice as a fifteen-year-old boy can muster. The subject was "The Atomic Bomb," and the opening passage was: *"A blinding burst of light. A tearing tide of sound. And within an instant, Hiroshima died as a city.*

Within the same instant, it was reborn as one of the most infamous slaughters in history."

I remember it so vividly and accurately because the giggles that gathered in the classroom were unmistakable, and made worse by the teacher trying to control her own mirth, shoulders a-shake. Never mind, I won. And I won the next level, too. And it was my brother, with his bombastic style, that helped me create that beautiful sentence which was so full of artful alliteration (or so I convinced myself). All of this stuff gave me a reputation in high school (secondary school for non-Canadians) as something of a smart cookie, and earned me some very welcome passes when my grades were less than stellar. Remember that I was in the midst of what was, for me, nearly an existential crisis, with my mood disorder in full-blown extremes, and I barely able to think, let alone work properly at school.

And so it went, until somewhere at the end of grade school, I learned from some of my friends, who also had siblings in high school, that Ranald was not well liked. Indeed, he was disliked by nearly everyone. I was gobsmacked and devastated. My hero, my big brother, not well liked? No, not even simply liked. This tore me up, and actually changed everything. I began to see him differently—his casual relationship with the truth, his boastful bombastic ways, and as time went on, more troubling things too. He married when he and his soon-to-be wife, Marley, were both quite young, and she pregnant. He dabbled in radio and TV, and then life insurance for a while, and that ended in a murky mess. He and Marley had two daughters some seven years apart, and despite their terrible home life and the chaos that followed Marley's divorce from Ranald, they somehow went on to become very successful, strong women. This is likely a result of how very bright they both are.

As Lily and I made our way through my law school years, and then my call to the bar, visits home to Copper Cliff became more and more painful. The chaos in Ranny's home was visible, the tension like a funk in the air. It was depressing, and I felt not only sad for him, but weirdly guilty too. It seemed wrong to me that I should have so much—a beautiful wife, law career, piping career on the rise—and Ranald should seem so lost. Worse happened, too. He landed a great job at INCO in Public Relations, a bonus arising from our family's friendship with a top guy at INCO who loved all things Scottish. He should have been set for life, but instead he was found out having an affair with his boss's wife or girlfriend (I can't remember which and it probably doesn't matter). In any event, he swore to me that this is what led to his dismissal. That's the story Ranald told and it may be true, or it might be another instance of his cavalier attitude to the truth, as well his inability to accept responsibility for what may have been misconduct or poor performance at work.

After the divorce he fought tooth and nail against his child support obligations. He had me bail him out of various scrapes, all of his own doing. He made me crazy. I was angry at him. I felt badly for him. He embarrassed me repeatedly with various antics in public. It was a very fraught relationship, and yet I came to his rescue time and again. There's a lot of water under that bridge certainly, but there's no compelling reason for me to drown in it. And now I can see things a little differently.

After Ranald died, there was an outpouring of personal calls and emails to me, as well as posts on the on-line magazine *Pipes|Drums*, all singing his praises, talking about what a wonderful fun guy he was, full of life, a lover of good food and a nice drink, and devoted to me completely. I can now see that public side of him, and that he did indeed enjoy his life a great deal. Yes, he made me crazy. Yes, I wished he were different. Yes he broke my heart. But all of these feelings and emotions arose because I loved him.

After Lily and I were married, my parents stayed on living at 18 Orford, and, as they said, "It's like it was when we started out—just the two of us." As we were leaving 18 Orford Street on the morning after our wedding, Mom and Dad were seeing us off to our new adventure in Toronto, tears welling up even in the eyes of my usually stoic father.

In 1972 Lily and I had been married for seven years. Mom and Dad had, some years earlier, become friends with a gentleman by the name of Keith Poff. Keith had been my history and phys-ed teacher throughout all of my 5 years of secondary school, and he was ranked by me as the best of all of my teachers. The friendship between Keith and his second wife Faye, and my parents was a little unusual given their age and educational differences, but it was marked by genuine affection and respect. Keith was an incredibly interesting and volatile guy. He was as ready to help and support his students, as he was willing to launch a piece of chalk, carefully aimed just over your head, if you were not "into" his lecture. A girl in our class had the dreadfully bad judgment to raise her hand during one of his verbal flights. Expecting an interesting question from a keen student, he acknowledged her hand, but alas, she asked permission to sharpen her pencil. "Of course," he said. Sharpen her pencil she did. He kept an ominous silence throughout the trip to the sharpener, the grinding of the lead and wood, and her return to her seat. After she sat down at her desk, he approached the pencil sharpener, ripped it from its moorings, and tossed it into the trash bin.

A different student, at another time, kept turning her head to look at the clock on the back wall of the classroom (when are we getting out of here?). School clock, meet pencil sharpener, as he dealt out the same fate. He left his spot at the front of the classroom, said nothing, marched purposefully to the back wall, climbed up on a chair and tore this innocent clock off the wall, hanging wires like entrails, and sent it to the garbage can.

I loved him—he was smart, a great raconteur and conversationalist, seemed to know something about everything, and lived only a few doors away from our home. He was a very good jazz musician, playing trombone, and made his way handily around a piano keyboard. He took a real interest in my first fumbling attempts to teach myself some piano skills. He became my friend after high school and to me it seemed pretty natural for that to happen, but I suppose it's fairly rare that a former student gets to be pals with his high school teacher.

There's at least one story about Keith that should be told. It was Christmas Day. Keith was wearing a new silky suit, of a hue somewhere between cream and brass. He had bright red hair and was a big guy: 6'1" and about 220 pounds. He had been banging away at the whisky for much of the day, and as so often happens with these occasions, things dragged on a bit too long, and by the time dinner was ready for the table, Keith was, as my father would say, rather *hors de combat*. (For those who don't feel like traipsing to the online dictionary, it means "out of action due to damage or injury"—I had to look it up myself so don't read any condescension into this translation.)

Anyway, back to Copper Cliff and the Poff dinner table at Christmastime. The turkey was done, its golden skin glistening as Keith mounted it on a carving board equipped with small spikes onto which the bird would be tethered to facilitate carving. As he entered the dining room bearing the bird, his foot caught on a carpet, he plunged forward out of control, the turkey leapt off the spikes and bounced off the table onto the floor, and the carving board flew out of his hands. The spikes attached themselves to his new suit, made a bow to gravity, and dragged down the front of the bespoke garment, trailing a pattern of torn exotic material behind them, highlighted by turkey grease and juices. Ho! Ho! Ho!

On August 5, 1972, my parents were enjoying a weekend at the Poffs' summer cottage, called, in Sudbury, a camp. It was a beautiful Northern Ontario August day—blue, blue sky, warm, bordering on hot —so it was into the cool lake and then into the sauna. Saunas in and around Sudbury were completely true to the Finnish model. A wood-burning stove was fed from an ante room, with the hot (HOT!) end of the stove pushing into the steam room. Sitting on the wooden benches, you drop very small cups of water on the stones. No steam appears, rather a quick and nearly silent *phsst* as the water vaporizes and the room temperature shoots skyward. Boil a while and then head to the Northern Ontario crystal water; back to the sauna, and back to the lake; repeat.

On one of these trips out of the lake, my mom, coming towards my dad who's holding his hand out to her, drops into the water, gets up, turns around and walks away from him towards the middle of the lake.

Everyone there knew this was a cerebral hemorrhage. There followed a mad ambulance dash to the Sudbury General Hospital, described by Dad as the worst hour of his life, with full life support initiated. Following this hemorrhagic stroke, there was no brain activity, so life support was shut down and she was gone.

While this was going on I was at George Campbell's house playing my pipes, and I got a call from Lily with the news. Home to Whitby and straight on to Sudbury, but by the time we arrived brain death had been declared. It was horrible for everyone, but no-one was more deeply injured by this than my dad.

He retired shortly afterward, and moved to Whitby where he was close to us, but he never recovered. He was diagnosed with permanent grief syndrome, and if there really is such a thing, he had it. He would fall into and out of great depressions. We would find him sitting alone weeping.

He ultimately did remarry and move to Hamilton, into his new wife's home, but none of this helped at all. His bouts of depression now took the form of two- to three-day bouts of binge drinking. He fell down countless times, putting himself in hospital with concussions and brutal facial injuries. He drove home (almost) one night, drunk as a lord, bounced off another car or two and crashed into a hydro pole. When approached by the police officer who arrived at the scene, he was asked where he was going. He drew himself up with the elaborate dignity that only the profoundly soused can muster, and said, "I'm going home." Well, not for a little while, said the cop.

I represented him on the resulting charge of impaired driving. As counsel introduced himself to the court with, "If it please Your Honour, my name is Livingstone, initial W., representing Mr. Wm Livingstone," the penny dropped and the judge's eyes revealed his immediate understanding of the situation. It is a fairly profound shift in the father/son relationship when that kind of thing happens.

He stopped drinking. He started. He stopped. All the while my brother Ranald, who also had remarried and who was living close to dad in Hamilton, became dad's enabler and drinking buddy, Ranald himself a raging alcoholic by now.

Time passed. My uncle Stuart died. My dad, Ranald and I travelled to Sudbury for Stuart's funeral. My father came undone. His wife gone, his brother-in-law and pal in the RCAF Pipe Band gone. He stayed on in Sudbury after the funeral until he succeeded in drinking himself to death. He was found in a hotel room (when repeated calls were not answered) by my cousin, Donald MacLennan. The autopsy report stated cryptically: "cause of death: cardiac insufficiency." Ain't that always the way, really? Reminds me of a remark of Lord Bertrand Russell when debating with a colleague: "That sir, is an obviousity."

Mildred, my mom, was a case unto herself. As I've said, she was bright, articulate, witty, and neurotic. She kept a home, the floors of which were so spotless, that one could eat off of them. Her cooking was beyond great. But she was violent about it. Pots and dishes clattered, flour was strewn all over the kitchen, pies were tossed into the oven with abandon and everything that came out of that kitchen was fabulous. In the dead of February, when temperatures could easily plunge to minus thirty degrees, she would decide that the house needed freshening up (notwithstanding that it was immaculate) and open all the doors in the place to "air it out." She killed the *Globe and Mail* crossword puzzle (very tough) in ten minutes, and was deeply and irretrievably neurotic—especially concerning her two boys, but I'm afraid most especially concerning me. No matter what be fell me— the usual childhood infections, colds, tonsillitis, mumps, swollen glands—she was an object lesson in how to freak out, and how to get her kid to do the same.

I think I may have been destined somehow to endure the emotional and psychological problems I encountered regardless, but still this was real schooling to help send me on a long journey of trouble. Because she died so young, when I was still in the woods (in fact nowhere close to getting out of them), all of the unresolved feelings and troubles lingered.

This is beginning to sound like I should be rending my garments. In fact she was a great lady, in many respects a great mother, and she instilled in me a love of words, reading and music. We were very close. Undoubtedly it's very hard to lose your mother say at age fifteen, but it can be just as hard for some to have that happen at thirty. I was one of those.

11

Look at Me Now

Deep lines down each side of my mouth, soon to migrate to full-blown wattles. Luckily a full head of hair, but that comes with all kinds of other unwanted hirsute complications: hair growing out of my nose and ears such that only relentless pruning can keep it in check. Feel the palms of my hands: those things are called Dupuytren's contractures. The tendons contract, get ropey and lumpy, and if not treated aggressively, they can pull the fingers into a claw shape. Thankfully, several thousand dollars of shock wave therapy has prevented that, but that expense, and discomfort, is not over; it will go on as long as I want to play.

The treatment works on a principle similar to that used to treat kidney stones, which in that application is called lithotripsy. Thousands of blasts in a few minutes to the affected area and *whammo!* chronic inflammation is converted to acute inflammation which, I am assured by my physiotherapist and doctor, the body can handle better. Two hundred and fifty bucks a pop, three times per week, and one week apart, and repeat as needed.

And this does nothing for the painful osteoarthritis in the joints of my fingers. That requires compulsive use of hot paraffin wax baths, hot gel packs, physiotherapy with ultrasound and topical anti-inflammatory steroids. Ultimately, maybe cortisone injections into those little joints. A home use ultrasound and hot wax bath completes the picture in our house, and Lily cracks that it's beginning to look like a rehabilitation facility. Good Lord, what I won't do to keep playing.

But I play. It's good. In some ways it's better than my last years on the boards—not the same pressure, I guess. But making a birl when you know that this movement, so completely at odds with the way the human finger has evolved to move and function, is going to produce a little stab of pain, is a bit of a challenge. But I do it. I started doing birls as a little kid, and I remember well my dad telling me that if in school things were quiet or boring, to pick up a ruler or a pencil and rattle off a hundred birls. I have no idea how many birls I've made but it must be a million. If that's not a recipe for overuse injury or arthritis, I'm not sure what is.

There's some real irony here. I have spent a lifetime running, playing squash, weight training in gyms, attending cardio classes and doing hard cycling—both mountain biking and road riding. In short, I've done everything I can to keep fit and healthy. As they say, if you want to give God a laugh, make a plan. So despite all this goal-directed effort, I was diagnosed in September of 2013 with high cholesterol, high blood pressure and atrial fibrillation. My array of medications requires planning to ensure I get them right every day, and they do seem to keep all of the problems in check. Blood pressure normal, cholesterol down, and atrial fibrillation fixed, at least for now. AFib is simply an irregular heartbeat, and while mine was described as "well controlled" (I asked my doctors, controlled by whom or what?—no answer), its collateral effect can be to cause blood clots in the heart. I was put on a drug called Pradaxa which thins the blood and effectively prevents clots. The side effect (there's always one) is that if you're injured in a car accident, run over by the big road brusher or knocked down on the bike, the drug can induce severe bleeding. There's no antidote to stop the anti-coagulant effect, so a big trauma would mean emergency surgery to find the bleed and stop it, as the drug's effect lasts for many hours. I was switched to a thing called Xarelto (gotta love those names) as there *may* be an antidote for it.

Anyway, there has been good news. I had a cardioversion; this is where they paddle you with big jolts of electricity, but below lethal levels, and the hope is the heart jumps back to normal rhythm. Mine did. Still is there. And I got off Xarelto and now just take Aspirin.

I still get to the gym five days a week, work with a personal trainer, ride the stationary bike, and from spring to fall do my cycling. So far it's all OK.

My only other major collision with the health care system, apart from my previously described crazies, was in 1982. After a very festive Christmas season and New Year celebration, with an excess of turkey, stuffing, mince meat pies and yes, wine, I was suffering some pretty serious pain in the solar plexus and upper chest. I went to my doc, a squash-playing buddy, and he thought it was maybe gall bladder trouble. He sent me for x-rays with the opaque dye showing the gall bladder and other organs. When the test was over the radiologist said, "Your gall bladder's fine, but I see an outgrowth of cells in your stomach." Press the switch for full-on hypochondriacal hysteria. Met with my doctor. He told me that judging by the location on the floor of the stomach, and the shape, nearly a perfect ping pong ball, it was likely a leiomyoma, a benign tumor similar to those that women get.

So it was off to the hospital for an endoscopy (camera tube down the throat) and biopsy of the lesion. The report read "normal stomach mucosa." What fools I thought they were. I *knew* this was completely unreliable because they never got past the mucosa into the body of the tumor. By this time I had just enough medical knowledge to be a danger to myself. There followed a week or two of anxiety in the stratospheric level. Of course surgery was required, and I met with the surgeon, an absolutely lovely man of Guyanese origin, who like my family doctor, was a client of our office. The meeting went something like this:

"So Bill, (in an elegant Caribbean accent) what's wrong with you?"

"Well Ray, I was rather hoping that you'd tell me."

"Well judging by the symptoms and biopsy, I would say it could be gall bladder, ulcers, indigestion, cancer or nothing at all."

CANCER!?

Looking back, I see he meant no harm at all, and in fact it's what these guys do: "Here, Mr. Patient, are the differential diagnoses." It's kind of funny now but it most definitely was not then. I had the surgery, Ray came to me the next day and said, "It's pretty hard to tell from a quick section biopsy, but I'm pretty sure, I'd say ninety-eight percent sure, that it's benign. We'll have to wait for the full detailed histology report." I replied, "Ray, that's OK for you, but I'd like you to fill in that other two percent."

Then the coup de gras. The lab technician who'd looked at all of my slides came into my hospital room a few days later (she the wife of another squash buddy) and was chatting away very comfortably and cheerily when she said, "Bill, are you OK? You don't seem very happy."

"I'm not. I still haven't heard the results of the full biopsy."

"You mean they didn't tell you? The report has been back for a few days and it's one hundred percent certain that it's a leiomyoma... non-cancerous." Jesus, what an experience. These guys crack me up.

Grampa John

Ranald, Andy Knox, the author

Ed Neigh, the author, Tomas Braunerhielma, Bill Sr.

The author, school picture, age 7

*Copper Cliff Highlanders Pipe Band front rank
from left: Bill Sr., the author (age 11), Ranald in P.Sgt. Position*

The author, age 8, playing at a Shrine Dinner with many dollar bills stuffed into the foxhead sporran

Baby pics. A friend of my mother's said of me "that baby is too good to live."

Inspection. From left to right: Robin Swain (note swagger stick), Bill Sr. (partially obscured), the author (age 7), Major General Chris Vokes, Ranald

Playing 'Scare of Fishing' for James Campbell on a roaring out of tune pipe at Oban...all 18 minutes of it.

Bill Sr. competing in the RCAF uniform in Nova Scotia in the early forties

Being presented with the Gold Clasp
1981, The Northern Meeting

The author being congratulated by
Bill Wotherspoon (second prize)
on winning the Gold Medal at
the Northern Meeting, 1977

An astonishing demonstration of eating lobster in New Brunswick after
a band workshop with St. Andrews Society of Fredricton Pipe Band.

1987 78th Frasers. Standing from left to right: the author, John Walsh, Doug Kirkwood, Ross Brown, Tim Murphy, Gord MacRae, Alec Patterson, Brian Pollock, Iain Donaldson, Chris Moran, Jake Watson, Syd Girling, Tom Anderson, Mike Grey, Jake Watson, Reid Maxwell, Luke Allan. Seated: Tom Bowen, Chris Barker, Bruce Gandy, Stu Liddell, Iain Symington, Scott Brown, Ron Rollo

The Glenfiddich 2000. Left to right: Stuart Liddell, Greg Wilson, Willie McCallum, Angus MacColl, Mike Rogers, Sandy Grant Gordon (Mr. Sandy) Gordon Walker, Mike Cusack, the author, Rab Wallace

*The Glenfiddich 1990. Standing left to right:
Gordon Walker, Mike Cusack, Willie McCallum,
Mr. Sandy, Murray Henderson, Greg Wilson, Brian Donaldson.
Seated left to right: Rab Wallace, Allan MacDonald, Colin MacLellan, the author*

The Glenfiddich 2001. Left to right: the author, Jack Lee, Alasdair Gillies, Gordon Walker, Colin MacLellan, Niall Mathieson, Angus MacColl, Greg Wilson, Willie McCallum, Chris Armstrong

Grier Coppins (cousin), the author, Lily, Bob Worrall and the late Scott MacAulay at the Argyllshire Gathering in the early 70's

Ev Hazzard and Lily, Cambridge Highland Games

The author bringing some much needed liquid refreshments to the troops after a band contest.

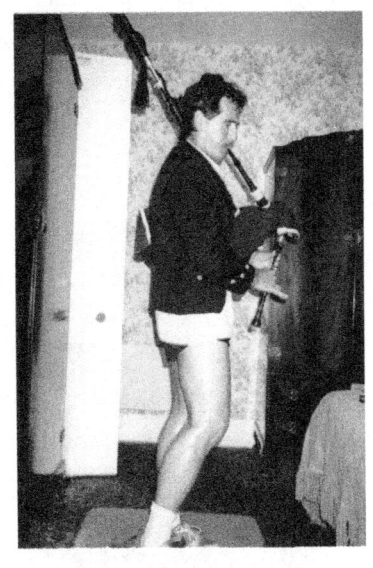

Practicing after a run wearing a jacket to try to get used to it.

The author with Andrew MacNeill on the grounds of Blair Castle at one of the author's 17 invitations to the event

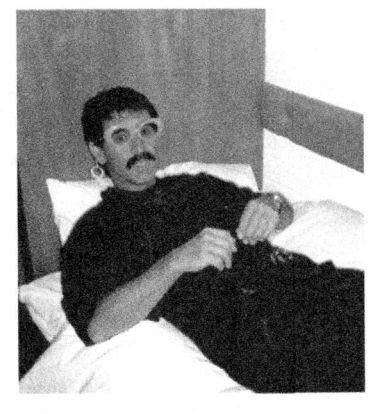

Acting the fool at the residence at Strathclyde University (Photo courtesy of Mike Grey)

Ranald at Cambridge Highland Games

Competing in the Former Winners' March, Strathspey & Reel at Oban

The 78th Frasers disastrous march on of the winning team at the MacDonald Brier in Kitchener, Ontario

The author, Lily, Bruce and Mike at Loch Carron on the way to Inverness.

Lily somewhere in the Highlands.

Mrs. Elsom, our wonderful landlady in Inverness, the author and Lily

The view looking east from 11 Evans Rd, the white house on the right.

Two orange creeks in Copper Cliff as they look today.

A "back yard" up the hill.

Lily talking with two wee Northern Irish boys as we were on a run near Ballymena

Competing at 'The Soo', age 14

John Walsh planting a kiss on the ear of the P/M after the World's win.

Reid Maxwell with the World Drumming Championship hardware.

Ranald in his role as Vice-President of the PPBSO.

Lily with Gerry Quigg.

The author, Reid and Mike at the after party 1987. Some glasses.

Top left: Bill Sr., Uncle John
Top right: Grampa John
Bottom: Grampa John, Bill Sr.

The RCAF Pipe Band in Nova Scotia. Top photo, Bill Sr. in the P/M's position, Uncle Stuart with the bass drum, Sam Laderoute kneeling in front of Bill Sr. Bottom photo, a kippers and beer party, with Bill Sr. holding up a plate and fork, and Uncle Stuart with loosened tie and wicked grin.

PART 2

12

Teachers and Tutors

I came onto a piping scene in 1970 that was in significant flux. Flux not only in one of its dictionary definitions connoting the "mixing of different elements," but also in the meaning of "flow or forward movement—any change, transition or modification." Previously, finding instruction, especially in piobaireachd, was driven in part by geography. By the time I became involved, it had been freed from that restriction. But in previous times, if you had to travel to learn, you would likely travel as short a distance as possible. I have argued that this geographical restraint had a lot to do with the development of "schools" of piobaireachd. Classic examples, of course, would be the adherents of John McDonald of Inverness and his forbears, although my understanding of this great figure is that he was a lot less rigid about stylistic issues and details of settings than some of his adherents, Robert Nicol being a notable example.

By 1970, air travel became affordable, piping broadcasts on BBC radio, still quaintly referred to as the "wireless", had become common, and the cassette tape recorder was everywhere. The result was that great figures like Robert Hardie, John McFadyen, Capt. John MacClellan, Seumas McNeil, R. U. Brown and others began travelling the world to teach at summer schools. This meant exposure to the many subtle and varied ways of performing this music, and for the keen and talented pupil, a broader education was suddenly available. It also meant that the traditional lip-to-ear method of instruction could be reasonably well duplicated and listened to by the pupil actually being taught, and even other students, over and over. For an interesting and the thorough discussion of these issues, see *The Highland Pipe and Scottish Society, 1750 to 1950,* by William Donaldson. The supposed lineage of pipers from the McCrimmons to the modern era is well described in Seumas McNeil's *Piobaireachd and Its Interpretation.* It is well beyond the scope of this memoir, which after all, you should forgive me, is about my experiences and stories about piping. As we say nowadays, it's all about me.

JOHN WILSON

So initially obeying the above-noted dictates of geography, I gravitated to the great John Wilson. John was a pupil of Roderick Campbell, composer of so many light music classics like the great 2/4 competition march "The Edinburgh City Police Pipe Band", and who himself was a pupil of the legendary Sandy Cameron. But Roddie Campbell seems to have been a very pragmatic and open-minded follower of the so-called Cameron school, for he taught John Wilson to play many tunes with distinctly McPherson-esque touches. Some examples spring to mind: John played, and taught me to play, the cadences in both the "Lament for the Viscount of Dundee" and the "Lament for Patrick Og MacCrimmon" with the first note long and the second short, or in Donald MacLeod's phrase, as an "and note"—a linking, connecting or passing note. This was anathema to Cameron folks, who pretty much insisted that the two notes be even at the very least, and often with the second one actually longer.

Certainly my experience with other adherents to the line of teaching now known as the Cameron School (in modern times funneled through Robert Reid) was that they showed a more slavish adherence to received wisdom, or dare I say dogma? Willie Connell, who taught and judged for many years in Canada, was a purveyor of this kind of ideological purity for a long time. There is of course no real surprise in this, since Willie worked with Reid making bagpipes for many years, and had more direct instruction from him than perhaps any other of Reid's pupils. It seems to me, though, that Willie developed a less rigid approach to Ceol Mor, the longer he judged in North America, and freely accepted interpretations from outside the Cameron/Reid methods, rewarding for consistency and musicality.

In any event, John Wilson seems to have been moulded by Roddie Campbell to be more generously minded about stylistic issues, never single-mindedly insisting that a "style" would prevail. In fact it became obvious to me over time, that what drove John's thinking about the tunes and their treatment was the musical context and structure of the piece in question, but always a framed by the teaching he got from Roddie.

John himself was a very practical man, and he taught piping in a simple and direct way. He demonstrated on the practice chanter how the piece was to be played and had the pupil play along with him until the match between them was as accurate as possible, or at least as close as it was ever going to be.

There was little or no discussion of the arcane language of medium/strong pulsing, or scansion of the lines of music in a piobaireachd. He demonstrated and the pupil copied as closely as possible—today we'd say "cloned"...and that was it. No intellectualizing, little pondering on the legends of the tunes, even ignoring something as wonderful as the bloodthirsty "A Flame of Wrath for Squinting Patrick," but rather simple, direct, straightforward instruction: "Here is how to play it."

He was, however, a true fanatic about technique. Perhaps because of the loss of his fingers and the way that forced him to (ahem) come to grips with the challenges of the fingerwork on the bagpipe, he developed an intense love of technique, which he produced as beautifully as any piper I have ever heard. He often said to me that good piping is "particular piping," repeatedly stressing the importance of the bottom hand. He even once had a "Eureka" moment when he announced that he finally understood the secret—it lay in the ability to accurately close the chanter and then produce the low G and D gracenotes which are the precursors of so much of the fabulous technique of the toarluath, lemluath and crunluath movements.

His practicality knew no limits. Raised in Scotland, he knew the weather could change in heartbeat—dress so you are prepared for suddenly different conditions. Layers, raingear, put it on, take it off as needed. So I did. Here are more snippets of his advice:

- If your hands get cold, slap your arms and hands around your torso frequently, and for many minutes at a time. Blood fills the hands and forearms and will get you past the stiffness.
- *Never* think about your bagpipe once you have started your tune. Just play the best you can—you don't know how the others have played, or if they've had the same bagpipe problems that you've had.
- Before you start a piobaireachd, picture the whole piece in your mind. As you play through it, make a mental check mark at the end of each line, and if the line is repeated put a cross through the check mark. This was the system he followed when judging, and it has pretty much become the system now employed universally in North America: three lines for each variation on the scoresheet, with check marks being placed at the end of each successful completion of every line.
- Start each of the technical variations carefully and deliberately— the first few movements should be very articulate and produced so that all gracenotes are very audible. Once you're in cleanly, you're away with it.
- Never look at the judge or the audience—eyes downcast in a completely self-contained bubble. I know, however, from some tales he told me that he did not always find it easy to follow his own advice when there were charming ladies in view. And this, maybe most amazing of all: when playing a piobaireachd always keep your feet in a sort of duck walk position—the feet in a "ten to two" position on a clock. You will never lose your balance,

even on some of the god-awful surfaces pipers are forced to play on.

John was not without some shortcomings and oddities. I believe his piobaireachd repertoire was rather limited. He told me more than once that he never really did well in the Clasp at Inverness because there were set tunes, most of which he didn't like, and he could not bother to learn them. I played at a competition in the 1970s and submitted "MacDougall's Gathering." John began flipping through the book, found the score, and instructed me to repeat the ground in its entirety "as the tune was so short."

He later explained that he was only looking at the score, and as it looked short, he called for the full ground to be repeated. When I played the tune, he was surprised that it was such a substantial piece. Normally one would have expected a top piper to have had MacDougall's well and truly locked into the repertoire.

On another occasion, he said that he had just learned "The Daughter's Lament" and pronounced it one of the most musically and technically difficult piobaireachds, if not the most difficult, piobaireachd he had ever played. John at this point was well past his competing years. Again it seems a curious omission from the repertoire of so accomplished a piper. Regardless of all of that, he may have had a much bigger repertoire than I was ever aware of—and it probably doesn't matter a whole lot, since the tunes he did play, he played beautifully.

When judging a pipe band he was not at all averse to inserting his head right into the circle between pipers, in order to get a better listen to the pipe section. This may have been the impetus for the creation of the outer circle, within which judges are prohibited from encroaching.

John sometimes seemed to be oblivious to the conventions around piping competitions. There was a solo piping contest in the Sergeant's Mess at Fort York Armouries in the early 1970s. A young man by the name of Chris Jensen was playing in the piobaireachd competition and produced a very light bagpipe. When he finished, and started to repeat the first line of the ground, John got up smartly from his table, approached Chris from behind, and passed his hands over all three of his drone tops. John addressed the audience before the prize giving and delivered a brief critique of all the playing. With no apology whatever, he explained that he simply had to check to see if Chris was playing three drones "since he had such a wee infant's bagpipe."

He was always outspoken and entertaining. To get a good sense of the man in this regard, it's worth trying to find his autobiography, *A Professional Piper in Peace and War*. The later sections contain many of his articles and letters to and from *The Piper and Dancer Bulletin*... blunt, direct, always utterly confident and unapologetic.

JOHN MACFADYEN

Sometime early in 1972, Ed Neigh suggested that I attend a summer school with John MacFadyen. I had played for him once at the Thousand Islands Highland Games. I delivered the "Lament for the Viscount of Dundee," and received a less than flattering score sheet ("slowing down badly in line two of the urlar....crunluath movement tight to the point of disappearance") but nevertheless approached him about attending his school. I don't know what my pals in the Ontario scene were like, but at this stage I was awestruck by these giant piping figures.

So for three or four years, Lily and I travelled to the farm of Mac Campbell some twenty miles south of Sarnia, Ontario, about four hours from home. We'd stay for a week in a resort town, Grand Bend on the shores of Lake Huron, and I drove every morning to the farm. Lil stayed home sunbathing and swimming in the pool while I sweltered in the incredible heat of July in southern Ontario, being tutored, cajoled, screamed at and generally subjected to the towering personality and intellect of John MacFadyen. The routine was something like this: in the morning, play on the pipes the tune you learned yesterday, without error, please; take up the practice chanter and go over with John the next piobaireachd on the agenda; return in the afternoon playing the new tune on the bagpipe, with John walking in the classic piobaireachd player's circular pattern, and with me following a few steps behind trying to follow his right hand, as he vigorously conducted with occasional shouts of dismay or approval. When I finally delivered a properly rippling crunluath movement, he screamed out, "THAT'S THE SOUND! THAT'S THE SOUND!"

Picture the scene: a hot, dusty gravel road, bordered by forest on one side and farm fields on the other. An old rural schoolhouse, a wooden structure, pretty rough with no comforts of home, and most of McFadyen's pupils using this as their quarters. No beds, just sleeping bags, and several of them jammed into this space. There was the sadly late Ed Neigh, and his brother Geoff, Jim McGillivray, David Martin and the late John Goodenow, the latter two living in Detroit, a reasonably short drive away. One hundred yards or so down the road stood the Campbell farmhouse, where Mrs. Campbell daily served us lunch.

Pipes were heard all over the farm as we all saw sought a relatively isolated place to practice. Often lessons were of the two birds with one stone variety, as we would be invited to audit another pupil's sweating efforts under the tyrannical gaze of MacFadyen. We loved it and we loved him.

He was a powerful character—imposing physically, fiercely intelligent, with a glittering command of the language, a man who could and did impose his will on your playing, causing you, forcing you, to produce music, especially piobaireachd, of which you were otherwise incapable. We all used our little cassette tape recorders for the sessions, and in the winter months I would listen to my playing from that summer and wonder at how he could extract stuff from me that by the following March I had lost. So the rule became: listen to the tape, listen again, and duplicate that.

What he gave to me, at least, was a sense of pace, power and assertiveness in piobaireachd playing. Even his delicate stuff, like "Lament for Mary MacLeod," was punctuated with pace, rhythmical complexity or surprise, and musical impact. He was certainly the most powerful influence on the general feel that I developed for the playing of piobaireachd. He taught me, without even articulating it, the value of the right tempo, and the sense of confidence and assertiveness, that even the most sorrowful of music demanded.

During my time with John MacFadyen, pipers could play in the Open Piobaireachd at Oban (now the Senior Piobaireachd) and the Gold Medals at Oban and Inverness. The Gold Medal contests of course had their own set lists usually requiring six submissions, and the Open a different set list usually four, if memory serves correctly. In addition, I could and did play at the Skye gathering, which demanded a list of McCrimmon tunes. I don't remember the number required, but I do recall that it was not unusual to be carrying a repertoire of 12 to 14 competition-ready piobaireachds. The salutary effect on memory and discipline could never be duplicated. When I hear current day pipers whining about the demands of learning set tunes, I simply scratch my head.

ANDREW MACNEILL

While I was just getting underway down this road, I played The "Battle of the Pass of Crieff" at Cowal Games for a bench composed of Bob Hardie and Andrew McNeill. While Hardie was the better known because of his strong solo career and legendary leadership of the Muirhead and Sons Pipe Band, both had great pedigrees, and from the same Cameron lineage. Andrew, a sheep farmer, lived with his wife Flora on the island of Colonsay and was regarded as one of the finest sheep dog men in Scotland.

It was 1973, and these two men awarded me third prize in the Open Piobaireachd at Cowal. This was a watershed event for me, as it was rare to the point of near nonexistence for a Canadian even to place in such a contest. But more importantly, it inspired me to think that I could really do this at this level. Even more significantly, Andrew struck up a correspondence with me which involved the exchange of cassette tapes where he would play tunes on the practice chanter as he had been taught them by Robert Reid, with full and colorful descriptions of Reid, his prickly personality and single-minded devotion to his Cameron teaching. This generosity of spirit was typical of Andrew, who loved good piping, was an excellent player himself and had a wicked and puckish wit. The story that I heard was that Reid had readied Andrew for the Gold Medals, but the Second World War intervened, and Andrew never did come back to competition. Whether that story is apocryphal or not, he was clearly a very fine player, and his willingness to share his knowledge with me added further gloss, or perhaps dimension, to my sense of piobaireachd and how to play it.

I recall one year at the Glenfiddich when the late Dr. John McCaskill teamed up with Andrew at the dinner and ceilidh that follows the contest. They were seen together as the last of stragglers called it a night and staggered off to bed in the wee hours of the morning. The Glenfiddich was always hazardous to one's health because it was held on the same day that the clocks went back to standard time, so at the witching hour more than one reveller said to himself, "It's not really midnight—we've just been given another hour,"—and the consequences were often disastrous.

But this particular year McNeill and McCaskill set a record, or at the very least a personal best, for they were still there at nine a.m. in the restaurant of Scotland's hotel, quaffing what I recall was peach schnapps or brandy and having not gone to bed at all. A truly heroic performance.

CAPTAIN JOHN MACLELLAN

In my quest for tuition, I approached Capt. John MacLellan, the director of the Army School of Piping, for some help. He had had a storied career, having won every prize there was to be had, and pulling off the remarkable feat of knocking down the "big four" all in one year: the Open Piobaireachd at Oban, the Former Winners March, Strathspey & Reel at Oban, the Clasp at Inverness, and the Former Winner's March,

Strathspey & Reel at Inverness. And he did this twice. As I said at the outset of this memoir, he was a very bold and direct player, and notwithstanding his military bearing and manner, he was a sensitive and kind man. When I wrote to him seeking tuition, he responded promptly, warmly and with real encouragement. He answered me by cassette tape and I recall his words, as I still have this tape and perhaps one hundred other tapes from all of my tutors from around this period.

"Bill you asked for tuition, but I think with your excellent bagpipe and technique you will just take from the listening"—and that's how our lessons went. I chose the tunes from the set lists, and he sent me tapes of him playing them, usually recorded on the bagpipe during his many years at the Army School. Bold, definitive playing, brisk in tempo, articulate crisp technique. He would precede the tune with some broad general guideline such as "the variations from here on must be kept moving, a good steady pushing into it."

As I write this, it occurs to me that this is likely the distinct difference in the performance style that I was taught by all of my tutors, from that which is heard today. Piobaireachd playing today can be very slow indeed, and it is a feature I find that I frequently comment on negatively when judging. I'm reminded of something my father said to me when I was fairly young, and playing a slow air at dirge speed: "Bill, come on, even grief has a tempo."

I rather took the piss out of Gen. Frank Richardson at the beginning of this memoir. But he was the author of a pungent remark about slow playing years ago. It was surely a never-seeming-to-end performance of a piobaireachd—a lament, which led Gen. Frank to write in a review of the tune a great line, that I confess to having purloined myself for use on more than one critique sheet: "The tune was played so slowly, as to be not merely sad but downright lugubrious." I hope I haven't mangled that too badly from memory.

So Capt. John and I carried on in this fashion for some time. He seemed to respect very much the player's treatment of the tune, or perhaps he was more liberal with players who had reached a certain level. For instance, after I had played the "Lament for the Harp Tree" at the Kingston Piping School, to which he had brought me on-board as an instructor, he suggested merely that there were passages in the ground and first variation (I played the Campbell cantaireachd version) where it might be appropriate to speed up and/or slow down. He asked if I would consider selecting, more or less at random, some of the high As and other notes that occurred to me, and extend them. It was quite an eye-opener, and I was heartened by the trust he placed in me. His advice was terrific. The tune soars with this treatment.

DONALD MACLEOD

Nothing needs to be said about the overall masterfulness of this remarkable piper and composer. As a teacher, however, he was in a league of his own. He also taught me by cassette tape, and he took the trouble to make them for me personally. I have Donald's entire collection of piobaireachd tutorial CDs, and it's pretty clear that the tunes he recorded for me, were for me, and not just a duplicate of the tapes that he made for general distribution.

He was the best pure teacher of piobaireachd I ever had. He explained the deficiencies in the printed scores found in the books, he explained and illustrated the frequent, but hidden, compound time passages in tunes written in simple time, he used his knowledge of the Gaelic language and song to extract the full beauty of the melody. He never made more of the piece than was in it. But he never made less.

He used a clear vocabulary:

"This is a little 'and' note."

"In this case, the first note is long and themal, the second a short 'and' note."

"This is a carryover high A, by which I mean, imagine picking it up lifting it up and over the fence, and putting it down gently on the other side."

He sang the tunes, in a very tuneful and expressive voice, second only to Bob Brown in that department, and then demonstrated on the practice chanter. He explained that singing it was the best way to get the "lights and shades," surely a John Mac Donald phrase because R. U. Brown used it a lot too.

Though I got to him when I was a pretty experienced player, he took no chances with me and re-taught me the crunluath movement as he had analyzed it: "Sound low G; make a D grace note; lift the low A finger; flush upon the low A make an E grace note, followed, after a very brief pause on low A, by an F grace note identical in size to the E grace note; allow a brief pause on low A and lift to E. This is not a toarluath plus something—it is a whole movement of its own. Practice this slowly, gradually increasing speed and maintaining the integrity of the movement as above described. Gradually slow back down, and then repeat the process. Finally, perform the same exercise adding the various theme notes with a G grace note on the theme note."

I follow this method with all of my pupils, no matter how advanced they are when they come to me. This method has saved me from ever developing a crunluath problem, as I will return to it if I sense an issue, and the movement self-corrects.

My lessons with Donald expanded to face-to-face sessions with him at the Grainger and Campbell shop on Argyle Street in Glasgow, where he worked and had an ownership interest. I perched on a stool playing the practice chanter, concealed from the public by a sort of a knee wall, facing Donald who would be sideways on to me. He would deal with customers coming in to buy reeds, music books, pipe bags and all the usual paraphernalia associated with bagpipes. He kept up a constant dialogue and chatter with the clientele, waving his left hand in a conducting fashion, which initially I was sure was absent-minded with no real attention to what I was playing. How wrong I was—any straying from the conducting, an error or technical flaw, brought the commerce conversation to a sudden halt, and a word of correction or advice from him. It was marvelous.

Aside from my father, these were the giants I learned from. I'm not sure that there's another piper of my generation who was under the influence of such an amazing, varied and rich group of leaders in the art. They were as different from one another as chalk is from cheese and wasn't, isn't, that the joy of it for me? I know it made me a more complete musician, and I hope, no I think, it makes me a better judge now that I work from that side of the bench.

13

Piping Guys I Have Known

The field was littered with fabulous characters of every type: people who were edgy, engaging, funny, envious, generous, sour, suspicious, good-natured, welcoming, forbidding and, on the pipe band side of things, paranoid purveyors of every nutty conspiracy theory that could be imagined in such a tiny, even cloistered, world as the microcosm of pipe bands truly is. It's astonishing to me that we can become so impassioned about something that only a tiny percentage of the world's population, likely measured in terms something like .0001 percent, has ever heard of, much less cares about. But *we* do. And I hopelessly admit that I am a member of that .0001 percent and will rail about my passion for the art, and the stuff I see wrong with it, for as long as I can put air into a Ross canister bag.

So my piping journey took me to, and through, Scotland, and what I have seen reminds me a great deal of what I saw in Canada, with our initial reaction to, and final acceptance of, Russian and other European hockey players. If you find it amusing that I resort to the obscure world of hockey (ice hockey as non-fans call it) to explain and elucidate the even more obscure and arcane world of piping, I ask your forgiveness and indulgence. I'm Canadian. I grew up with hockey as well as piping. As the Italians say with a Romanesque shrug, "Whadda ya gonna do?"

I don't want to give the impression that the initial reaction from all pipers in Scotland was negative and condescending. It was not. But that attitude was very much in the air, at least in the air around me.

Maybe it was just me, but I doubt that. It could go beyond negative to downright insulting.

Here is a little example from the West End Hotel in Edinburgh. This was sometime in the early 1970s and there had been a wonderful event at the Leith Town Hall—the Eagle Pipers Recital. It was really a contest featuring some of the best: Iain Morrisson, Norman Gillies, David Hutton, Jimmy McGregor and others now lost to memory. The format was a March, Strathspey & Reel, Hornpipe and Jig. The playing was phenomenal, Ian Morrison won the day and provided a short recital after he was announced as the winner. (This event, incidentally, was the inspiration for the creation by my dad, who was with me there, of the William Livingstone Invitational, now "The Livingstone.")

I recorded the performances, and spent many hours in the years afterwards trying to clone what I had heard, especially from Iain's playing. I never did completely get there but the effort led me to a better place in my light music. I idolized Iain's playing and to this day regard him as one of the most beautiful light music players I have ever heard. Interestingly, given what I'm about to reveal below, Pipe Major Angus McDonald of the Scots Guards was a close second. For those who would complain that I've omitted some other greats in this judgment, I agree that Roddy MacLeod, Alasdair Gillies, Stuart Liddell and others share this distinction. But I have competed against at least two generations of pipers, and what I'm describing is the effect on my own playing, of the guys who helped shape it, while it was still being formed. These two (Iain and Angus) were entirely different in approach, with Iain producing delicate, refined musicality, elegant technique and a sweet bagpipe. He was the first and best exponent of the round reel—or is it better termed the straight reel? Whatever, it was unique and captivating.

Angus, on the other hand, had a bold direct style, hammering technique, and as befits a big man, a big robust pipe.

The West End Hotel in Edinburgh was a famous hangout for pipers, and could be counted on to draw the curtains of the bar after what was then an uncivilized closing hour, and allow the ceilidh and fun to carry on until the partiers themselves decided to end it. After the Eagle Pipers event my father and I were somehow invited to the West End, likely at the behest of Norrie Gillies. Norrie, father of the famous and tragic late Alasdair, was a great guy, and the first Scottish piper to befriend me and offer a welcome into the club. He was a terrific piper in his own right, and as good a march player as I've ever heard—almost certainly where Alasdair got his great march playing

After we had settled in the bar and had a dram or two, Pipe Major Angus, and Pipe Major Ian MacLeod, leader of the Edinburgh Police Pipe Band, arrived in "full huff and puff" as my dad called it, having just finished performing in the Edinburgh tattoo. The two then launched into a conversation, with me and my dad no more than a couple of feet away, wherein they began slagging "these Canadian boys."

"These guys are all technique, and don't know how to produce any music at all. I'll tell you Iain, I'd much rather hear a boy playing a good musical tune with a few technical blemishes, than one of these with nothing but technique alone."

You can see the insult and condescension intended. They knew exactly who I was, and set about doing this deliberately. It certainly created an impact, for I was very hurt by the assessment, and remember it 40 years later.

But these were the earliest days, and attitudes later softened. At the Argyllshire gathering in 1976, I played "Millbank Cottage" in the March competition. Pipe Major Angus was listening, and complimented me on my tune, saying that though my top hand was a bit flat, "you will still be all right." Indeed I was, winning the event.

And Angus, a legendary wit, and roguish raconteur, was a very funny guy. Tom Speirs was telling the story of how the Clasp he'd won at Inverness had been lifted... stolen. Tom related how he'd had to have a replacement struck and paid for by himself. Angus eyed him and said, "That's the second time that Clasp was stolen." Ouch.

Or when Angus was terminally ill and he remarked, "What am I going to do if the doctor tells me I have only three minutes to live? Boil an egg?"

It's a truism to me that the Scottish sense of humor, generously distributed amongst Scottish pipers, is a unique, dark and fabulous take on the absurdities of life. Billy Connolly, Craig Ferguson and many others don't come by this stuff by accident—it comes with the genetic material, the wonderful subversive nature of much of Scottish society, and perhaps as well the weird and troubling stuff that goes on every day and night in Glasgow, Edinburgh and almost every town of reasonable size.

THE MAN-SPACE INCIDENT

I started going round the games in Scotland without the slightest clue about the "rules," or at least the protocol. I travelled everywhere with Lillian. When I went to the games park, she came with me. I had no idea that none of the Scottish guys did this. They travelled alone. When I consider it now, it may have been a function of raw geography. In Scotland, competing at a contest staged as part of a Highland Games, or even as a major stand-alone event, seems generally to involve a round trip completed easily in a matter of hours, and certainly a day. Maybe that's a contributing factor, and maybe not—it might simply be the custom—but universally it seemed that wives did not accompany their piping husbands to contests. Lily always came with me—she did so at home, where a one-way trip to a contest could exceed four or five hours, and she did so in Scotland. It seemed a perfectly natural sharing of something important to us both. The fact that my colleagues at the time of the events described below ("colleagues" is perhaps too enthusiastic a description of them, at least as they were in those days) frowned on this practice was made exquisitely, painfully clear at the Portree Games, this in the early years.

The Isle of Skye Games, as they are formally known, are staged over two days, a Tuesday and Wednesday if I recall, with the piping events held on the first day. The Games occupy Wednesday and are held in the most beautiful Brigadoonish setting: a natural amphitheater called, in English rather sadly, "The Lump." It's a promontory of rock that juts into Loch Portree with its panoramic view of the Black Cuillins, with the Town of Portree a precipitous plunge below. And Games they are—all the classic heavy events, kid's races, hill races and of course Highland dancing.

The tradition was that the winning pipers from the previous day's competitions had to play for the Highland dancing. Now this quaint custom seemed to proceed from the notion that all good pipers know how to play for Highland dancing. Well, it's not true—or certainly not in my case. So imagine the amazingly picturesque scene of Portree Bay—high on a hill, overlooking the sea, or what would be the sea if it were not obscured by rain, fog and other phenomena only described in the meteorologist's handbook.

I was required to play for one of the Highland dancing events—I don't know which one and it doesn't matter. I didn't know what to do then and would know less so today. It was very cold and wet. There was a capacious tent set up, perhaps for the athletes or maybe for the pipers to tune up in. I discovered this tent—*aha!* Some place dry and a little warm for Lil and me to repair to while I try to tune my soggy pipe, and release my frozen digits. So in we went. I struck up my pipe, and like every piper who ever lived I turned my back to folks around me and began flailing away with some tuning notes, and the strathspey or whatever it was that someone told me I had to play.

I had no idea that I had violated a treasured man-space. Scattered around the sides of the tent were little shrines or totems of pipe cases, cans of lager, folded rain capes and Glengarrys and Balmorals. Each of these little piles belonged to one of the winning pipers. As I struck up and began to prepare for the godawful "playing for the dancing," I invited Lily into the warm and comforting precinct of The Tent.

JEEZ-Oh! as they say. There was soon a display of male micturition—kilt-lifted urination and nearly canine marking of territory as would give an anthropologist material for a doctoral paper. Lily got the point. No kidding. She fled in the face of this rather bizarre display of male dominance, and never ventured near another piper's tent again. And I don't think I did either.

ROBERT U. BROWN

You didn't have to search very hard to find folk on the generous side of the ledger. My first Argyllshire Gathering ("Oban") was in August 1972, my mother having died suddenly several weeks earlier. The investment in a trip to Scotland for Lil and me, as well as for my dad who'd planned to travel with my mother, was a hefty chunk for a young struggling lawyer and a smelter worker from Copper Cliff. Despite my mother's death we decided to press on with it, since staying at home would change nothing, and at least we would all be together.

This was right at the beginning of my career and I was as raw and green as you could imagine. The tune requirements for the Gold Medal Competition demanded a list of six piobaireachds.

I was scheduled to play last in the event, and I believe I was to be competitor number forty. It was close to eight p.m. as my time approached, and I entered the stage of the quaint Dunollie Hall wearing an outfit that only a dork from Ontario could have donned. It consisted of a McLaughlin tartan kilt, a gaudy concoction of startling red and green that was the kilt worn by the General Motors Pipe Band of Oshawa. This city is, and was even more so then, completely driven by the automobile industry, with huge GM assembly plants driving the heart of the economy and providing the majority of the jobs. The band wore the McLaughlin tartan in tribute to Colonel R. S. McLaughlin ("Col. Sam"), who had founded the McLaughlin Motor Car Company in Oshawa and later sold it to General Motors.

My ensemble was completed by a waistcoat, a fancy jacket with special metal buttons, a drummer's plaid tied around the waist and draped up and into an epaulet on the left shoulder, fastened there with a cairngorm brooch the size of a dinner plate. Headgear was almost certainly a Balmoral but I think, mercifully, it did not sport a feather.

I walked over to the judge's bench, looked into the twinkling eyes of R. U. Brown (Robert Urquhart Brown), one of the "Bobs of Balmoral." His faint smile was not unkind, but I could see him taking the measure of this fellow with the woefully unfashionable garb, and rendering a silent judgment that was not going to be helpful to me.

He gave me my tune, "Struan Robertson's Salute," and I was off. Pipe sounding well, in fairly good control of the nerves, but disappointed in the choice of tune given me—I had much better stuff on my list. I don't recall what the others were, but I remember thinking that this was the weakest tune of the six, both in terms of length and inherent quality, as well as my own preparation.

So I launched into it; it started well, the repeated first line continued in steady fashion, and then I began to play the first line for a third and fatal time. When a piper does this sort of thing, there's a mental jolt—"How the hell did I manage that?" All that's left is to wave a pitiful salute to the bench, exit stage right, take the pipes apart and have a drink. So I did just that with Lil and my dad. Several, in fact.

The next day, following the light music competitions at the games field, I was with Lil and my dad in one of the nice downtown hotels in the "lounge bar." This was how they still quaintly referred to the "nice bar" as compared with the public bar and the riff raff that might accumulate there. R. U. Brown was sitting there with some piping friends, almost certainly fellow judges. He caught my eye, summoned me over to their table and spoke to me in the kindest manner imaginable:

"Struan Robertson was in your list as your last choice because you needed it as your sixth tune, am I right?"

"Yes, you are."

"Well, we're very sorry, because the minute you blew up your bagpipe, we knew we had made a mistake. Don't be discouraged by what happened."

Not many judges would make such a wonderful gesture—it was incredibly heartening coming from a legendary figure and I was entirely uplifted. I replayed those words many times over the next few years. My direct interaction with Bob Brown was very limited, but what little there was always confirmed my impression of him as a very warm-hearted person. Of course, like most serious piobaireachd players, I have the entire collection of the *Masters of Piobaireachd* CDs and every time I listen to Bob Brown, I regret not having had one-on-one tuition with him. It is obvious from these recordings that he was a very beautiful piobaireachd player, and capable of extracting the most exquisite musical touches from the tunes, touches that seem to elude almost everyone else.

In particular for me, there is a prized recording of Brown, said by Malcom MacRae, himself a Gold Medallist and now a senior judge, to have been done in 1968, with him playing "The Lament for Mary MacLeod" on a BBC broadcast, done live from a studio in Aberdeen. This performance opened my eyes to what was possible in this already beautiful tune. I played "Mary MacLeod" in Oban in 1979 and won the Gold Medal with it. I have a cassette recording of this performance, and while it evokes some of Brown's treatment, clearly I was still not completely invested in it, or more likely lacked the confidence to just run with it.

His rendering of "The Lament for Mary MacLeod" features long sustained theme notes, well beyond what is typically heard, contrasted with very short, although not hacked, connecting notes. He plays with tempo and pace, showing great willingness to increase and then relax the feel. He takes control of the poignant passages, and unusually in the variations, he stretches them to the utmost in expression. His variations never fall into the somewhat dull and excessively metered or "march-like" feel so often heard with current performance style. As I play the tune now, it's obvious that Bob Brown put a whole new gloss on my understanding of it—which is not to say that it's a clone of his playing. I likely couldn't do it just like him anyway, but he truly opened a door to a new way.

R.B.NICOL

Now for the other of the Bobs of Balmoral. Here's the scene: the Braemar Highland Gathering in the period 1972 to 1976. R. B. Nicol sits in the middle as the senior man in a bench of three, in a tiny little three-sided tent, judging the piobaireachd competition. It's always an early start for this event at Braemar, the third coldest city in the U.K., sometimes with frost on the ground at the beginning of it. The judges are wrapped in multiple layers with a care that would have made proud the Egyptian guys who prepared the pharaohs for their journey to the never-never. Kilts, jackets, vests, sweaters, all somehow nestled in there, plus Balmorals (what else?), capes, shawls and great tartan blankets draped from the waist over the knees to the brogue-encapsulated feet. And the contest went on. Forty pipers, more or less.

And here's the magical thing—the wonder. There's not a music book in sight for these judges—no *Piobaireachd Society Collection*, no *Kilberry*, no... nothing, apparently, but their faultless, nearly digital memory of the three hundred or so tunes that comprise the piobaireachd repertoire. Not to fret, however, since all the pipers knew that Bob Nicol and these disciples of his on the bench had learned all this stuff so well that there would be no possibility of a mistake. Even then, at my relatively adolescent stage of understanding, I knew this had to be complete bull feathers—the potential for hubris arising from judging some forty pipers without any reference guide to determine who was on the tune or off it was high, indeed a recipe for disaster. Not that they may not have "known" the tunes in a broad way, but rather that following the score is a much better way for the judge to keep his head in the game.

And so it came to pass (biblical reference just there for stylistic sarcasm) that Bob Nicol and his team presided over some fairly spectacular judging screw-ups. I know I started this memoir with a tale of a judging fiasco that affected me—but the Braemar Specials, as my teacher John Wilson called them, exceeded almost anything that one could anticipate. Here's how John described what happened one year at Braemar:

"*I listened with pleasure to John MacDougall playing the 'Blue Ribbon'... I met him coming out of the competition area and I told him that I had enjoyed his performance very much. 'Ach,' he said, 'I missed out a whole variation.'... When the result was announced, it was a 'Braemar Special': First prize—John MacDougall.*"

Wilson then goes on to describe his three-line method of judging, ticking off each line and always having the *Piobaireachd Society Collection* at hand. He points out that by this method, a "Braemar Special" is practically impossible. He writes in *A Professional Piper in Peace and War*:

"*When the very competitors who have assiduously practiced their tunes for the current season, can, and do, make major mistakes, how on earth can a judge expect, or be expected, to memorise perfectly a large number of piobaireachds, some of which he hasn't played or heard for donkey's years, or possibly knows only by name? The whole thing is just ridiculous...*" John then finishes with a recommendation that the Piobaireachd Society mandate that judges carry the books. My experience today (noting, however, that I have never judged at Braemar and expect never to be asked and so can't speak to that contest) is that no judge would dream of judging without the book open in front of him.

For me the coups de grace with R .B. Nicol came after the piobaireachd contest at Aboyne. I had played "The Bells of Perth." Well. On a fine pipe. As was customary for me with Bob Nicol, I got not a sausage. I'd encountered him before at the games in the northeast—Braemar, Aboyne, Ballater etc.—and was not surprised at the result. At the end of the day I was in the beer tent having a dram with fellow pipers, talking the nonsense typical in such a group, when Mr. Nicol made his way across the tent, apparently to speak to me. It was obvious as he was pretty much up in my face. I had not approached him to discuss my tune; indeed, I had never approached him on such a matter at any time. (This is how I remember it. Jack Taylor, who saw it all, says I asked him about my tune—an apparent no-no at the time. Jack may be right about that, but it's not how I recollect it. In any event Jack and I agree on the substance of the verbal exchange that took place.)

His opening gambit was, "Your 'Bells of Perth' was all wrong, right from the very first note."

Gawdawmighty, shades of General Frank—why this? I asked, "What do you mean—in what way?"

"The first E of the ground is long, and you played it short, right to the low G."

By this time I had been around enough piobaireachd dogma preachers to have some views, so I expressed them: "That just fries my ass. That fries my ass to a goddam tee."

Picture here a demeanor drifting between astonished and nearly apoplectic

"Uh...wu...well Well, where did you get that tune?"

And now my own axe fell: "From John Wilson of Edinburgh." Of course Mr. Nicol would register that name like a thunderclap, for John was the fellow who ruled the boards in the twenties and thirties, when Mr. Nicol and most others competed against him with less than stellar success.

The story took on a life of its own, likely because it was true, and witnessed by many onlookers. I've been reminded of it many times, and it always seems to evoke a chuckle at the piercing of the piñata, and the outspoken take-no-horseshit Canadian who was not in the thrall of rigid thinking about our music, and its sometimes self-appointed torch bearers.

This also was an event too enticing to escape the barbs of John Wilson's pen. Writing in *A Professional Piper in Peace and War*, John observes that *"Donald Morrison, one of the judges and a great player in his own right, had Bill first, but Bob Nicol wouldn't have him in the prize list. Nicol said, in the presence of Morrison, that his playing of The Bells of Perth wasn't in the traditional way that he had got it from John MacDonald of Inverness: that the Es in the urlar were too short."* Wilson goes on: *"Roddie Campbell told me that when John MacDonald first heard him competing, he asked Roddie who his teacher was and Roddie replied, Sandy Cameron. MacDonald said he would go to Sandy Cameron for lessons too, and he did."*

Wilson writes: *"MacDonald knew both the Cameron and MacPherson styles and would never have been so small-minded and bigoted as to penalize either style. I received many a first prize from John MacDonald, even in front of his own pupils, and when I judge, I try to be as just, impartial and fair-minded as I always found MacDonald to be... a judge who is bigoted and dogmatic is a danger to piping."*

However, all was not a crap shoot from the so-called Balmoral School of piobaireachd. Jack Taylor is a perfect example. A lovely guy to begin with (always a good start), and steeped in the teaching of the Bobs of Balmoral. But not a shred of dogma or rigidity to be found in him. His approach to the music seems to be based in humility, and he is open, broad-minded, and always ready to reward a thoughtful, musical and committed approach.

A very good friend of mine, a fine piper and a serious student of ceol mor and its attendant history, has ruminated on this subject. His thinking considers how the teaching and education in the art of piobaireachd resided for a long time with the "common folk" such as Bob Brown and Bob Nicol. From that point there seems to have been a movement to pass the thinking of these two men to many members of the professional class. The result seems to be something of a professional class condescension in the matter of ceol mor. His thesis is that without the intervention of "society," piobaireachd today might still be dead as an art of compositional creativity, but it might be vastly more wonderful as music than it is today.

To be sure, there were many great guys on the Scottish scene. Angus J. Maclellan, Pipe Sergeant of the Glasgow, later Strathclyde Police Pipe Band, befriended me and made me welcome from the very start. A fine and powerful player, pipe held on the right shoulder, he was a big guy with a wicked wit and willing to share what he knew. And what he knew was a great deal, most of it derived from Donald MacLeod. Angus sat in our first home on Lupin Drive in Whitby, and doctored up my Kilberry book with the amendments to "Glengarry's Gathering," to put it into the style in which he played it to win a Gold Medal. We became lifelong friends; he was one of Wee Donald's greatest pupils and had an encyclopedic knowledge of the repertoire, both ceol mor and light music.

I cannot be certain of the year, 1974 approximately, when he played in forty-seven separate events and won forty-two prizes. Remarkable.

Bob Hardie (yes the great R. G. Hardie), Colin Drummond and his brother, Jimmy, took various trailers, caravanettes and portable living arrangements and camped here and there at various Highland games. Bob Hardie was a very modest and shy man, never going on about his dazzling status as a piper, and sincere to his boots. In the World Pipe Band Championship in 1984 the Frasers had placed third. This was only the second trip to the Worlds, the band having only adopted the name The 78th Fraser Highlanders in 1981. I was in the habit in those days of waiting out the interminable pointless march past and prize giving, by sitting on the grass with my pipes beside me. When our third place was announced, one of our pipers gave a shriek and a jubilant leap skyward, only to come down on the top joint of the bass drone of my 1925 vintage Hendersons, which barked out a sickening crack as the tuning pin gave way. With the top joint of my bass drone hanging like a victim of Loreena Bobbit, I made my way to Bob Hardie's shop in Glasgow where, while I waited no more than thirty minutes, he crafted an identical replacement in matching black wood, installed it in the big drone, and I was on my way.

Once at the Cowal Games in Dunoon, Bob Hardie, the Drummonds and the Livingstones were camped at the top of the rise opposite the grandstand, talking over a dram, when several rifle shots broke out from the housing development behind us. With bullets seeming to whiz and whir by us far too closely, there ensued a dress rehearsal for a rapid lights out, and a scramble to the floor. We all escaped unharmed, but I gained a newfound respect for, if not outright fear of Dunoon and the Cowal Highland Gathering.

And here is one final, if slightly grotesque, footnote to what could go wrong in Dunoon. This place is a very picturesque spot at the south end of the Cowal peninsula—it's somewhere between a large village and a small town. On the second day of the games, when the pipe band competitions and Highland dancing are held, thousands of revelers flood the streets—flood being an unfortunate term here.

The main street leading from the games park to the ferry dock is lined several rows deep with folks who have been partying all day long, dropping emptied cans of lager everywhere. The pubs have been filled to overflowing for hours (more unfortunate liquid imagery) and the whole place is, by about six p.m., quite out of control, verging on chaos.

The Frasers in this particular year made the traditional march down to the dock to catch the ferry back to the mainland. We had a fair wait before we could board the next available boat, so we took the opportunity to stock up on fish suppers. We loosely assembled around a stone fence or dyke, using it as a makeshift table for the consumption of this classic, though humble, treat. We munched away, oblivious to the ominous rumblings that must have been going on underfoot. Suddenly, no more than twenty or thirty feet away, one of the great round iron covers that allow access to the sewer system for maintenance, in an earlier, less politically correct time called manhole covers, was launched into the air, did a flip like a coin being tossed at the start of a sporting event, and crashed to the pavement with a metallic ring like a bell. It needs to be said that the sewer system of Dunoon was undoubtedly overtaxed beyond the point of endurance by the thousands of patrons drinking, and yes, voiding into that system. The manhole cover rattled and clanged to a stop. I shall not describe in detail what happened next. Just imagine any underground liquidish system overloaded to the point of explosion. A geyser of raw sewage is a frightening possibility. That's what happened, and half the group of Frasers lost their fish suppers. Had I not been there to see it, I would not have believed it.

SEUMAS MACNEILL

I have met some interesting and difficult piping folks over the years—many quite elegant and refined as they slammed you to the mat, and others decidedly less so. Here is an example of the former.

Seaumas MacNeill, was the Principal of the College of Piping in Glasgow. He invented the institution so one should not cavil too much about the self-appointment to the position of Principal. Tall, thin, with something of the aesthete about him, he was very well educated, and with a vocabulary and acerbic wit that made him a perfectly suited radio host on the BBC piping programs, but which, in terms of his international reputation, served him best as the editor of the *Piping Times*. This publication made its way right around the piping world—it was subscribed to and read wherever the pipes were played. I had more than one run-in with Seumas. Seumas was referred to in dismissive and derogatory tones by Willie Connell as having been originally called Jim MacNeill—true? not true? I don't know, but the cynical and blunt-spoken Willie Connell certainly made his views about the famous Seumas known to all who'd listen.

I had won the Brymay Trophy at the Cowal games for the first of five consecutive times. This trophy is awarded to the piper who accumulates the best overall results in the March, the Strathspey & Reel and Piobaireachd events. Seumas wrote in the *Piping Times*, or perhaps said on the air on the BBC piping show, that this achievement could be safely ignored, for "as everyone knows, the best pipers don't go to Cowal any more." This was said at a time when Mr. MacNeill was travelling regularly to the U.S. and Canada, earning what was likely not an insignificant supplement, in cash perhaps, to his salary as a lecturer at the University of Glasgow. One would have thought that a little harmless boost, or at the least the avoidance of a deliberate insult to a North American piper, would have served him better.

Then there was my performance of the "Big Nameless" tune in the Open Piobaireachd at Oban. As mentioned earlier, pipers in these days could compete in this event, even if they had not won the Gold Medal.

Of my performance, Seumas had something like this to say (accurate quote unavailable to me):

"Bill Livingstone played the 'Big Nameless' tune and demonstrated that the great tunes would be better left to the masters, and the others should stick to the potboilers which win most contests".

Pass the bandages please.

I reminded Seumas of this a few years later at the after-party following the Glenfiddich Competiton. He said, "Did I really say that? That's terrible." All done with a sly grin on his face.

I was invited to compete at the 200th anniversary of the Falkirk Tryst piping competition. The Tryst has a storied place in piping lore, representing, as it does, the first piping competition in history, at least as we now understand competition. Some background here: I have fought a lifelong battle with the problem of the bag slipping down my side as I play. One year at the Glenfiddich I was moving confidently towards a major prize in the piobaireachd event when the bag began its inexorable descent to my hip, heading ultimately for the knee. By the toarluath doubling of the "Pass of Crieff" there began to emerge some micro squeaks and chokes as my bodily grip on the instrument was failing. By the crunluath variation it was a horror show. Now the thing is, in an invitational event such as this, the expectations are very high, and the contest runs on a schedule which, while not laid out, is very well understood by the pipers. So most pipers will, out of consideration for those to follow, even in this hopeless situation, soldier on to the bitter, squeaky, chokey end. I did.

But I vowed to find a solution, and years later I did. I cut a round hole in the left side of my jacket, and a long oblong hole in the left arm of the jacket and was thus able to play in what approximated shirtsleeves. I won't try to recount the waste of money and jackets this entailed, but it was considerable, because not only did I mutilate the jacket I played in, but I also had to have another one that was intact, for walking around in when not playing, otherwise I'd have looked as though I'd fended off an attack by a hungry Doberman. It was only after a few early attempts that I learned to have the job done properly and neatly by a tailor.

Now to the Falkirk Tryst. I had not yet devised the jacket-wrecking scheme, but I was in need of a fix. I had won the Clasp that September at Inverness playing the "Lament for the Laird of Annapool," the monster of all piobaireachds, and with all the practice, preparation and rehearsal for that event, my sheepskin bag had turned into something resembling a chamois that's been used to wash the car. So I tied on a brand-new sheepskin bag. When I tested it after the usual and now only dimly remembered ritual with the bag seasoning, the new skin adhered to my side like it was glued there. Voila! Slippage problem solved, gone, forgotten—never again to torment me. Snowy white, unblemished, virginal even—I thought it looked beautiful.

As I strode into the competition area, a very dignified rotunda suitable for town Council meetings, I noticed nothing unusual. My head was totally into the game and fierce concentration on the task at hand— i.e. playing piobaireachd. So I struck up and gave as good a rendition of "Rory Macloude's Lament" of which I was capable. I took a bit of a risk with the grand first variation and its doubling, which is written as the first variation of "In Praise of Morag." The first variation of Morag has undergone some bending over time, and of course it's now perfectly acceptable to play it in an even style, with all three notes of the three note groups roughly even, but with, as Capt. John schooled me, a slight swelling of the first of the three as though you can imagine it being played more loudly than the others. So I did that on a fine pipe and with technique from the top drawer, start to finish—only to learn that I didn't qualify for any prize in the list of five places. Ditto for the March, Strathspey & Reel. By this time I had become accustomed to the vagaries of prize awarding in Scottish piping events, and I just vowed to suck it up and keep on keeping on.

It was not long before the problem became painfully transparent. Seumas wrote the thing up in the *Piping Times*. I don't have a copy of the article anymore, so I can't quote it verbatim, but I can share with you that it was, in Seumas' frequently unfortunate style, an ill-informed and denigrating piece. His tone seemed to be that I had deliberately set out to insult the organizers of the Falkirk trust. I had played without a bag cover, the naked skin of the brand-new sheepskin bag being flaunted white and unashamed in front of the audience!

And that transgression committed after this organization had actually "paid my way!" to be there. No interview with me at all, no question about why the lack of a bag cover, just the arrogant assumption of certainty and correctness in all things piping. It's little wonder his reputation and legacy is a decidedly mixed one.

I for one, however, think his contribution to piping was towering. I don't like, but I don't terribly mind, that I was the object of several mean-spirited if not vicious barbs. It must be remembered that he created the idea of piping journalism, which to the present day thrives in the great piping publications that we all read assiduously. And he led the way to the creation of the National Piping Centre; these are huge contributions. Sadly for him, he was somewhat overlooked when it came to appointing a Director of the Centre. There were efforts to accommodate him with some role in the new institution, but they were unsatisfactory to him

And anyway as one wag said, you're nobody until you've been slagged by Seumas.

And here's a delightful postscript to this story. There was a film being produced by the BBC in and around the events. It ended up being called *The Glorious Effect* and it featured film of me getting off the plane in Prestwick, where I had landed on my way to play at the Falkirk Tryst, and followed me into a taxi. As part of the process of filming I had been interviewed during the Northern Meeting on the banks of the Ness River ("Do you get nervous?" "No, of course not," with this last accompanied by a huge exhalation of cigarette smoke giving the lie to this denial). But the best part of the video is the footage of the judges at the Falkirk Tryst as I made my way into the Council Chambers to play, sheepskin bag exposed for all to see. The judges nudged and harrumphed at one another about this terrible affront.

Seumas was right—they did pay my way. But if he had thought to give some context (oh, that old journalistic watchword), he might have asked me for an explanation of the reasons, musical or otherwise, for what I did. And he might also have seen that while this particular trip was indeed on their dime, I had likely, by this time, spent $70,000 or more of my own money in travelling to Scotland to compete.

I guess that I could have played "Rory McLeod" like Patrick Og McCrimmon himself, and the result for me would have been the same.

BOB SHEPHERD

Now we come to R. T. Shepherd—Bob Shepherd frae Fyfe. It's not easy to select from the many anecdotes about this fellow, but I'll relate two. From about 1979 through to 1982, when the Frasers came into existence, I had been variously the Pipe Major of Caber Feidh, then of the General Motors Pipe Band, which ultimately transitioned within a couple of years into the 78th Fraser Highlanders Pipe Band. We were playing some pretty revolutionary stuff, and creating a lot of buzz. These were the days when we had John Walsh, Ian Anderson and other good players contributing to the repertoire. But principally, in these early days we had Gerry Quigg. He was and is the embodiment of cool. If you're old enough to remember the TV show *WKRP in Cincinnati*, think Dr. Johnny Fever and you'll get a glimpse of the style of Gerry Quigg: droll, laid-back, smart as hell and a wizard at musical ideas.

He was born in Bryn Mawr, Pennsylvania and lived for some years in Northern Ireland, which was his dad's home ground. The resultant accent is a unique if somewhat mystifying combination of Pennsylvania twang and Northern Ireland brogue.

He immigrated to Canada following his stint in the U.S. Air Force Pipe Band, a gig that kept him out of Vietnam. After noodling around Caber Feidh and the GM band with me, he stayed on board when we became the 78th Frasers. When Gerry and I played together in Caber Feidh, it was clear to me that he was a fountainhead of ideas. Sadly, however, Caber Feidh was in a sorry state of internal strife with some of the younger members pressing for organizational revolution—doing away with the title of Pipe Major and replacing it with something called a Prime Motivator (I guess because the initials PM lined up), dropping the focus on competition and so on. They drew up a whole manifesto, which got rejected. They left. Despite feeble efforts to carry on, the band folded. So I presided over the demise of this fine pipe band that had such a strong history and tradition. Clearly not everything I've done in piping has been a success.

But back to Gerry. During the period of transition from Caber Feidh to GM to the Frasers, we had brought out "Laggan Love Song," "The Mason's Apron" and "The Little Cascade" as well as other innovative music not typically heard in pipe bands, and certainly not typically heard as *we* played this stuff. Each of these had a different genesis, "Laggan Love" from the Irish group Horslips, "The Mason's Apron" from the Boys of the Lough, and "The Little Cascade" in a Bossa Nova rhythm with some delicate, and distinctly non-pipe-bandy touches in the timing of certain bits. (Read Gerry's interview in *Pipes|Drums* from July 2011 where he describes in detail these sources along with actual recordings of them.)

Now enter Mr. Shepherd. He had taken the Dysart and Dundonald band to the World Pipe Band Championship in 1977 and 1978. As a result, he had become a hot commodity, and was sought out to judge in Ontario, and did so on a few occasions while the Caber Feidh/GM/ Frasers were showcasing all of this fresh new stuff, in the various iterations of this group that was really the same band.

It was later reported that Mr. Shepherd had kept a tape recorder on his person while judging and recorded us. I was told this by several sources who had seen it, although I did not notice it at the time as I was engaged in conducting these bands. Clearly he did something that enabled him to get our ideas and music recorded for his and his band's purposes. And the result was that our innovations suddenly and magically appeared in Dysart and Dundonald's repertoire. It was maddening. Not only was there no acknowledgement of the source of these things—and remember that innovation in pipe bands is pretty much anathema, so those who do it might be forgiven for being territorial about their creativity—but Dysart's and Mr. Shepherd's use of this music was frankly was not just a rip-off but a cheesy one at that, losing, in my opinion, the integrity of the approach we had adopted to these pieces. So he robbed the Frasers of the chance to debut this material in Scotland. It would not have been a debut, and we would have been accused of ripping off Mr. Shepherd and his band. But the truth of the origin of this stuff is spelled out in exquisite fashion by the aforesaid Gerry Quigg. Here's how he told the story to Andrew Berthoff of *Pipes|Drums*:

> BERTHOFF: *The 78th Frasers and the tail end of GM, the cusp of that transition. The music was **allegedly** lifted by people like Bob Shepherd——who may have taken credit for some of the ideas. Considering you had a lot to do with the genesis of both ideas, how did that make you feel?*
>
> *(Note: above emphasis added by Andrew Bertoff)*
>
> QUIGG: *I guess ambivalent might be one way of saying it. I mean it was nice that we were almost getting a compliment, by the fact that he was playing some of the things that he had heard when he came over here and judged us. But I kind of did resent that he never acknowledged the genesis of his ideas. But that's neither here nor there. He and Ronnie (Rollo) are good friends and I know that Ronnie got as much as an admission from him as he ever will or could and that's good enough for me.*

And then came the final insult on top of the initial injury. In 1983 and 1984 there were great pipe band competitions in Chicago at Grant Park on the shores of Lake Michigan. A spectacular setting and event. Anyone who was there remembers it as one of the grandest parties of all time, as everyone involved stayed at what was then the Conrad Hilton Hotel. This grand old place, eighteen stories tall and with some seven or so towers seeming to be independent structures but in fact joined together, was a hotbed of nearly maniacal fun. Parties broke out everywhere, in the rooms and just as frequently in the grand lobbies onto which the elevators opened at every floor stop. Filled with over-stuffed couches and chairs and elegantly carpeted, these places became irresistible gathering points.

My luck was such that I ended up in a group folks in the lobby of one of the floors up in the teens, where Bob Shepherd appeared—or maybe he was already there and I had not noticed him, else I would have skedaddled. So Mr. Sheppard, unbidden by me, launched into this story, delivered in that hilariously imitable Fyfe accent: "See Bill I was in Ireland doing a school and workshop, when someone brought a recording of a piece of music, "My Laggan Love," and I was so taken with it, I scribbled it out on the blackboard right then and there, and that's how I found it." Unable to speak in the face of this brazen story I snorted, sneered and disappeared.

On August 11, 1988, just two days before the World Pipe Band Championship, the 78th Frasers staged a concert in one of the main halls of the Assembly Rooms in Edinburgh. Michael Grey, Bruce Gandy and I went away for a "pre-game" meal and returned to the venue about two hours prior to showtime, which was seven-thirty. We were stunned to see a lineup of people stretching around the block to gain admission to the venue. It was both exhilarating and daunting; we joked about the rock star feeling.

This place is a magnificent piece of architecture and a grand venue for a pipe band concert. The place was packed and we had a tremendous time playing, receiving standing ovations and demands for encores. At the after-party I was approached by several of the greatest names in pipe band history, and told that Bob Shepherd had sat in the bar throughout most if not all of the show, offering to all and sundry, whether they wanted to hear it or not, his view that we were "a load of shite, and they'll get fuck all on Saturday.".

Inasmuch as he was scheduled to judge Grade 1 on Saturday, I could not let this go unchallenged. I contacted the then head of the RSPBA, Robert Nicol, and gave him the details of what happened, and identified by name all of the completely unassailable sources of the reports. I demanded some form of action and penalty.

All that was done was to remove Shepherd from judging the Grade 1 bands on Saturday—not nearly enough. He continued as an RSPBA adjudicator, judging countless major championships, including the Worlds, many times. A figure-skating judge behaving in the same way would likely receive a lifetime ban.

Still though, the fairly poisonous relationship between us has produced some funny moments. The guys in the Frasers were well aware of my feelings towards the man from the Kingdom of Fife and his history of slagging the band. In full knowledge of this context, they pulled a prank on me that initially had me shuddering in embarrassment. Mike Grey told the story on the 60th birthday website that folks affectionately created for me. Here is how he described it:

> Driving home from band practice in one weeknight evening, the carload of us were, as usual, feeling particularly troublesome. With the novelty of the cellular phone still fresh and almost exciting we—well maybe it was me—decided to call Bill up on his own luxuriant car phone, for gawd knows what real reason. Speeding along Highway 401, we connected with Bill: Bill's answering machine, that is. He had his car phone forwarded to his office and that was where I ended up. If opportunity knocks—answer the door! And that is what was done. On went his machine: "You have reached the offices of Coath Livingstone, etc." At the sound of the machine I launched into my very best Cardenden brogue (well practised, ken, thanks to years hanging around J. Reid Maxwell): "Hello Bull Livin'stun Boab Shepherd frae Cardenden, can ye gee me a ring bock, ut's very important ken." After hanging up

we all laughed and never thought much of it until the next day, when Bill called me at work somewhat a-flutter. His Dundee-born receptionist had cleared the strange message from Bob Shepherd, assuring Bill it was genuine, you see, as she could spot genuine Fife anywhere. With that Bill had called Bob up in Fife. Bob didn't know what the hell Bill was talking about and they both figured—rightly—some prankster was up to no good. Anyway the band— and Bill—had a good laugh, that day and years later.

The ending was not quite as innocuous as Mike describes it. When Shepherd's phone rang, his wife answered. I'm sure I didn't misread the tone of astonishment when she called out, "Boab, it's Bull Livin'ston frae Cahnadah." Nor was there any mistaking the cautious sense of inquiry in his voice when he took the phone.

"Bob, it's Bill Livingstone. I had a message at my office to call you."

"No Bull, I didnee call ye."

Ah shit. The penny dropped. Here I was tricked into calling a man I had little desire to speak to, and I'm sure that he had precisely the same feeling about me. If we'd had Skype then, he would have seen the flush of embarrassment creeping up my face.

It was, however, very funny after the fact. As are many other equally devious pranks that have been pulled on me. It seems pretty obvious that I am a gullible bonehead when it comes to this stuff, but as Kurt Vonnegut says over and over: "I had to laugh."

BOB WORRALL

When the new schedule came out each year, I'd grab it and circle the Boston games. To me it was The Two and the other 80. (Magic Johnson)

The first thing I would do every morning was look at the box scores to see what Magic did. I didn't care about anything else. (Larry Bird)

...Typically, associated with competition is the drive to win, or defeat one's opponents. However not all opponents are alike. Certain competitors or rivals can instill a motivation that goes beyond an ordinary competitive spirit or the objective stakes of the contest. It is clear from the opening quotes that Magic Johnson and Larry Bird viewed contests against the other as far more significant than games against other teams and players and that they were heavily focused on, indeed almost obsessed with, their relative levels of performance.

...prior interaction is central to rivalry as relationships are generally formed over time...we believe that competitive experiences can leave a lasting psychological residue that may influence competitive behaviours even long after the contests have been resolved.

(Source: Academy of Management Journal, 2010 Vol 53, No. 5, 943-969)

Bob Worrall grew up in Teeswater Ontario, a small town in Bruce County south western Ontario, near the shores of Lake Huron. It abounds with place names like Kincardine, Lucknow, Cromarty, Greenock and Glammis. His father was the editor of the local newspaper, and undertook the running of highland games in Teeswater for a couple of years. Bob started piping lessons with Bill Millar, a very fine piper from Northern Ireland who likely imbued Bob with the terrific clarity of technique so common in pipers from Ulster, and very much in evidence in Bob's playing. He is almost exactly nine years younger than I am, and we came onto the Ontario piping scene at roughly the same time. I started in the "Open" as it was then called in 1969, and Bob migrated to the Open a year later at age 18.

From the outset we were pitted against one another. We each took part in John Wilson's group lessons at the Fort York Armouries. When I graduated to private lessons with John, he reminded me more than once that I was doing very well, but still had a way to go to catch Bob.

In Ontario in these days there were many competitions throughout the summer games season, and Bob and I would knock heads nearly every weekend. He was a tough guy to beat, especially in light music, and his work ethic and practice discipline were faultless. I had an edge in piobaireachd, perhaps because I loved that music so much, and devoted a lot of energy to expanding my repertoire of tunes each year, whereas Bob seemed content to work within a smaller selection of tunes. Our rivalry was for quite a long time, a feature of the Ontario circuit, and frequently the topic of conversation on Games day…"who won the March?… what about the piobaireachd?… who was "Piper of the Day?"

Then we began to play together in the General Motors Pipe Band. We became friends, and in fact palled around together quite a lot. Then something happened. I can't be sure I know what it was, but it was not great from either one of us. Our friendship soured and turned into something brittle. Bob had gone on to great success at Inverness, winning both the March and the Strathspey and Reel in 1977, but never competed in the Former Winners' March Strathspey and Reel at Inverness. I have asked him why that happened, and why even more strangely he gave up competing entirely in 1983. Following his breakthrough at the Northern Meeting, Bob, who had completed post graduate studies to become a teacher, landed work teaching high school. The school year started immediately after Labour Day, which put his work and career in direct conflict with Oban and Inverness. He continued to compete on the Ontario circuit until 1983 and then hung them up and took up judging and teaching bagpipes.

The real reasons for his retirement are surely more complex. Still a young man, Bob was dealing with his own identity and sexual orientation. He was struggling with the death of his father. He was living in what at least in those times, was the fiercely macho world of piping and pipe bands. With our renewed friendship and ease with each other we've talked about how he dealt with this, and he's very clear that he "simply did it". He and Todd have been together for 25 years, and married for 15 of those. It's a pretty courageous story.

After retiring from competition, Bob took up judging in a serious way, judging bands and solos all over the world where pipes are played. He's clearly an auto-didact, and has educated himself thoroughly in all aspects of pipe band performance, and in particular in the art of piobaireachd, his mastery of ceol beag never in question.

As for my side of this business, for a large segment of the time that we were, if not estranged, then at least somewhat strained, I was struggling with my own issues brought on by my depression and anxiety. I can't offer this as a complete excuse for my part in it, but I certainly was not firing properly on all cylinders during these times. I asked him recently what he thought might have contributed to our frosty relationship. He said that he believed that if he had stayed with me in the General Motors band, and then we had gone on playing together in the 78th Frasers, things likely wouldn't have gone off the rails. I think there's a lot to that, because playing together in a band creates a camaraderie that is pervasive, and nearly demands bonding and friendship. Bruce Gandy and Mike Grey were similar rivals, but they played together in the Frasers, and what happened between Bob and me, did not happen to them.

I started this discussion with a reference to the great rivalry that existed between the two players who changed the game of basketball forever...Larry Bird and Magic Johnson. After they retired from playing, these rivals became great friends. They wrote a book together, made countless joint appearances, and had a Broadway play staged about their amazing careers. Recall the importance of relationships in forging rivalries. Magic and Bird were about the same height, they turned pro in the same year following Magic's team beating Bird's team in the NCAA Championship, which set the tone for the annual March

Madness of college basketball thereafter. As Rich Reilly of ESPN has said, "they were so inflamed to beat each other that it pushed them to heights they might not have otherwise achieved".

I may be accused of a touch of overstatement in comparing two Canadian pipers to two of the legends of basketball, but rivalry is the same, no matter what the field of endeavor. Bob and I have similar relational backgrounds…we came on the scene at nearly the same time, we took lessons together from the same man, and we faced each other nearly every weekend, in the same limited arena. As Magic said of himself and Bird "Both Larry and I are very strong, strong willed and strong minded". The same is true of Bob and me. No wonder we had the relationship we did.

And that past tense is the key. Like the basketball players, we now find ourselves in a place of mutual affection and respect. It's a place we're both happy with.

14

The 78th Fraser Highlanders Pipe Band

My early career in pipe bands would not have led anyone to predict that I would become the leader of a band as successful, and as many have remarked, game changing as the 78th Frasers. In 1970 I was giving a small recital at the regular monthly meeting of the Toronto Branch of the Pipers' Society of Ontario. George Campbell, who had just immigrated to Ontario from Glasgow, was in the audience, and remarked to a mate, "See that guy playing over there? Well I'm going to get him in the band." The band he was referring to was the General Motors Pipe Band based in Oshawa, and George was its Pipe Major. And more to the point, Lily and I were living in Oshawa. He invited me to come out to a practice, I accepted, and soon enough joined the band.

It was a Grade 2 band, and typical of the times fielded some ten pipers and a similarly small drum section. Compare that with today's sections of up to twenty-four pipers, ten snare drummers, six tenors and a bass. The band had some very good players, and also typical of the times, some journeymen whose talent was to be able to "blend." That, too, is creature long gone extinct, at least in the Grade 1 and 2 ranks. Now you must be a good piper, period. The pipe corps was strengthened by George himself, Bob Worrall, Johnnie MacKenzie and me. We went along for a few years, got better, got to be pretty good, added John Kerr as the leading drummer, replaced him with Jimmy Agnew from St. Catharines, added my cousin, Grier Coppins, and his mate Pat O'Gorman to the pipe corps, and seemed to be headed for some good things. But behind the curtain not all was well. George had fallen in love with booze, and it took his already electric, energetic personality over the top. I left the band.

Next in my peripatetic wanderings, I became the Pipe Major of the Caber Feidh Pipe Band in Toronto. This was my introduction to Gerry Quigg, mentioned elsewhere in these pages; also in the pipe section were Grier Coppins, Pat O'Gorman, Ian Goodfellow, and Brian Pollock. We had the great Luke Allan on bass drum, with John Kerr as the leading drummer and Trevor Ferrier and other disciples of the Kerr style making up the drum corps. It was not to last very long. Grier, Trevor, Pat, and Ian had a plan, which I describe in more detail elsewhere in these pages. No Pipe Major—that post to become Prime Motivator—less emphasis on competition, more experimental music and other "peace, love and brotherhood" ideas as I came to call them. Their plan was rejected, and they all left the band, which led to the collapse of Caber Feidh. Grier, Ian, Pat and Trevor went on to form Na Caber Feidh, lived in Britanny for a year, returned with a whole new set of sounds and ideas arising out of their exposure to Breton music, and became a well-known Celtic/Folk/ Rock band. That later morphed into Rare Air, and Grier is still make his living as a musician under the rubric Grier Coppins and Taxi Chain.

Sickened with pipe bands, I turned my back on the whole idea, and focused all of my piping energy on my solo piping career. That didn't last long. In 1981, George Campbell and Johnnie MacKenzie paid me a visit, pleading with me to take the reins of the still-existing General Motors band. By this time I had my first Clasp, and all the light music at Oban and Inverness, and I succumbed to their pleas. And so I became the Pipe Major of the General Motors Pipe Band at age thirty-nine. As we'll see, that changed in a very short time.

I have often been asked to describe the how and the why of the 78th Frasers Pipe Band and to explain the "method" that I used to have it work as it did. Here's a small anecdote that might illustrate the process. I recall in, I think, 1989, Mike Grey and I had dinner with Richard Parkes at the Dickens restaurant in Inverness. We were there for the

Northern Meeting. Dinner turned out to be a fairly heavy affair, with Richard being very earnest and serious and in full cross-examination mode. We had recently won the World Championship and he was on a quest to do the same thing. He peppered us with many questions about how we did this or that, or what the motivation for X was, how did we decide and fix on certain pieces of music, what were our practice and tuning techniques. Richard at this stage was clearly a guy who wanted to fashion a world championship band, and was looking for formulaic systems to achieve that.

In fact, the Frasers didn't start in that way, and never became anything like that. It was all very organic—what developed was not a willful, thoughtful creation, but a function of the people involved, their talents, and their intense focus on the music.

If it's not excessively glamourizing it, we were concerned with what we saw as the artistic element—it was not about setting the chess pieces in the right positions to assure victories. We of course were thrilled to win, but the intensity of the band—and there was a huge amount of that—was directed at what we could do in musical terms. I always thought of it as a petri dish of musical invention and creativity, with ideas appearing from many corners. It is not disingenuous to say that it was all about the music, not the prize. I always felt, and said, that if we do what we want, and do it well, the prize will take care of itself. It was incredibly liberating, and created this rich atmosphere of musical adventure and pushing the boundaries.

I know I was quoted in interviews after our 1987 win, as saying that we had a five-year plan and blah blah blah: "We first had to prove ourselves as I learned in my solo career in Scotland, plus we simply had to get good enough." I was flying at the time and felt the need to say something pithy. No five-year plan ever existed. What I really meant was that it would take us five years to get to where we wanted to be. But oh my, the number of times I have since heard pipe majors comment on their own three- or five-year plans can't be counted. But indeed, there was a certain arc over the five years leading to the Frasers capturing the World Championship. From 1983 to 1987, in each of those succeeding years, the band was placed fifth, third, fourth, second and finally first. Topping it off with the Live in Ireland concert and recording in the same year as we won the Worlds gave the band a unique cachet and place in pipe band lore. This was a singular achievement for a newly formed band—such a meteoric rise was unheard of.

The way that the original 78th Frasers Pipe Band tartan came about is sort of a metaphor for the rise of the band. In 1967, the year of Canada's Centennial, the David Stewart Museum in Montréal fostered a re-enactment of the 78th Regiment of Foot, which fought at the Plains of Abraham. Simon Fraser, Lord Lovat, the chieftain of the Clan Fraser, enlisted the cream of the Jacobite gentry, many of whom had fought at Culloden. It appears that a swatch of the original tartan from the 1760s had survived and was given to a weaver, who was asked to reproduce this tartan for the kilts to be worn by the re-raised regiment. The weaver tossed the sample on the shelf where it remained for a considerable period, resting in the sunlight. By the time he got around to weaving it, the reds had faded to orange and the instantly recognizable and unique tartan was born. Unplanned. Organic.

To take up the story of the abandonment of the General Motors tag, and get to the founding of the 78th Frasers, this is what happened. Iain Symington was in the GM band and he had some connection with members of the Toronto garrison of the 78th Frasers Regiment. They needed pipers from time to time for their functions, and called on Iain. One thing led to another and before long there was talk of the band become becoming associated with what was originally The 78th Regiment of Foot, and later become known as The 78th Fraser Highlanders. It brought us instant cachet, historical significance, and more to the point, new uniforms, even if the orange-hued kilt earned us some scorn as "the Halloween Highlanders" and "the Pumpkin Pipe Band."

The initial arrangement was to last for five years. It did not survive beyond that time. But the Regiment was great, and allowed us to carry on as the 78th Fraser Highlanders Pipe Band. Unique branding is a hard thing to establish in the pipe band world, and I was fiercely proud of the fact that there was no need to go further in that world than to say "the 78ths" or "the Frasers" to know who was being talked about, and for a pipe band fan to know the kind of music we played.

So when Roderick MacLean, Pipe Major of the Halifax Police Pipe Band and former 78th Fraser himself, called me in 2001 to tell me that the Halifax police could no longer sponsor the band and the Citadel had taken them over, changing the band's name to "The 78th Highlanders," I was deeply offended and angry. The phone call went something like this:

Roderick: "Hi Bill. I have some good news... well, maybe you won't think so. We're no longer with the Halifax Police, we're with the Citadel and it has changed the name of the band to The 78th Highlanders."

Bill: "Jesus Christ, Roderick, how could they do that and how could you be part of it? They just come along and scoop the product of twenty years of my life's work?"

It went downhill from there, with justifications about some old regiment called the 78th Highlanders having some association with Halifax or the Citadel or Nova Scotia, and "orders from on high" etc., etc. I was so steamed I couldn't remember the justification, and later had to go and look up some history to see if the story stood up. Justified by their local history or not, in the pipe band world a unique brand and image is valuable in every sense of the word, and I am still not happy about what was done and have told them so.

Yet there was some satisfaction to be had. One year at the Worlds, we were in the final tuning area, and the 78th Highlanders "Halifax Citadel" (this latter I guess guiltily added after the initial name change), who were slotted to play ahead of us, were announced as entering the arena. A voice behind talking to his mate said, "Bloody - nonsense—there's only one 78th." I did chuckle.

Many years have passed since then, and my feelings have mellowed somewhat. As one who was in charge of a world-class band for twenty-nine years, it is not lost on me that financial support for a pipe band is a valuable thing indeed. The Frasers struggled throughout our entire existence with the challenge of being completely self-supporting, and it was a hell of a burden. Indeed our band manager at a certain period, the wonderful Ev Hazzard, had posted debt on the band's behalf to her credit cards in a staggering amount—something like $70,000. She did this out of love for the band, but it was simply insupportable, especially since the true state of affairs was not known to the leadership. Once this terrible situation came to light, it had to be fixed. With the careful stewardship of John Cairns, the Pipe Sergeant at the time, the debt to Ev was finally paid off.

While I see the need to compromise things in order to gain some funding, my understanding is that the financial support in return for naming the band with a title so similar to the Frasers was less than stellar, which still makes me wonder what actually is the extent of the sponsorship. I hope it was substantial. It takes some $60,000 to $70,000 a year, more or less, to run a pipe band in Canada, especially one that travels to Scotland to compete. I'd love to know the amount they got/get.

But to return to the story of the original 78th Frasers—"my" Frasers—the band began its steady rise in 1983. By then we had Michael Grey and Bruce Gandy, who were composing music, as was I. We had John Walsh and Ian Anderson, both of whom had experience in the Celtic folk world and access to music from that world not yet heard in pipe bands.

In those days we had the anchor team of J. Reid Maxwell ("Coffee"), Luke Allan and me. Reid and I were perfectly suited at that time—both very aggressive players devoted to high speed and energy. I hear recordings from these days and want to shout and cheer. And while Luke couldn't read a note of music, he was the best bass drummer on the planet and had an intuitive understanding of the rhythms of Afro-Cuban music and of the Brazilian variants of it. He knew where silence was a tasteful musical choice, and had a great knack for getting a great bass drone supplementing sound from his drum. It's true he could be a little undisciplined and unpredictable, but that didn't prevent Alex Duthart from once calling him the best pipe band drummer in the world.

Reid was a very special case. Young, brash, arrogant and full of self-confidence, he had recently emigrated from Scotland with two world championships with Dysart and Dundonald under his belt. Mike Grey initially brought him to the band. His first appearance at band practice was classic Reid—black and white judgments and all laid out in his Fife accent, so reminiscent of his former Pipe Major Bob Shepherd. He pronounced that our drummers played "a load of shite." Familiar ring to it?

I asked him how he would drum to "The Mason's Apron." By this time we were well into round reels, and the U.K. bands had not fully caught on. So I played "The Mason's Apron" on the practice chanter, and he accompanied me on sticks and pad. It was a bit of a setup, and I heard what I had expected to hear—a dot and cut style of drumming out of sync with the smooth flow of a round, or perhaps better stated, straight, reel. I turned him down, as much for attitude as anything else.

But our drumming was not good. *Really* not good. So Mike went to work on Reid and talked to him about the stuff I couldn't tolerate. He came back to me offering a chastened Coffee Maxwell and so it happened that he became our leading drummer and it was great for a long time—but not for all time.

Still it was a great run together. We were both in love with the front end of the beat, and the mesh was magical. Forward motion, excitement, and because of our natural affinity for this style of play, the ensemble presentation was captivating. On top of all of that, Reid was able to write scores that captured the stuff in the melodies that needed to be highlighted, and seemed able to make drumming easy for his corps. He has gone on with SFU to show conclusively that this is no accident.

With all the full-throttle talent in the room, not to mention no shortage of huge egos, often incongruously accompanied by great sensitivity and thin skin, you would have thought it would be a chaotic mess. It was not. It was an unusual mixture of collaboration but in a perversely highly competitive environment.

I suppose part of the secret was that I was not threatened by any of it—by which I mean all the high-voltage talent. I was happy to have such a strong team around me, but felt that I was the right guy to make final musical decisions. Ideas came from everywhere, and we worked in collaboration towards a final decision—usually mine, but quite frequently as a group. I doubt there was anything like it before and there may not have been since.

Let me assure you that I don't view those days through rose-colored glasses. I'm not a Pollyanna and managing this juggernaut was a full-time task. The pipe section was riddled with high-powered talent and outsized egos to match. The simple act of bringing new music to the party could be an exercise in self- flagellation. Tunes could be treated with shrugging indifference, whole-hearted guffaws, comments like "Are you serious?" and the great ability that all pipers seem to possess, of singing a piece of music, even a great one, in the most demeaning, insulting sing-song fashion imaginable.

The pipe section developed, without any deliberate intention, a two-tiered character, and this fact alone gave rise to mutterings and discontent. In the first tier, of course, were the most talented players and composers. It was perfectly natural that we would gravitate to each other, because if you've got some people with superior talent, skill and creativity, they're the ones to whom the leader will look principally for consultation and input. But none of these guys was a shrinking violet, and they made life challenging for me from time to time.

John Walsh was born and raised in Bradford in the north of England, and was brought to the band by Ronnie Rollo. John is a self-taught piper, a stunning achievement in itself. He found himself in the Shotts and Dykehead Pipe Band and then in the British Caledonia Airways Pipe Band, a unique experiment not unlike the Invergordon Distillery Band of a generation or two before.

In "B-Cal" John became friends with, and likely much influenced by, Allan MacDonald and Pipe Major Angus, these great MacDonald guys being cousins. They left a huge imprint on John's playing, both in terms of repertoire and style. He is a lovely player of light music, in particular jigs and reels. Smooth as silk, seemingly effortless, with an uncanny sense of time, everything in rhythmical proportion, and all delivered with fingers that appear hardly to move at all. This last feature made it difficult for the pipe section to follow if I was not playing, for John as the Pipe Sergeant would be leading the pipers.

John is one of those guys who I felt was beyond talented. I know a lot of talented players, but he had a gift. I always thought, and I have told him directly, that he could have had everything that can be had by a piper, but that his ambition was not fevered enough. He was somewhat like Scott MacAuley in that regard. Had either of them pursued piping the way that I did, or Jack Lee or Mike Cusack, their achievements would have been legendary. It may have just been too easy for him.

For all of John's apparent confidence, he is very sensitive, and easily hurt. He left the 78th Frasers, moved to Nova Scotia, his wife Jean's home, and established his business of manufacturing shuttle pipes, Highland pipes, practice chanters and pipe chanters. He had a background in what used to be called tool and dye making, and he applied his considerable skills to the very well-made instruments he crafted.

After some time away, he returned to the Frasers, and we enjoyed several fine seasons together again. By this time Iain Donaldson was the Pipe Sergeant of the band, and had become the owner of a business started by his dad, the British Shop in Buffalo N.Y. Iain is an aggressive businessman, and with his encouragement, John invested a great deal of time, energy, and undoubtedly capital in the design and production of a new pipe chanter. The band played the chanter but with mixed, or even less-than-stellar results.

One year I called a practice on the Sunday after the Maxville Games. It was held in Kingston, Ontario, a town about halfway home to Toronto. Neither John nor Iain was there, which was a real shame given what happened. We had been in possession of a set of new chanters, made by a different pipe maker, for some time and we tried them out at this practice. We universally agreed that they gave us a much better pipe sound, especially on the top hand. I decided to switch to them.

With only a few days left before the band left for Scotland for the Worlds, there was no time to handle the change diplomatically, although I doubt that any amount of diplomacy could have mitigated the feelings that the sudden change engendered.

Upon arrival in Scotland, John confronted me on the stairwell of the university residence we were staying in and told me that he was deeply hurt by what I had done. The words I remember were something like, "Bill we have known each other for twenty years, and you couldn't have hurt me more if you'd stuck a knife right in my guts." God, I felt awful, but while the PM's job is to be aware of the sensitivities of the individuals, his primary obligation is to the team of thirty or more musicians.

In any event, we lost both John and Iain Donaldson to Shotts, where they both played as long distance guest pipers, gathering another World's title in the process.

These were not the only sensitivities I had to try to understand and "deal with," if that's the right term. Michael Grey comes immediately to mind. I met Mike in his sixteenth year when he started coming to me for instruction. An assiduous student with a work ethic similar to my own, his quick mind, natural talent and serious passion for piping was obvious from the start. His withering and often daunting wit appeared a bit later, as he gained confidence and some maturity.

We launched into a mentoring relationship that over time matured into a friendship, which continues to this day. Indeed we had problems, particularly around the time that Mike was becoming discontented with the Frasers, which ultimately led to his leaving the band. I'm not sure even now what happened, but I *suspect* that at that time he was having his own ambitions, and thinking that it was time for me to retire and open the door for him. But at the same time, Mike is a notoriously impatient guy, and perhaps he just felt it was time to move on because it was no longer fun.

By the time he left we were playing a significant chunk of his output as a composer, and I only learned after the fact that this caused resentment.

His impatience was something to behold. Because he's so bright, he soon loses interest in those who are not up to the repartee. He quickly becomes bored when some project, whether it be learning new tunes, selecting reeds, or working on the sound doesn't go as smartly as he hopes. His impatience is palpable on these occasions. Here's an example:

Mike had discovered the story of Donald Morrison, The Mégantic Outlaw. This tale was important to him because Mégantic is in the Eastern townships in Québec, where Mike was born and raised through his early years. His idea was to use the general theme of Morrison's story as the skeleton upon which to hang a musical version of the legend—or as they call it in opera, the libretto.

Mike, Bruce Gandy and I met at my house in Whitby to get the project of creating "The Megantic Outlaw" underway. We made a pretty good start that night, getting a good opening tune completed, a bright and cheerful jig to be used in an appropriate spot, and a few other ideas sketched out for the piece. Not a bad night's work. But Mike was completely annoyed: "This is taking far too long—we should have had this whole thing finished by now."

We broke up the brainstorming session and met a few days later. Mike walked in, slapped the entire completed score for the suite on the table, with harmonies built, complex and terrific shifts from reel to jig time and back again—a real marvel of musical ingenuity.

And of course, Mike went on to compose pipe music in the most prolific way. His output of original pipe music is likely second only to that of Donald MacLeod, and he was never shy about bringing his stuff to the band. It was only after he left that I heard about the resentment that this caused, and how much I was seen to be at fault for indulging him.

And it needs to be said: as much as I am fond of him, he could be a very difficult guy. Smart, quick witted, and as they say, one not to suffer fools gladly. Still he's one of my favorite guys in piping—he makes me laugh, I make him laugh, and we share some fundamental ideas about our art. Our conversations are wide ranging, pretty much everywhere and not just piping. The craic is terrific, and like all of us I suppose, with passing years comes more maturity. I love him and I'm sure the feeling is reciprocal. He got me back into pipe bands after I left the Frasers; reached out to me and said, "Bill, just come and play—no bother, no psychotherapy sessions with pipers—just fun." I accepted and here I am in the Toronto Police Pipe Band, while ironically Mike left the band after my first two seasons in it. Still we continue to be the best of friends.

Bruce Gandy was, and is, a different character altogether. In those days he was a very fine, nearly electric player of light music, and now in the later stages of his career, of ceol mor as well. Bruce is also a prolific composer with a great knack for playing and writing reels—big ones and little ones. He also has some weird kind of musical intelligence.

At a two-day band practice at my house one lovely summer weekend, he sat on the grassy slope under a tree and played both sets of march, strathspey and reel straight through without flaw on the practice chanter. But here's how he played them:

"Argyllshire Gathering," part 1
"Brigadier Cheape," part 1

"Argyllshire Gathering," part 2
"Birgadier Cheape," part 2

... and so on, in that fashion, through "Blair Drummond" and "Bogan Lochan" to "John Morrison of Assynt House" and "Charlie's Welcome," alternating each part of the respective tunes as he went. He made it right to the second-last part of "Charlie's Welcome" before crashing and burning. The rest of us sat around gobsmacked.

Bruce was not without his spiky bits and sharp edges, either. He comes from a large family and lost his father Ray, a piper too, when he was still quite young. Growing up in Victoria, B.C., he was of course drawn to the City of Victoria Pipe Band, and there came under the influence of its PM, Jamie Troy. Jamie, never known to be overly soft-hearted and certainly not bashful, is a very fine piper and pipe major. His City of Victoria band produced beautiful tone and playing, which I'm sure left a clear impression in Bruce's mind about pipe bands, and he was not backward about coming forward with his thoughts.

Bruce is a plainspoken, direct fellow who leaves little room for doubt about his views. But for all the tension among us all, we cajoled, insulted, joked, and traded barbs with great good humor and laughter.

There was a significant amount of discontent amongst the pipers who were not part of this leadership group, a group somewhat snottily memorialized by Iain Symington in his tune, "The Piobaireachd Club." The sarcasm is implicit in the title. The complaints were fairly typical I think—the infantry feeling they were not informed as well as they wanted to be. Syd Girling once told me I was the master of the mushroom style of leadership: "feed them bullshit and keep them in the dark."

I was aware of the bitching, because a lot of it was made directly at, or to me. Barry Ewen, a terrific piper and a great guy, was a frequent caller after a band practice. Fresh from his stint in Nova Scotia, where he led the Scotia Legion Pipe Band, he was not averse to repeated calls offering unsolicited advice on everything from tune selection, playing styles and tonal issues to leadership deficiencies. Ross Brown was a frequent caller as well—also with the same broad range of suggestions or complaints. Others were less forthright, but the whinging went on amongst themselves, and was later reported to me—but we survived it all and went from strength to strength with ever-increasing success.

Earlier in this section I talked about how the orange-hued tartan came about. Sadly, we were to make a mistake and lose the strange distinction of wearing that kilt. Andrew Berthoff had the idea of creating a specific pipe band tartan for the 78th Frasers. The intention was to create a riff on the garish orange color with some tweaking here and there... to continue with a reflection of the tartan that symbolized a singular pipe band. Iain Donaldson ran with the idea as he was invested in the notion through his business, the British Shop, but ended up creating a fairly nondescript tartan that made the band look more or less like all pipe bands—and so the metaphor comes full circle.

I am not a harsh leader, and I was not a tough pipe major. Pipers were dropped from the circle with a gentle, but clearly dismissive, wave of the hand—arm extended, back of the hand facing the piper, a gentle flip or two of all fingers up in the direction of the piper who was being sat down. This, at least, is how it has been described to me, and memorialized by Iain Symington's tune "A Distant Wave."

Never a screamer, I always believed that it was not possible to beat people into being better musicians. But I was usually surrounded by a coterie of extremely talented players, who had an incredible focus and attention to the detail of the style I wanted. Jim McGillivray once wrote of me that he could never understand how I could run a Grade 1 pipe band the way I did. It was contrary to everything he knew about or believed in regarding bands, but it "somehow worked."

I'm often amused by people coming to me and mentioning supposed incidents that happened in the band, usually involving some harsh measure by, or comment from, me. Almost always these tales are apocryphal. It really didn't happen that way. Indeed, I was very intense, but then again so was pretty well everyone around me. Tom Bowen, one of the original pipers in the band, recounts a story of how the band was in Scotland practicing for the Worlds, and it was not going well. He swears that my admonition, my instruction, my cross and bad-tempered direction to them was, "Jesus guys, c'mon,—play better."

Again, as told to me by band members, I had a habit of taking both hands and rubbing my hair with my fingers—always taken as a sign that I wasn't happy with how things were going. Seems to me a lot better than getting up into a piper's face, voice at volume ten, spittle flying while berating someone as a useless or lying sack of shit.

The answer to the question of how music was chosen is composed of several parts. There is no explanation needed for the stuff that came from the well-understood heart of the bagpipe repertoire. But what about the outliers for which we became known? The first test was whether the melody was coherently reproducible with respect to the tonality of the bagpipe. Inherent in that broad consideration was whether the piece could be fitted within the bagpipe scale (well, scales, really, because there are a few) and in particular with respect to the unique intervals of the chanter.

It was required that there should be some broad Celtic, Highland, or Gaelic connection with the tune. It could, indeed, be a modern composition, but if it captured the feel, it was in. Think, for example, of Mike Grey's "The Eastern Townships," Bruce Gandy's "Frasers Lullaby" or my own "Ashes on the Afton."

This thinking led us into traditional Irish music, a field that we mined early and often. It also sent us, with Mike Grey in the lead, to Cape Breton, a repository of Highland and Gaelic stuff. While the parameters were pretty much fixed and respected, there were still times when common sense said this is too good to leave out, so a compromise for a note that was outside our range would be made by substituting something from our bagpipe scale. The test was, did it mutilate the tune? If not, we'd run with it A good example of this is our treatment of "The Sea Maiden".

A final standard for inclusion was to ask if the tune had been played on the bagpipe before, but was not well known. Or was it played or playable on a fiddle, whether Shetland, Highland or Irish? Or was it played on Uilleann pipes. We also looked at the source: was it an old source, old tune or Gaelic song?

All of this, for most of the time I was at the helm, took place in the face of organizational adversity. After the first five years, we were completely on our own: no sponsorship, no money, completely self-sustaining. We had no band hall or practice facility—we were always finding a place to practice that cost money we didn't have.

Pipers and drummers were travelling miles and miles to practice. We had players from Ottawa (a four-hour drive one way), players from Barrie (a two-hour drive), players from London (a two-hour drive), players from New York (a three-hour drive), players from Cleveland, Ohio (three-and-a-half hours) and even, during the 90s, players from Scotland and Australia. And all of this was done without any financial help from the band, because we simply couldn't afford it. It was quite an honor to have people make these sacrifices to play in the Frasers.

That's the measure of commitment that we had, and it stands in contrast to the situation with many Scottish bands, where geography usually dictates what band a piper or drummer will play with—it has to be a relatively short drive. Then again, this kind of thing is not entirely foreign to Ontario bands. The Toronto Police Pipe Band, where I'm playing as at this writing, has a contingent of players who come from Montréal, Ottawa, Pittsburgh and the middle of the Michigan mitt, as well as other far-flung places. North America is huge. Distances are immense, and I guess we may just be used to it.

We made the travel of part of the fun. The 80s and 90s were the heyday of Highland games in Ontario. These were the Halcyon days of pipe banding in this province. There were anywhere between eight to fifteen contests over the summer and they covered areas from Ottawa and Montréal in the east, to Brantford, Cobourg and Fergus in central Ontario, and Kingsville and Sarnia in the southwest. There were sporadic sproutings of contests in the smoky places, Hamilton and Toronto, and beloved ancient and quaint farming towns like Embro. We, and many of our friends, had camper trailers—the kind of flattened trailer that gets hauled behind your vehicle. When you arrive at your spot, the clamps holding the top down are released, and the whole affair is cranked up to reveal screened-in sides, plastic drapes for rain protection, a bed or two and a little kitchen and some cupboards.

We'd gather at a spot, erect these things, have a couple of adult beverages, and then have supper cooked on a propane gas Coleman stove. Our favourite was mince and tatties—simple Scottish fare, which laid a good foundation for the frivolity to follow. Inevitably there were campfires, whisky (blended in those days) bagpipes, fiddles, accordions and singing... a natural ceilidh.

If the scent of the mince and tatties grabbed you the night before, it was hardly a patch on the smell of bacon frying, toast browning on the open flame, and coffee brewing in an enamel pot—all of this usually in the lovely warm morning light in high summer in Ontario. But I confess there were near-drownings on some of those mornings when a heat-driven thunderstorm would crash and rattle through. Breakfast was followed by a hair wash and ablution of the body under the ice-cold water dispensed from a standpipe, and then out with the pipes to play in the solos.

There were many of these affairs over the years, and while they could be raucous indeed, I loved every minute of them. And so did Lily—as always, with me, and sharing in the wonderful nutty fun.

We had done this camping thing many times at the Fergus Highland Games, right from General Motors days, but one year is burned into my memory: 1987. The old Fergus Games field (the new one is a sterile "modern" facility) was bordered on the south side by a fairly steep hill, which was heavily shaded by tall pines planted in rows.

Preparing for the Grade 1 contest, I had the band set up in an open spot, and once we were making some good sound we played "Journey to Skye," opening pipe solo and all, including the great drumming break that had been scrambled together only a short time previously. Of course we knew we were going to play it in Ireland about a week later, but this was the first public airing of the piece.

By this time the Frasers were quite accustomed to attracting a large audience to their tune-ups, but this reaction was of a different order altogether. People—pipers, bandsmen, and pipe band enthusiasts—began to materialize amongst the trees. This is not a short piece of music—it's nearly seven minutes in length. Hardly anyone moved. There was none of the noisy chatter that usually surrounds a band warming up. Silent attentiveness, watchful eyes—an obvious connection between performers and listeners even though it was only a warm-up. They burst into spontaneous applause at the end—lots of it. I was utterly relieved and gratified.

From the beginning, getting "Journey to Skye" off the ground was a challenge. Here's how it started. Jim Blackley was a top drummer in Scotland who had come to Canada many years before. He had stayed at my parents' home for a short while on his way to Vancouver when I was fourteen or fifteen. So I knew him, and as a kid I could see he was unique—intense, driven and cool—no ordinary guy. By the 1960s, Jim had come to Toronto, bringing with him a great reputation as a jazz drummer, but mostly as a hugely sought-after teacher. Some of the best drummers on the planet came to study with him. I was not aware that he was in the Toronto area when these events happened: he approached me at the Fergus Games in 1986, white knitted skullcap in place, and identified himself. He is not an easily forgotten man and it all clicked right away. Small talk, memories revisited, and then to what I think was the reason for the visit and the reconnection.

"Bill, do you know Don Thompson?"

"No, I don't think I do."

"Well he is a great all-around jazz musician. Plays piano, drums, vibraphone and bass. Multiple Juno award-winner (Canada's top music awards). His wife Norma is from Vancouver—a piper and a piobaireachd player. He has composed an orchestral piece for pipe band, calling it "Journey to Skye." He understands the tonality and scale of pipes, and I think this is a great piece for your band to consider. I'd like you to meet him and hear the piece—just see how that goes."

Arrangements were made and I travelled into Toronto to meet Don. A most unassuming guy, shy even. In his basement he had a grand piano, drum set fully assembled, a vibraphone and a double bass resting in a stand. There was a glass partition or window through which I could see a complete recording studio. And then to the business at hand—he sat down at the piano and played the entire piece through from start to finish, playing the well-known lead melodies with his right hand, and the countermelodies with the left, even using his hands on the wooden ledge that sits above the key board to demonstrate how he heard the percussion. It was, of course, riveting. I asked him to play it again. And again. As we listened, we talked about how the piece might sound in its final form, with questions from me about how much liberty I'd have in the final arrangement of it.

Not that I had any ideas at that point—I was completely blown away by the whole concept, and it just seemed obvious that some translation to the pipe band idiom would be needed. In fact that turned out to be too pessimistic—all that really happened in changing from the original was the shifting around of various sections internally within the piece, reprising some bits, constructing the percussion break and building the climactic ending. But that was nothing more than rearranging the bits of the whole that Don had created.

It's hard to overstate the impact on pipe banding that this amazing piece produced. First, it was tonally beautiful—rooted in the key of D (our D, not the piano D, actually more akin to E flat on the piano with a strong pull towards low A) and weaving subsequent variations of the initial beautiful motif into many time signatures, with the composer's imagination boldly on display, stringing these new structures on the original melodic skeleton. In short, a complete tour de force, which prepared the ground for a previously unexplored approach to composition for pipes.

Funny how it did not come easily to the band. Don Thompson showed up at a band practice with the piece completely scored out. We circulated it around the pipers, who sat dumbfounded looking at it. We simply couldn't read it. It was written in what I now know was a dumbed-downed version of scoring for orchestral musicians, with Don hoping, I think, that we would at least be able to get the idea. Didn't happen. It featured double staves, joined, with melody and counter-melodies or simple harmonies switching from the top to the bottom staves and back again. We had never seen music like it, and there was a fair level of embarrassment among us for our lack of knowledge, and a considerable amount of dismissive snickering at the whole idea.

Don was extremely patient. He walked around the table, singing the individual sections, helping with the reading of the music and getting us through it all. There was a lot of resistance—nothing like this had ever been attempted and the whole notion was so foreign that the instinctive reaction of many was outright dismissal of the whole idea. But Bruce Gandy was my ally in this, and he joined me in pushing and shoving to get the thing figured out, and then to play it. It was a big challenge, and one we eventually met. By the time we could play all the parts on the pipes, it was suddenly clear that the piece was beautiful and utterly unique. At that point we began the actual arrangement, getting the sections linked, and the finish put together. Of course, much of the piece was played on pipes only—no drums. But there was a need for drums and it was not happening. With Ballymena and a live recording only a couple of weeks away, and my hair now close to being torn out, Alan Savage took the bull by the horns and worked up some terrific percussion, which we converted to a mini drum fanfare in the last two-thirds of the piece, with the pipes getting out of the way, and leaving drummers showing off beautifully on center-stage.

What an incredible feeling it was to play "Journey to Skye." I never tired of it, and I played it in every version of the Frasers until I stepped down after twenty-nine years as Pipe Major. However for me, the performance at Ballymena remains the most thrilling and moving. Just as the band, a year previously, had never encountered anything like this before, here was a wildly enthusiastic packed house of pipe band fanatics on its feet, roaring with approval at this new form of music for our idiom.

This piece was instrumental in inspiring a new generation of piping composition—thematic, with circular cohesion, sometimes based on a narrative and sometimes just a musical adventure. It opened Mike Grey's creativity to produce what is almost a tone poem in narrative style, depicting the story of Donald Morrison, "The Megantic Outlaw." Think, too, of Michael's "Immigrant's Suite"—how do you tell the story of the desperation and final triumph of Scottish immigrants to Canada within the strictures of a pipe band? Listen to this piece and you'll see how. My own composition efforts also drifted into this sphere with "In Celtic Times" and, later, my "Tribute to Johnny Rowan."

Others have dipped toes in the water, and while I may reserve judgment on the musical merits of some of these efforts (they shall remain nameless), it's clear to me that this wonderful field of experimentation would never have happened without "Journey to Skye" to open the door to a whole new way.

15

The Northern Ireland Adventure

With our fondness for the music of Ireland we had made friends and fans in the Northern Ireland pipe band community. However, we were extremely surprised when the Graham Memorial Pipe Band extended an invitation to the band to perform a concert in Ballymena in August 1987, a few days before the Worlds. We leapt at the chance. We learned many years later how it all came about. Graham Memorial had earlier hosted concerts featuring Boghall and Bathgate, Dysart and Dundonald, Vale of Atholl and Polkemmet pipe bands. One evening at Graham's band practice, their bass drummer, a great fan of Luke Allan, the Fraser's bass drummer, floated the idea that they should bring us to the County Hall in Ballymena to stage a concert. It was an idea that struck a chord with their members, and they ran with it.

Word of this previously unattempted, crazy venture began to circulate, and eventually found the ear of Ronnie Simpson. Ronnie was the head honcho at Lismor records and we had worked with him previously on band albums, and also on solo projects. We came to an agreement in which Lismor would produce a live recording of the event. Ronnie had on board the incomparable Bob MacDowall to engineer and produce it. Thank "somebody" for that one. You've heard my views on theism—I fall somewhere between Richard Dawkins and Christopher Hitchens in this regard—so "somebody" is the best I can do here.

Now a word about these guys. Ronnie was an impresario who brought The Who to Wembley Stadium. Pretty good cred, I'd say. He was and is, also a wonderful, irreverent and flamboyant character who really knew a lot of "stuff." Bob MacDowall is a terrific engineer and producer, with an incredible ear for the bagpipe and pipe bands generally and a guy who struggled with recurrent little lesions on the tongue from years of playing trombone. When you think of it, a trombone guy (another instrument that people joke about, although not with the same vicious edge as the bagpipe gets) recording a pipe band concert, has a certain weird sense about it. When you listen to *Live in Ireland*, remember that this was recorded in 1987, with technology that would now be seen as coming from the Pleistocene Age. And again, thanks for that very fact—two inch tape, vinyl record—it was a great capture of the real sound of the band. I don't know how he did it. We played on a hardwood stage in a room that was pretty much just an auditorium or high school gym, with echo and reverb bouncing everywhere, and snare drums rattling the windows. The record does not sound like that. It has a warm tonal quality, and if you listen to it from start to finish, you can hear the band gradually settling into the moment, with MacDowall's great skill capturing the subtle shift in the quality of the band's tone and the gathering refinement of its playing.

At the interval, the band congregated in the tuning room, a cavern-like space, and frantically pulled through drones, dried reeds with tissues, and reassembled the pipes. It was a close and sultry night, and it was raining and raining and raining. As I was priming myself for the second half, Lillian appeared. She had been in the audience. I saw her and started whinging and complaining that I didn't think it was going well at all. She laughed: "Are you crazy? They're on their feet, and angling for better views of the stage—they're having a great time." What a relief.

We retuned the pipes, which were now rich, stable and booming. The second half opened with three 6/8 marches and suddenly it was all there—tone, swing, precision and balls-to-the-wall commitment. The last few tracks on the record are the ones people usually refer to as the cream of the thing—and indeed, listening to "Journey to Skye" followed by "The Fair Maid of Barra," "The Gold Ring" and "The Clumsy Lover" still produces a thrill in me. Ian Duncan, of Vale of Athol fame, was sitting in the front row, as were many other scary luminaries, and he told me after the Worlds that he knew we were going to win it when he heard the tone of the pipe section in "The Fair Maid of Barra." Our playing of "The Fair Maid" is incidentally a good example of how we sourced material. I had heard the fabulous Allan MacDonald play it at the piper's ceilidh at the Northern Meeting, where he reversed the parts and added some delicate touches and figures to the beautiful melody. It stuck with me and found its way into the band repertoire.

While the album cover is a shocking and nasty green color (Ireland I guess), it continues to be the largest-selling pipe band record of all time. It's pretty gratifying to have people come up to me even now and say something like, "I was there in Ballymena and (a) that concert changed my life or (b) that's the greatest pipe band I have ever heard or (c) I redoubled my efforts on the pipes and still play to this day," and so on. This has happened so often that I wonder if it's possible that all of these folks could have been in the Ballymena County Hall that August 12, 1987.

It was a stunning experience for us and it would seem too, for the audience. Here's a review of it from the self-described "Ulster's Newspaper" (*The Times*):

> *Unforgettable scenes followed an-all too short musical and ambassadorial visit to the borough, as enthusiasts from all over Ulster, from Dublin, Cork and even from England, Scotland and North America, paid a massively moving tribute to what they simply termed the best pipe band they had ever heard.*
>
> *Sheer exhaustion eventually compelled piping genius Bill Livingstone to take the 78th Fraser Highlanders band off*

stage—an environment which under the lights had at times reached the nineties.

A sweat-soaked "pipey" assisted by big, bearded Englishman Pipe Sgt. John Walsh led his men finally backstage to the second—or was it the third—standing ovation from a deliriously happy capacity audience of mainly Ulster-Scots...

To try to describe the two hour plus musical extravaganza would be a futile exercise; adjectives are superfluous; the reputation of the world's most entertaining tartan ensemble was truly vindicated. In fact, they possibly surpass the brilliance of previous performances in an environment which must surely now be recognized as the mecca of pipe band concert presentation... This was pipe banding taken into a new orbit; a sphere which more than complemented visits of Boghall and Bathgate, Dysart and Dundonald , Polkemmet and Vail of Athol. Many argue that the 78th even surpassed the contributions of their Caledonia cousins.

What savoir-faire was embodied in the ebbing and flowing of Donald Thompson's haunting, musically meandering Journey to Skye—undoubtedly the pinnacle piece of the concert. The superb integration of pipe and drum with an educational performance for all percussionists by bass drummer Luke Allen—the perfect link man. No histrionics here... the 78th *have always been regarded as the trailblazers and in the vanguard of the newest wave of pipe and music, the éclat of Ireland's most discerning tartan audience left the communicative Canadians in no doubt as to their prowess...*

> *There were the new compositions—many by the bands own personnel—with their mystical harmonies and minor key signatures; the brilliance of the soloists which every band member seemed to be... Completing it all was the explosive drum accompaniment of John Reid Maxwell's "backend"—the former Dysart snare man and a pupil of the great Willie Bell in tribute to his former tutor...*
>
> *Encore? What else but the 78th eternally popular triangular—The Fair Maid of Barra, the Gold Ring and the Clumsy Lover. Magical!!*

The Graham Memorial pipe band hosted us in fine style. We stayed at the Tullymore House, a hotel in a fairly isolated countryside setting. It had been closed for a while but arrangements were made to bring back the kitchen and bar staff. We ate like kings, and I'm not afraid to admit that we partied at night like college kids. It was here that I learned the delightful Northern Ireland nickname for Grouse Whisky—"I'll have a Low Flyer please." It's my favorite blended Scotch to this day—maybe the charm of the name, pronounced as only a true Ulster man can do, rubbed off permanently.

Lily and I were fairly fanatical runners at that time and every day saw us on a ramble on narrow roads through beautiful rolling countryside. It puzzled us a bit that no matter where we were in the run, someone from the Graham Memorial band, or the hotel staff, would pass us on the road, give a wave or stop for a wee chat and a "how're ye doin" and be off.

One of these jaunts down the road is especially memorable. Coffee Maxwell (Maxwell House Coffee—get it?), now the formidable J. Reid Maxwell, holder of several World Championships with three bands, had taken up running and joined us one day. Sadly my inner compass came a-cropper and we ran for a very long and unintended way.

One kilometer after another, cresting a rise, no, that's not it, rounding a corner, ah we're here—shite! No, we're not—where are we? Two little red-haired boys at the side of some stretch of road, looked on at the people running on their road, clearly from some other part of the world, and asked, "What're ye doin'? Why are yez runnin' arouind like this?" It was a great experience, leaving us all weary but exhilarated. Reid and I were at the peak of our friendship and musical journey, and it was all too grand.

This was 1987 and the Troubles were still erupting in full force. We were billeted, we were later told, at the Tullymore House, because it was a place where it was easy to see who was coming and going, with only one main entrance into the environs of the hotel, surrounded by a stone wall on all sides which made it easy to protect us. It was only on leaving Northern Ireland that we learned that we were all under the protective eyes of our hosts and their friends. We were being protected but with great discretion and subtlety—we were never aware of it.

There was a singular event, though, which brought home to this bunch of naïve Canadians the nature of the godawful mess in Northern Ireland. We were being treated to a tour of, and luncheon at, the brewery which brewed Bass Ale and Tennent's Lager, and had been loaded into a bus for the trip to Belfast. We had come to a complete stop in a traffic jam which I recall as being on the infamous Falls Road. True recollection or fanciful memory I'm not sure—I *am* sure though of what happened. We were entertaining ourselves with boisterous songs of questionable taste, laughter and cans of Tennent's, when an armored vehicle went past us going in the opposite direction. On its top were four British soldiers (kids it looked like) dressed in full camouflage, posted on the four corners of the vehicle, with hands on the triggers of automatic weapons, pointed in all four directions of the compass, the barrels and business ends of which passed us at eye level.

A serious hush descended on the previously raucous crowd in the bus, and it remained that way until we were moving again and well out of the situation. A sobering experience for young men and women raised principally in Ontario, far away from anything remotely like this business of staring into the barrel of a deadly weapon.

Of course we escaped unharmed. At the Brewery, we were feted in an elegant room, treated to Irish whisky and of course Bass and Tennent's, and we heard for the first time the wizardry of Davey Spillane on Uilleann pipe, as his band Moving Hearts was played through the sound system. We were stunned by the hospitality, and by Spillane's music, which became a compositional inspiration for Bruce Gandy, and a style of playing for the 78th.

We were also taken to a glittering formal reception with the Lord Mayor of Belfast, Dixie Gilmore OBE, with the whole band invited. This kind of thing doesn't happen any longer, and more's the pity.

We left Ulster on Friday morning, travelling by bus to Larne, and then taking the ferry to Stranraer in Ayrshire Scotland, and a further bus to Glasgow. The whole journey was on the order of eight hours, and it was during this time that the overall head man of the Ballymena event told us of all the precautions that had been put in place to protect us. This head man was the illustrious Tom McCarrol, who later went on to the top job at the Royal Scottish Pipe Band Association (RSPBA)—where he once distinguished himself at the prize giving at the World Championship by congratulating "all of the winners, but all you losers too." It was a hilarious gaffe for a North American, "loser" being a common term of derision (what a loser you are... a worthless fool) but Tom was so well intentioned and heartfelt that he can't have meant it as we took it.

Still that may not be the funniest thing I have heard on Glasgow Green, where the World Championships have been held for a long while. In 1990 The RSPBA staged a Jubilee Contest on the Sunday after the Worlds to celebrate the 60th anniversary of the organization. Perhaps it was being required to march off in strict formation to Scotland the Brave, or the unrelenting rain, that made folk churlish. Regardless, the Jubilee Contest maintained the same interminable ceremonies and prize giving as at the Worlds itself.

All of the names that follow here are imaginary and drawn from a fictional hat—I have no information that any of these bands ever existed, or if they did that they were involved in this exchange, so I have simply cobbled together some names that may have a vaguely familiar rhythm, to illustrate the way this stuff can, and did, go down—this really happened:

"And in first place in the Grade 5 B competition, with the South of England RSPBA Trophy, The Isle of Colonsay Shield, and the Black Isle Whisky Charger to be held for six months, The Heddington Junior and Juvenile Combined Pipe Band!"

From the bitterly disappointed runners-up, who had fully expected to march off with all that hardware, came the following riposte, shouted into the now mysteriously quiet air:

"SUCK MY COCK!"

Funniest thing ever heard at the Worlds.

Back to Tom McCarrol, who told us the full story. He himself had slept for years with a gun under his pillow. He had security surrounding the 78th at every minute, special officers on the bus to the concert venue and back to the Tullymore House, with a bomb threat posted for our return from the concert to the hotel. We were stopped from boarding the bus, while two officers went and fetched a tray of cold pints, and others took sniffer dogs through the coach. Mysteriously and naively, we didn't twig to the truth. At the ferry dock at Larne, however, we saw real evidence of what was going on: British soldiers crouched down everywhere, camouflage and protective gear and weapons at the ready. To call it sobering doesn't quite capture the feeling at the time.

We arrived in Glasgow at our digs at Woolfson Hall in a smir, soon to be real rain—though it's hard to tell in Glasgow since it seems to come from the ground up sometimes. We had a quick run through two sets and the medley, and I called a halt to further practice. We had played so much in the last week that I knew the pipes would be fine. I gathered the band together and gave what I hoped would be a meaningful pep talk. I wish I could claim credit for the thinking in it but I cannot. It came from my dearly loved friend, Andrew MacNeill of Colonsay—I talked about him earlier.

It was the year I won the Gold Medal at Oban, playing "The Lament for Mary MacLeod." Andrew dragged Lily and me into the Rowan Tree

Restaurant and demanded that we have lunch with him. This involved a couple of steadying drams, and a lecture to me about what I complained was a terrible case of nerves. I was meant to play behind several pipers following the lunch break, and I was in extreme performance anxiety mode. Andrew spoke to me quietly, affectionately, firmly, but with a touch of annoyance in his tone. "You silly arse, do you not know that everyone else is afraid that *you're* here? You should be afraid of nothing—they're the ones who ought to be nervous."

So I took the sheepskin bag apart from the rest of the pipe, went into the men's washroom (toilet is a word that causes Canadians to feel squeamish), and blow-dried the bag inside and out with the electric hand dryer. I had played earlier in the Open Piobaireachd, as it was then called, and the bag was as soaked as a chamois after washing the car with it.

Bag dried, courage boosted by the aforementioned wee drop o' the crater, it was off to the Corran Halls for the 1979 Argyllshire Gathering Gold Medal competition. Pipes up. Sounding fine and stable, safely away into "The Lament for Mary MacLeod," I walked too close to the curtain for Capt. John's comfort, as he later told me ("God man, you were close to shutting off your outside tenor on it") and with the watery product of a head cold trying to invade my moustache, I did it—my second Highland Society of London Gold Medal.

So now back to Woolfson Hall—I gave the 78th Frasers the same speech, modified for pipe band purposes, that Andrew had given me in 1979. "Right, guys... don't be nervous. Don't be afraid. They're the ones who are worrying. This may be history in the making—make the most of it—bold, confident, even arrogant if you feel it. We have nothing to lose—they have a great deal, if not everything."

So after some diligent bagpipe maintenance (water had been a problem all week long), it was to off bed and then to Bellahouston Park in the morning. There was little rush as we were slotted to play last in both events. In these days the medley was played first, there was a tuning area between the Medley and March, Strathspey & Reel arenas with about twenty minutes between these events.

Though the bus ride was relaxed, with some sleeping and Bruce Gandy playing practice chanter, the minute we broached the gates one could feel the tension and increased blood pressure kick in. It was a murderous wait—the day was cold and wet, with on-and-off showers, and the issue of timing the set-up of the pipes crucial. The tension was fierce, with many close to the point of freaking out altogether. While we waited and waited to start, I sent one of the pipers over to where Simon Fraser University was tuning up, to get an idea of their pitch—tuning meters were by now routinely used. It's amusing to think that the report came back that they were at 474cps—amusing because today a pitch of 484 to 486 is pretty common. In fact in Ontario in August, at 88 degrees F., 488 to 490 is not unheard of—and there's nothing to be done to drop it.

Anyway, the Frasers' pipe corps was not at 474, and by quite a long way. We knew SFU was in a purple patch, and going great guns, and felt we simply had to be within range. So hemp was adjusted, reeds were sunk, pinched and warmed, and we managed to get the model pipes (mine and John Walsh's) to the pitch.

Our warm-up took place on a paved path with trees lining either side, providing dubious shelter from the intermittent rain. We managed to peak the sound at just the right moment, despite the electric angst-riddled atmosphere, with some on the verge of losing composure. We marched to the first arena for the medley event, the crowd parting before us. We got away well, and hope for perfection surged until one piper lost it, playing a high G instead of F in the second part of the opening tune, "Up to the Line." Shrieking discord. But we survived and pressed on, going well through the tricky reel arrangement of "Bundle and Go," with the rain now lashing down, and undeterred we finished with "The Foxhunters" in waltz time going great guns. An eruption of applause exploded at the sounding of the last note.

In those times, the Medley and March, Strathspey & Reel events ran consecutively about twenty minutes apart, with a tuning circle between the two arenas. These were twenty frenzied minutes. My own pipes were drenched, with water running down the drone bores. I, and others, had to tear them down, dry them with brushes, re-assemble them, all with the rain hosing down—it seemed futile and redundant but it worked. Bagpipe laundry accomplished, we re-assembled as a band and brought the pipes back up to pitch. Since we were the last to play, this frantic exercise was carried out in eerie quiet, with no other bands behind us, and everyone ahead of us finished with their March, Strathspey & Reel.

We formed up and entered the second arena through another parting of the crowd. By the fifth part of "Blair Drummond" I was convinced that we were on track to do what a few years earlier was unthinkable. Still though, the daunting challenge of eight parts of "Charlie's Welcome" loomed ahead—with chanters drenched and pipers trying not to squeal with every gracenote or birl. God knows how the drummers held onto their sticks. But we got home and dry— well, home anyway—with no disasters.

We didn't have long to wait for the result as we had been last to play. The sick tension before the announcement and the joyful celebration after it will never be forgotten. Reid Maxwell charged towards me like a scene from a movie, leapt on me, and wrapped his legs around me like a monkey—his corps had the top prize in drumming as well.

The rest of the day and night is pretty much a blur. The bus ride back was pure cacophony and riotous joy. We partied at Woolfson Hall with the guys from St. Laurence O'Toole, and listened gobsmacked to Terry Tully playing a seemingly limitless repertoire of tunes with dazzling rhythm and musicality. Some were hoarse and voiceless from all the celebratory screaming.

It was an amazing day—a triumph against terrible odds, and as it turned out, a watershed in pipe band history. It also was a one-off experience. It's one that no other band can have, the mould having been broken on that day.

It's important to put this event into full context. As *Pipes|Drums* magazine put it, "In the twenty-five years since the 78th Frasers gained the title, the Worlds has been won 16 times by a band not from Scotland [now 18 times as at this writing]—one cannot see this as anything other than a sea change in the world of pipe bands."

The truth likely is that the Frasers should have won in 1986 and 1988 as well. A review of the recordings for these years will probably confirm that these would have been the correct results. Reid Maxwell has recently reminded me that the 1988 medley was even more groundbreaking than anything that had been done previously. Take a listen to the layering of time signatures and melodic interplay; since then, this has become a much-copied feature in Grade 1 medleys. In fact, there's a funny story about the judge who it was felt single-handedly sunk us in 1988. He was a Canadian, and his rather idiosyncratic placing of the band was blamed, within the pipe band itself at least, for our failure to win again. As the band members were gathered around the coach for the disappointed return to their quarters, the suspect judge approached the group seeking a ride back with the band on the bus.

Exactly at the moment of his arrival, one of the pipers was engaging in a less-than-flattering description of the judge in question, referring to him as a "#$&%!head" (here supply your own insulting and vulgar prefix). As luck had it, the term had a somewhat audible similarity and resonance with the name of the judge in question. Whatever—it was a tense moment for us, but it seems not to have been heard and it all passed with, so far as I know, no permanent damage to relationships. (Since this was written my great friend and very fine piper Ed Neigh has sadly died. He was the judge in question. The full story is that as Ed approached the gathered band members, one of our pipers, furious with Ed's burying of us in his placement of the band, referred to him as "a fuckhead". On seeing Ed, and trying to save the day, he turned it into a sort of "hail fellow well met" greeting with "Fuck! Ed!)

16

Bagpipe Follies: A Potpourri of Funny Incidents

THE ASSEMBLY ROOMS EDINBURGH

The Frasers did a concert at The Assembly Rooms in Edinburgh, the one I earlier described in which Bob Shepherd ran his mouth in such an unseemly—no, completely unprofessional—way. After the show there was a grand reception for the band and the pipe band luminaries who had been in the audience. As part of the affair, there was a delightful buffet set up (a boofee, as it is sometimes pronounced in Scotland).

Lillian was moving along the tables displaying the repast, gathering some samplings of the tasty offerings, when behind her a gentleman (yeah, right) approached her very closely and reached around her waist and groped her in the most shocking way. Since she couldn't imagine anyone else doing this, she turned sharply around and launched into a scolding: "Billy, what are you—?" Of course it was not me. It was a very well-known piper who may have made too many trips to the bar, and who, it seems, had some psychological issues. Seeing the anger and shock in her eyes, he quickly dashed away.

So my lovely bride, all 105 pounds of her, bided her time while she worked out a strategy. It came to her. After asking a reluctant Mike Grey to watch out for her, she left the area and went to the entrance hall immediately adjacent. She made eye contact with the groper, raised her hand, and waggled a crooked index finger, beckoning him to join her. I can imagine the flush of feverish excitement that coursed through him as he thought, "my God, I've struck it rich—who'd have thought?" As he came within arms' reach of the little Ukrainian dynamo, she clocked him with a wicked right hand and a "Don't you ever touch me again!" He spent the rest of the evening complaining that "Bill Livingstone's wife is crazy. She whacked me for no reason at all."

Of course I will not divulge his name, but it's a one-hundred-percent true story. And damn it, how proud of her I was.

HATS OFF

In the days of the General Motors Pipe Band, George Campbell and I were the greatest of pals. He is truly one of the brightest, funniest, most engaging men I have ever known. We were not especially good for each other, as in those times we were both pretty hyperactive, and George was having a wicked romance with booze. He has long since stopped drinking completely, stopped smoking, reformed his life, made amends and blah blah about the 12 steps. He had taken in his Spanish teacher in a selfless act of kindness, while the fellow struggled through the awful ravages of esophageal cancer, ultimately succumbing to it. He started running. Suddenly it was many miles a day. His relationships failed. He carried on and started new ones. He lost his eldest son Stephen to a terrible case of diabetes, which made itself known on a trip home from the Maxville Highland Games when Stephen was about seven or eight, stopping every fifteen minutes to pee. Lorraine, Stephen's mom and a physiotherapist, knew instantly what was wrong. Lorraine was a fine accordion player, and was a central figure in all of the ceilidhs that I've described.

George is totally great now—crazy with a lust for life, and maybe just a bit crazy. I don't care, he's terrific. I know I'm wandering but just a quick anecdote about George Campbell. He was having lunch at work at GM, sitting with a much younger man, and George reached for an artificial sweetener for his tea. The young man said, "You know, George, you shouldn't use that stuff, it isn't very good for you." To which George replied, with the deadly Glasgow inflection he has never lost, "Son, I've given up more things in my life than you have ever started."

The Hat Scandal—the precise date is lost, but it's sometime in 1975 at some Highland games on the Ontario circuit —features the General Motors Pipe Band in which I played, and of which George was Pipe Major. In Ontario, all Highland games and pipe band contests end with the massed bands. It's a hated feature of the games, but the Pipers and Pipe Band Society, which manages all the contests, provides the judges and stewards for the competitions, receives a generous fee, and agrees to present two massed band performances, one at noon at the opening ceremonies and the other at the prize-giving and closing ceremony. Between the end of the competitions and the final massed bands, the routine is pretty much as it is in Scotland. Bandsmen gather in the beer tents or their own little enclaves, and await with dread the call to muster for the massed bands. Things get mislaid, bonnets get lost and even bagpipes have been known to disappear. What happened arose solely as a result of the author (at this time Pipe Sergeant of the GM band) marching on with the massed bands, without a proper head covering. It led to a hilarious prosecution of the band by the Pipers and Pipe Society of Ontario (PPBSO), but funny now or not, it also led to some pretty severe penalties.

The evidence in support of the prosecution was weirdly similar to the opening narrative of Long John Baldry in his wonderful "Don't Try to Lay no Boogie Woogie on the King Rock and Roll." That's with soft, not hard G's in boogie woogie. If you haven't heard it go to the internet and download it. Over a terrific piano rumble he describes being arrested on the streets of London in 1957, for disturbing the public peace by sitting on his amp and playing blues. He has to appear in court and he describes the arresting officer's evidence, in all of its nutty Monty Python detail, and delivered in a South London accent. Here's the evidence mounted against us by the PPBSO, in that same accent with the same deadly earnestness of that poor cop in Long John Baldry's droll send-up:

"On the occaizhun in question M'lud, I wuz on patrol in me capacity as chief steward, keepin' a watchful eye on the massed bands performance, lookin' for floutin' of the rules yeah. M'lud, it appeared to this witness, which is to sie me, that the Pipe Sergeant of the GM pipe band, one William Livingstone, had marched onto the field for thee foinal massed bands, bareheaded M'lud—as in no hat—no Glengarry, nor even Balmoral. And this, in my opinion M'Lord, in spoite of, and indeed in open defiance of the rule requiring all members performing in the massed bands to appear appropriately attired, including headgear. Well M'lud, in furtherance of me duties as chief steward, I approached the aforesaid gentleman, and while remaining at least an arm's length away from 'im, gestured vigorously with me finger to the top of me 'ead, to draw attention to this grievous uniform violation by Mr. Livingstone, yeah.

"'E reached out in attempt to strike me M'lud and it was only me nimble reaction and fear of injury that permitted me to jump back out of 'is range... and that's the truf M'lud."

And now for the facts. Indeed I did appear in the massed bands sans bonnet—it got lost, mislaid or otherwise disappeared. It seemed at the time to be unimportant since I was at least participating in the hated barbaric torture of massed bands. As the band was executing a left wheel, Norm Brown, the aforesaid witness, accompanied by John Watson (Jake's dad) approached me, with a fairly enraged demeanour that would have been hilarious were it not so crazy, and began gesturing furiously to his head, and berating me in a loud voice. Embarrassed and feeling centered out in front of the public and the other bandsmen, I responded with the only gesture available on such short notice, and also made more challenging as we were on the move marching. I proffered my right hand, middle finger extended.

When the band came to a halt in our position, George asked me what the hell that was all about. I told him. In a dazzling display of insolence, and as later would become evident, bad judgment, he ordered the entire band to remove their headgear, and we performed thusly for the remainder of the massed bands spectacle.

Reports were duly made by Messrs. Brown and Watson concerning my sullen disobedience, my attempt to assault Norm Brown, and the heinous behavior of the PM and the entire band for so flagrantly flouting the rules. I suppose it was all more or less true, but so disproportionately inflated—especially the part about my attempt to assault Norm Brown. A more cowardly, peace-loving guy than me likely does not exist. Anyway, the result was completely unexpected. The band and all the soloists in it, which included Bob Worrall and me, were suspended for three contests, included in which was Ottawa, the home at the time of the Piobaireachd Society Gold Medal.

This couldn't stand. Andy Knox, another lawyer in the band, a very fine gentleman and the son of Rachael Knox, who held a huge position in The Law Society of Upper Canada (the governing body for Ontario lawyers) exercised his considerable clout and arranged a meeting with Garry Smith, one of the premier lawyers in Toronto specializing in Administrative Law. This branch of the law deals with how administrative bodies such as boards, tribunals and government agencies must conduct themselves. The same general approach also applies to the governing bodies of private organizations.

Central to this area of the law are the Rules of Natural Justice. These provide that a body must render decisions in an unbiased way, that parties receive clear and unambiguous notice of the allegations against them, and that all parties affected have equal opportunities to present evidence and reply to the allegations. These Rules also enshrine the principle that no one ought to be a judge in his own case. It is mandatory that even the appearance of bias be avoided.

Cleary the entire procedure violated every one of these rules. There was no notice, no opportunity to be heard or to present evidence, and the "Tribunal" itself was the executive of the PPBSO (recall the Rule, "No one should be a judge in his own case"). So we demanded a review of the decision, which would involve a face-to-face with the executive of what was still the Piper's Society of Ontario. This meeting was held during a summer evening on the back deck of Sandy Keith's home in Hamilton. Sandy was still a detective in the Hamilton Police

Department. You can guess the degree of tolerance he would have had for arguments from a defence lawyer based on something as arcane as the Rules of Natural Justice.

Still, armed with a complete legal brief, citing previously decided cases, and advancing our own demolition of the preposterous lies of Norm Brown, we met them. We gave our side. We persuaded. We lost. Outraged, we considered a lawsuit against the Society, which may well have destroyed it. Common sense and a cooling-off period came to the rescue. We served our suspension like chastened good boys, and life carried on.

Some good came of this tempest, however. I drafted, and succeeded in getting passed, a code for the disciplining of members, which imposed a strict set of rules that would ensure that a railroading like this could not happen again. Here it is, edited to remove some of the eye-glazing legalese:

There shall be a Discipline committee composed of the President, Vice President and Secretary with one other appointed by the President.

The Discipline Committee shall meet at the request of three members of the Society, or one member of the executive.

The Committee is empowered to deal with individual or band members who are alleged to have committed a breach of the Rules.

The Committee may levy the following sanctions:
- *reprimand*
- *fine*
- *suspension*
- *expulsion*

No disciplinary action may be taken without written notice to the member setting out:
- *the date time and place of the meeting*

- *the nature of the charges*
- *a warning that failure to attend will allow the meeting to proceed in his absence*
- *that the notice must be received seven days prior to the meeting*

A FLAME OF WRATH

We presented a concert in 1997 entitled a Flame of Wrath, called of course after the famous piobaireachd of the same name. It commemorates a gruesome event in Highland and piping history. The great piper Donald Mor Macrimmon had a brother called Squinting Patrick because he had a defect in one eye. He was murdered by his foster brother, who ultimately fled to Kintail in the Highlands. When justice was not done within a year as promised to him, Donald Mor pursued the villain to Kintail, where the villagers concealed him. So Donald Mor set fire to eighteen of their houses, killing many of their inhabitants in the process. He then composed the wild and striking piece, "A Flame of Wrath for Squinting Patrick." It appears that these Highlanders were not a gentle and forgiving bunch, and it surely gives some limited insight into the hatreds, resentments and grudges that we, in the pipe band world at least, harbor to this day. Still, sharp words and insults are a significant improvement over pyromaniacal massacre.

The idea for this concert and the band's performance of this great piobaireachd, replete with percussion, as the signature piece, came from Andrew Berthoff. Ronnie Simpson of Lismor Records was taken with the idea, and agreed to finance a video of the entire show. Sadly, the outfit chosen to fulfil this task seemed (seemed?!) to lack the requisite skills, equipment and personnel to do the job properly. They failed to light the stage or even to recognize that lighting was going to be a problem. The result was a gloomy video with most of the great visuals, including some terrific dance sequences, lost in a foggy blur. The dance sequences had to be reshot in their studio, with the contrast between the well-lit and viewable footage and the rest of the video creating a jarring reminder of what was, and what could have been.

This cost Ronnie Simpson and Lismor some 20,000 GBP in unrecoverable outlays. But there was worse—the crew had failed to master the critically important business of synchronizing the audio and video. The result was pretty much terrible, and would have been hilarious if it wasn't so obvious that the video could be showing the whole pipe section apparently playing a D throw, while the audio sounded a sustained high A, and so on interminably. I spent about two full months in the studio, three to four days a week, doing my best to guide the technicians in synchronizing what the eye saw with what the ear heard. If you're going to indulge in this kind of non-compensable time wasting, it's best to be self-employed... the unfortunate corollary of which is that if you don't work, you don't get any money.

THE QUEEN'S HALL STANDOFF

The 78th Fraser Highlanders were booked to play "Live at Queen's Hall, Edinburgh—one night only." This concert was organized and promoted by the late Bruce Campbell, who died suddenly in 2014. Amidst a flurry of warnings from others about the high probability of not getting paid, I insisted, on the afternoon of the event, that I have a meeting with Bruce to confront the issue of payment for the band. Sure enough, he told me that he planned to pay us from the gate receipts. This of course is a recipe for—no actually, it's nearly a guarantee of—getting stiffed, and many a performer has learned this the hard way.

So I girded my loins and, with complete determination, advised him that unless we received a bank draft for the agreed fee prior to show time, the curtain would rise, if at all, on an empty stage. I'm not sure how he managed it, as it was a Saturday and few if any banks would have been open, but we were indeed paid in full before show time. Still, it was a very unpleasant thing to have to do, because it revealed my complete lack of trust, and must have seemed quite insulting to him.

But I had learned this lesson in my days playing in bars and clubs, and was not about to subject my team, who were counting on the money to defray their costs, to a risk like that.

BRING ON THE MUSCLE

A gentleman who had become engaged in the manufacture and distribution of reproduction vintage bagpipes had "loaned" a set of these pipes to a prominent soloist in the 78th. I'm not entirely sure of the arrangement, but I believe it was something along the lines of, "Play this pipe in the major solo competitions, and it's yours," or yours at our cost, or something similar.

Whatever the deal, when we landed in Scotland for the Worlds, we received communication from this fellow that he needed to have this bagpipe back. It quickly became evident, with rumors flying everywhere, that his firm was in the throes of going under—that is, it was in bankruptcy, and returning the pipe to him personally could, and likely would, have presented a problem having serious legal implications. A bankrupt firm must disclose to the trustee in bankruptcy all of the property and assets that are available to satisfy, in whole or in part, the debts of the company.

So we demurred (after consultation amongst us—"us" being the piper in question, me the legal eagle, and the band manager, a senior police officer in Sarnia Ontario and a black belt in Judo). One never knows when that kind of help may be needed, as we almost learned. Our reluctance to hand over this silver and ivory pipe was seemingly not well received, for the next day, the erstwhile purveyor of these bagpipes appeared unannounced at our digs at the university. He was tense, wound very tight, aggressive and demanding. He was accompanied by a chap who most surely was the muscle—a big threatening guy, looming and scowling. He reminded me of Mario Puzo's description of the character Luca Brazzi in The Godfather—the killer who had a facial complexion the color and texture of raw veal.

We staved off the threat of violence, (thank you, Judo meister) and headed the next morning to the offices of the bankruptcy trustee that was handling the affairs of the failed company. Sure enough, the set of pipes, with silver mounts and having considerable value, had not been disclosed as an asset of the corporation, which would have made them available for payment, at least in part, of the debts of the company. We had brought the pipes with us and delivered them into the grateful hands of the trustee, and I have not seen or heard of this man (or his henchman) since.

THE MASSEY HALL TURNAROUND

To the Toronto music fan, Massey Hall has iconic status. Its construction was financed by Hart Massey of Massey-Harris fame, later Massey-Ferguson, manufacturers of the greatest line of farm machinery of its time. It was finished in 1894, and has been the stage upon which many of the greats have performed: Caruso, Gordon Lightfoot, Horowitz, Gershwin, Neil Young, Charlie Parker, Dizzy Gillespie, and The Band. It's renowned for its acoustics and the natural warmth of its sound. In 1988 an idea came along that the Frasers would stage a concert in Massey Hall. It seats 3,500 people, so the task of filling it was a monumental, if not downright silly, challenge. I had become friendly with the Senior Regional Justice in our area, Justice Jack Jenkins. I had also become friendly with an amazing lawyer and character, Rodney Hull Q.C. These two took it upon themselves to see that this concert would be a sell-out. Rodney knew every judge on the Ontario Court of Appeal bench, and Jack was an arm-twister of the first order.

Between these two, almost every lawyer, judge or person connected to the justice system was... um... persuaded to buy tickets for the show. These folks were additions to our already burgeoning group of fans. The concert took place on Sept. 24, 1988, a date never to be forgotten as it was the day that Ben Johnston of Canada won the Gold Medal in the 100-meter sprint at the Seoul Olympics.

Curtain time arrived. A sold-out house. I was as nervous as a cat when the neighbor's Doberman is off the leash. My job initially was to open the show with a solo rendition of "Lord Lovat's Lament." Recall that Lovat is the Chieftain of the Clan Fraser, so the choice of opener was fitting—and it's also a simple and welcoming pipe tune for the many in the audience who knew less than nothing about piping.

I was sharing my anxiety with Mike Grey about going out solo in front of what, for a pipe band, was a dauntingly huge audience, and setting the show off with " Lovat's Lament." Mike, in a classic touch of mind bending (there is another word I could use), said, "For gawdsakes, don't worry, you'll probably play 'The Green Hills' anyway." All pipers reading this know that the first three notes of these two tunes are identical, and thereafter they diverge pretty drastically.

The curtain rose, the lights came up slowly with dramatic effect, I struck up the pipes, and I launched (oh Mike, how can I thank you?) into "The Green Hills," familiar to all pipers and non-aficionados alike as "The Scottish Soldier." I did the classic bail-out of every piper who finds his feet planted in the excrement—I went to a long high A, pretended to tune my drones, and scoured and raked through my hard drive for the correct tune. I did finally find it, but the sweat was puddling at my feet by that time.

Usually a piper humbles himself by messing up in front of the few hardy souls willing to sit through a solo piping contest—not 3500 folks. Mike was tickled pink with the result of the prank. And the show did go extremely well—we knew our audience and delivered "Amazing Grace" with pipers stationed all around the great room. Standing O. Mike wrote a fine tune in honor of the occasion—"The Massey Hall Turnaround"—it *was* a turnaround as we needed the lift after failing to repeat as World Champions. This provided it. We put money in the bank, and saw that our music was accessible to, and very much liked by, ordinary listeners... meaning decidedly not pipe band people.

CURLING YOUR HAIR

It's a frequent jibe that Scotland has given so many obtuse inventions and pursuits: curling, golf and bagpipes. Of course the naysayers never focus on the great things we all owe to Scottish ingenuity. Consider if you will that Scotland and its sons and daughters have given us the following:

The steam engine
Macadamized roads
Ivanhoe
Anesthetics
The decimal point
Reaping machines ("Darling it's someone here about the reaping"—in tattered grave-stained shroud, scythe in hand
–*Monty Python*)
Dolly the cloned sheep
Antisepsis (now you don't have die after surgery, though you still may—see later)
Penicillin
Radar
The telephone
Dr. Jekyll and Mr. Hyde
Whisky
Television
Fax machines
Harry Potter
The indoor toilet (where would we be without it?)
The cash machine
The pin #
And yes—bagpipes, golf and curling.

In Canada we became fascinated with the last three, and thousands of us flock to strike in mad frustration at the impossibly silly ball, with the ridiculous club (although now graphite-laden and titanium-metaled beyond its original structure) on golf courses which strive to look and play nicely in the thirty-degree Celsius heat of summer in Canada followed by five months of snowbound winter.

Of the bagpipes no more need be said.

But of curling it must be observed that Canada has plunged headlong into a passionate affair with this somewhat arcane game. It's played on ice. The ice is pebbled. This is achieved by a person walking up and down the sheets, as they're called, waving back and forth a wand from which water droplets are sprayed onto the smooth ice surface, where they freeze into little pebble-like bumps. This pebbling is the magic that allows the curling stones or rocks to bend around various obstacles, typically the stones of the opposition team, called in Canada, rather quaintly, the "rink." There are two launching places in the frozen ice, at each end of the sheet, which allows both right- and left-handed throwers to choose their most comfortable one. The curler places his chosen foot into the recessed slot, and delivers the stone. These things, the launching places, are referred to as "the hacks"—no kidding.

All of this plays out, at least in my days of doing it (yes, I was what was called a "schoolboy curler") in a hellhole of a cold damp curling rink. The central feature of most curling events (called bonspiels) is that after the frigid contest is done, during which no amount of sweeping, now known as brushing, can increase body heat, all the combatants get together and drink fairly alarming quantities of booze. In fact, when curling became an Olympic sport, the IOC looked at the body types of most of the participants and decreed that curlers should adopt a more healthful lifestyle. They were required to meet certain weight and body mass index parameters. This of necessity involved some significant adjustments. Now I don't know about you, but the thought of the IOC laying down guidelines for rules to live by seems a bit of a stretch.

OK... to get to the point. At some point in the 80s, the Brier—it's had many names, but I think when we did the gig described below it was still the MacDonald Brier, sponsored by one of the great cigarette manufacturing companies in Canada. This was finally stopped, as the government, after having taken untold billions in tax revenue from the cancer conglomerate, yielded to pressure and called a halt to tobacco companies sponsoring sporting or other events.

So it was the Canadian National Men's Curling Championship. In 1986 it was held in a southern Ontario town called Kitchener. Its name had been changed from Berlin, as it had been the home of a great influx of Lutheran and Mennonite Germans. It was renamed in honor of the first Earl of Kitchener. And that reminds me of a delightful anecdote—not to do with "Kitchener's Army," the pipe tune, but rather the better-known tune, "King George the Fifth's Army." I was judging an amateur piping contest somewhere in the U.S., when a fresh-faced lad approached my table and announced, in a pronounced southern drawl, that he would play "King George Versus Army" in the March contest. After some head scratching, I diagnosed his problem. America is football mad. Not soccer; American football. The college leagues have storied teams… Army, Navy, Grambling. This young man was obviously a fan. He translated the tune title "King George V's Army" as some famous football game. Impossible not to giggle.

I did say back to the Brier, didn't I? OK then.

The deal was we were to lead the winning rink onto the frozen ice surface after the final game had been concluded and the champion determined. If you haven't tried to march on a sheet of ice while playing a bagpipe or a drum, I can only say that the experience is fraught with risk. This presentation ceremony was being broadcast live coast to coast to coast (as we now say in this amazingly monstrous country) and we received very careful instructions. Owing to the nature of the venue (a hockey arena converted to several parallel sheets of curling ice), we were lined up in single file, more or less in the bowels of the arena. It was a long way back from where I was, situated at the head of the line, to the drummers at the back end. The instructions from the producer were clear and simple. Not apparently, clear and simple enough. I passed these instructions along, stopping every five or six feet to repeat them to the bandsmen. We would be given a hand signal from the producer, at which point I would step out so as to be visible to the single file of pipers and drummers, and relay the signal for the band to strike up. No word of command, just the signal. There could be no delay. Everyone must be ready at the drop.

Our time arrived. I got the signal from the producer, stepped out and relayed it to the group, bringing my right hand down in a definitive chopping motion. But somehow I was missed—either I didn't step out far enough, or trying to operate as a unit in single file was simply a sure-fire recipe for trouble. The result was that the front half of the band stepped off smartly, left foot leading, and fully expecting the two heavy, full-throated three-pace rolls of the drum section. Instead we got a half-hearted attempt by one side drummer to execute a roll (as John Kerr used to say, "sounds like tatties rollin' off a table) and a couple of uncertain beats from the bass drum. In the space, the silent space, normally separating the two rolls, a frustrated, embarrassed and very pissed off Pipe Major filled the void with a vigorous declamation: "JESUS CHRIST!" It was live TV, I'm afraid, and the offending words were broadcast loud and clear to the whole nation.

Lily told me when I got home, that the phone began to ring instantly. "Did you hear what he said!?" and the offending blasphemy repeated. "No, no" said she, quick as a wink. "He said, 'Play it twice.'" Not the first, and not the last time she saved me from myself.

DON'T TOUCH ME

In the years of the Caber Feidh Pipe Band, our membership included many rebels and subversives. We're talking here about flower children, people left over from the sixties, the sexual revolution, the upheaval over Vietnam and the general distrust of authority. Not bomb makers by any stretch, but certainly licked with a faint hint of the paint brush of civil disobedience and challenge of authority, especially of the military or quasi-military variety.

The band attended Cowal Games in perhaps 1977 or 1978. We were, of course, expected and required to participate in the March Past at day's end, with all bands trudging past the reviewing stand, and then being herded into a sort of hollow square formation. All of this may have looked impressive from the grandstand (which structure has physical echoes in the grandstand at the Maxville Highland Games), but down at ground level there was a fair bit of disarray. Many of the bands of those days still wore the Number 1 dress tunics, waist belts, cross belts, plaids and feather bonnets. Very grand, but often as not, concealed in the feather bonnet was a beer or flask of whisky, a packet of smokes, some Swan Vesta matches and even the occasional meat pie.

The team of drum majors, or whatever they were, behaving like a team of sheepdogs, managed to herd us all into a semblance of organization and shape us into the hollow square. And then, one of their number, brandishing a military moustache and carrying a swagger stick (ever wonder why it's called that?) approached one of my pipers, and taking the stick out from under his arm, used it to tap, in a horizontal motion, this young man on the shoulder, and instructed him to shift to the left and to get in line. The young Canadian, having no knowledge at all of military tradition and custom, and even less of the connection between pipe bands and the Scottish military, exclaimed rather loudly, "Don't touch me with that thing again, or I'll knock you down." Welcome, sir, to the Canadian way of thinking.

MORE SWAGGER STICK KICKS

The swagger stick was an implement used by military officers for the purpose of directing troops, and in its earlier incarnations, starting in Roman times, employed in dispensing discipline—that's right—whacking folks with it to improve behavior. Even without a thorough understanding of the history of the swagger stick, it took little thinking to see that the person brandishing it was declaring himself to be superior, and to be in charge. The typical approach of the bearer of the stick was to advance upon his chosen subject (see "victim") and remove the stick from its resting place in the oxter of the wearer. The effect was meant to instill instant contrition and a falling into complete obedience.

It was about 1994 and we were competing at the World Pipe Band Championships with a medley which opened with waulking songs. This is highly authentic and traditional Gaelic music, which was invented to accompany the tedious work of waulking, or shrinking and thickening the newly woven tweed. This form of singing flourished in the Hebrides until the 1950s.

The typical song follows a call and answer pattern, and is delivered in a highly rhythmical and pleasing way, with verses sung in both Gaelic and Gaelic-sounding vocables. The rhythm is pronounced and very strong in order to help co-ordinate the beating of the tweed with both hands and feet. Have a listen to the Frasers on YouTube—WPBC 1994—it's great stuff. We were aware that opening a medley with this music was likely to cause some jaws to drop. In order to comply with the rules, we realized that we would have to start with two three-pace rolls and an introductory "E," and so we did. Of course to be true to the ancient idiom, we had to play in 2/4 time at about 60 bpm. I found it thrilling and absolutely captivating to march into the circle at that pace, looking and feeling for all the world like a dignified group of French Foreign Legionnaires.

After our performance, the hours passed, we had some fun and laughs together, and then as the sun was sinking another swagger-stick man (not the same one, but cut from the same stiff cloth) came striding up to our bus, where the entire band was gathered in preparation for heading over to the March Past. This fellow approached me and in a fairly booming Sergeant Major's voice declared, "Well Pipe Major, you'll be pleased to know your band was not disqualified." Baffled, I asked how such a step could even be considered. "Well, your introduction and opening tunes."

"REALLY!? That's crazy—we played two three-pace rolls and an introductory "E," as required"

"Yes, well, the decision stands—your band will not be disqualified."

Now my question was then, as it is now, if we're not disqualified, why this need to come to me and announce a negative finding? The answer of course is that the RSPBA makes the rules, and any perceived attempt to skirt them will be squashed, and will be *seen* to be squashed.

There's a bit more to this story. It reflects the attitude of the RSPBA and its complete failure to honor its mandate—to promote and encourage the culture and advancement of pipe-band music. The unfortunate corollary to this is that the role of the World Pipe Band Championships has taken on a stultifying influence on pipe bands and their music. The relentless pursuit of the Worlds has pipe-band music becoming ever more narrow, formulaic, unimaginative and risk averse.

There is a wonderful postscript here. There is now a specific rule in the books following the waulking song fiasco of 1994. The rule provides that a medley performance "shall be adjudicated from the first strike of the first roll on the quick march... the introductory tempo shall not be less than 60 paces per minute." So the irony is complete. The RSPBA toyed with the idea of disqualifying the Frasers, and then passed a new rule that enshrines as the required standard, precisely what we did in 1994. You can imagine their thinking—a DQ would have led to controversy and a thorough and transparent debate about freedom of musical choice. The RSPBA is not good at this kind of thing. So they chose something more punitive—not just for our band but for all bands. They sent a clear signal—"stuff like this is rubbish—play by our narrow rules or get buried."

We lost another opportunity to confront this thinking when we chickened out of playing "The Megantic Outlaw" at the Worlds some years later. Of course we were chastened by the whole waulking song episode, and after a real debate within the band, opted to play a standard medley. Playing this terrific piece of music would have forced a real conversation, many years before the Toronto Police band at Cowal received what seemed to be a carefully planned drubbing, with Andrew Wright pronouncing that particular medley "mumbo jumbo."

CENTRED OUT AT THE CENTREPOINT

The Centrepoint Theatre is a beautiful concert venue located in Nepean, one of the tonier neighborhoods in Ottawa. The band was staging a concert there, and we must have had the evil eye turned on us that night. The show opener was a wonderful piece composed by Bruce Gandy, building in tempo and shifting in and out of various time signatures until finally we tore into "The Lark in the Morning" at full warp speed and delivered nine minutes of terrific jig playing. We gave Bruce's piece the title "Starburst" because the narrated introduction evoked that image, and because the voice that I used on the electronic keyboard in the opener was called Starburst.

I did not play pipes in this set—I was the keyboard man. In the piece following the opener, I was to lead it off with a solo on the pipes. To ensure the pipe would stay in tune, I put one of the pipers in a dressing room, equipped with a video feed from the stage, which was meant to be used by performers to check on the progress of the play, the ballet or the concert, and to ensure that they were ready for their cue.

As I walked onto the stage to take my chair front and center stage at the keys, I was struck by the advanced age of the audience, and by the fact that several in the front row already had their hands clapped over their ears. So nonplussed was I by this, that as I took my seat at the keyboard, I miscalculated my position, with the result that my sporran clunked down on the keys with a thundering discordant racket, all in that Starburst voicing.

Ah, but there was more fun to be had. As the number ended, I stepped forward to acknowledge the audience and the applause, then turned around to face the band arranged in concert formation (which we invented), expecting to see my loyal yeoman coming onstage with my bagpipe in hand, and in tune. Nothing. No sign. No sound of ghillie brogues running. Seconds passed. Then minutes. An eternity of dreaded dead air, it seemed. I finally fled the stage, and ran to the dressing room, there to see my faithful retainer with his back to the TV screen blissfully unaware of what was happening, or rather not happening, on stage, and playing Lochanside. I roared at him, grabbed my pipes, tore back to the stage pouring sweat and out of breath, and tried to brazen it out. Strangely the guys in the front row stayed for the whole concert, and never did take their hands from their ears all night. The manager of the Centrepoint scolded us later, saying we clearly were not used to performing in a "plush seat" theatre.

EARLY ADVENTURES IN SCOTLAND

When Lil and I started our trips to Scotland, we were young and poor—we had thousands of crushing dollars in student loans to repay and were living on my income, such as it was, as a very junior lawyer. Lily had stopped working as a radiographer in 1972, having worked very hard since our marriage putting me through law school. Our trips required careful planning and scrupulous budgeting. In these days Oban and Inverness were separated by two weeks or more, and the trip to compete could stretch to three weeks if you wanted play at both, as well as Cowal and Braemar.

The solution was found by having a vehicle that we could live in as well as drive around the country. These were like Volkswagon vans and were called caravanettes. The roof opened and lifted up much as an accordion unfolds. There was a propane stove (the fuel was called calor gas in Scotland), a sink, running water, and of course a bed. Showers could be had at the campgrounds we often frequented, but these were not always located where we needed them.

When we stayed in Oban, we parked the caravanette at the north end of the Corran Halls car park, next to a trail or pathway that led up the hill and on to the houses behind the Corran Halls, site of the Gold Medal competition. Morning rituals and ablutions were conducted in the men's washroom (recall how I mentioned that in North America, we shudder at use of the word toilet), including a shampoo, shave and general body sponge bath.

At least once a day, Big Ronnie Lawrie would pass us either going up or coming down that same path which led to his home. Often, on the streets of Oban, Ronnie would be headed to MacTavish's Kitchen where he performed on the pipes nightly, and sweep Lil and I up in his enormous arms and drag us along for the show.

We also parked the caravanette outside the entrance to the hall in Portree where the piping events were held. It reminds me of a church hall but I believe it's actually the Skye Gathering Hall. Once we were awakened on the second day of the Gathering by pipers tuning up—outside, of course, there being no tuning rooms in the hall. I recall struggling out of the vehicle fairly weary and unkempt. I somehow won the March that morning, playing one of the tunes set by the piping committee, which routinely required the pipers to play tunes composed by Isle of Skye pipers. I watched the great John D. Burgess that morning, with a sheet of music and practice chanter, doing his best to memorize one of these unmemorable tunes. It boggled my mind to see this legend, a towering talent and piping figure, submit to this... what could you call it? I had, and have, no words to capture my feelings of seeing him in this situation. Imagine the silliness of asking a guy like John D. to play a piece of crap march, when they could have heard his masterful, and idiosyncratic playing of "The Highland Wedding."

At one of the contests in the northeast, likely Aboyne, it was so cold that there was nothing for it but to raise the accordion roof, light all four burners on the stove, and play with the bass drone scraping the ceiling. The temperature inside soon shot to a blazing eighty-five degrees Fahrenheit, with condensation streaming down the walls and windows. But the heat wouldn't stay with me—once outside, I began to shiver again. Horrible conditions in which to play music, or maintain stability in an instrument notorious for instantly changing with temperature and humidity.

I had a similar, but more successful, attempt at dealing with the cold weather at the Argyllshire Gathering in 1979. I was meant to play last in the Strathspey & Reel and the day was fairly typical of Argyllshire weather: overcast, with occasional drizzle, and cool. With the size of the entry I had a long wait—what to do about my cold and stiffening hands? There was a refreshment stand with a giant vat of water being kept hot by a gas burner beneath it. The burner had a couple of square stacks running on the outside of the vat up to the top of it, presumably to carry away fumes and excess heat. As I waited and waited to play, I'd park at this spot, push up my sleeves, and heat my hands and forearms over the open ends of the stacks—dash away and play a bit—and then repeat the process. It worked, as my mitts were warm and flexible enough to allow me to play "Delvinside" and "The Ness Pipers" well enough to win the Strathspey & Reel. The downside was that I had no hair left on my hands, forearms and eyebrows. A small price to pay, since it surely would grow back, although I did smell vaguely like roasted suckling pig for a while.

HOW I MET MY BAGPIPES

Early in my legal career, I did a lot of criminal defense work. I was contacted in that capacity by a young man who knew of me from piping, to assist in his defense of a charge of what was then called rape, but what is now known by the more generic term sexual assault. It appeared that my client and a friend were returning from an out-of-town construction job, and got caught in a blizzard. They had to pull off the highway, and took a room in a local hotel. There they made the acquaintance of a young lady, and the three of them frolicked away the evening, and thereafter repaired to their room. I needn't describe the ensuing events in any detail, but suffice it to say that the aforesaid young lady, who had consented to the party, suddenly developed buyer's remorse and complained to the police.

It was a pretty flimsy case for the Crown (the prosecutor for the American reader) and I was able to negotiate a plea of guilty to common assault in return for a conditional discharge and six months of probation. As the defense bar might say, this was "a kiss."

I rendered an account to the young man in an amount that I thought was commensurate with the value of my services to him, which was considerable. Many weeks went by without payment, when one day he arrived at my office unannounced. He said "Bill, I haven't paid your account yet."

I said, "I'm aware of that." He asked me to follow him, and we went down to the street where he'd parked. He opened the trunk (boot) of his car to reveal what looked to be a pipe case. He opened the case, and I was looking at what I would later learn was a vintage 1925 set of silver and ivory Hendersons.

"Would you accept these as payment of your account?"

"Yes," said I. And so I came into possession of one of the finest bagpipes in the world. All of this is supported by a formal bill of sale, a document I required to establish ownership should there ever be a question about the transaction in the future. It may yet turn out to be helpful in crossing borders with the pipes, mounted as they are with very old ivory, as the bill of sale long predates the international ban on ivory and would likely be helpful in demonstrating the antiquity of it. Old ivory material is exempted from the regulations that control what is now the shameful slaughter of elephants for their ivory. I keep a copy of the bill of sale with my pipes, but I have not had a problem at a border as yet.

As great as this bagpipe is, it went through a rough period that had me worried that it was somehow ruined. I was in New Zealand judging their national pipe band championships several years ago, and while there I performed a series of recitals. The pipe had been a little fussy before going down there, but it went completely wacky once I was there. It was embarrassing to play a recital with a pipe that simply would not stay in tune. At one of these events, I was chatting with a man by the name of Jack Phillips and moaning about how unreliable the pipes had become. He said, "I think I know what's wrong with them. Do you find yourself selecting and rejecting drone reeds because they're unstable? Do you find that as you bring the top joint down on the tuning pin that they get tight or stick?" My answer was "yes" to both.

He said that the bores had likely come out of parallel and he could fix them by re-boring them. He had a bagpipe workshop at his home and invited me to come over and he'd fix them up. Before I agreed, I checked around with some good pipers and they all said he was an extremely good and careful craftsman, and had fixed Dr. Angus MacDonald's pipes, as well as Stewart Finlayson's and Brian Switalla's too—both excellent pipers from New Zealand.

So off I went to Jack's home, where he greeted me at the front door, took me out back to the little shed housing his lathe and various tools, mounted the first section of a tenor drone, clamped it in place and started the lathe. He picked up a reamer and advanced on the spinning drone, which to my eyes looked as though it was spinning with a significant wobble. In went the reamer, out came slivers, shavings and chunks of black wood, looking like chocolate bits for the top of a cake. I couldn't watch. With an exclamation of "Jesus Christ" (yes, yet again), I left the shed and returned when all sections had been under the knife. Then, install the same old drone reeds back into the pipes, strike them up, tune them and play. Ahh... just like days of old. I later learned that Jack was a deeply religious guy, and my outburst could not have pleased him.

DONALD MACPHERSON—AN ENIGMA

I didn't know Donald really well, but I did have some interesting interactions with him. In the year or two before my first trip to Scotland, I had no idea who he was, which in itself is very interesting. I certainly knew of Donald MacLeod, Willie Ross, G. S. MacLennan and others, but I now realize that it was because of their stature as composers and collectors. Andrew Wright has offered the opinion that the most important pipers are the composers because they leave a tangible legacy. Mike Grey, the most prolific living composer of pipe music, said in a *Pipes|Drums* interview that in life, the pipers are the most important, but in death the composers are. That seems to be tacit agreement with Andrew's opinion, with Mike adding that merely piling on prize after prize doesn't keep something evergreen.

This incident would have occurred in 1972 or 1973—I know I was still incredibly green, but my old pal George Campbell back in Ontario had filled me in on the wonders of the "prize-winning machine" that was Donald MacPherson, and the undisputed magic of his bagpipe. The setting was the Argyllshire Gathering and what was then called the Open Piobaireachd (now the Senior Piobaireachd), held in the dark, dank, cold and gloomy Phoenix Cinema. Donald was about to play and I entered the theatre and took a seat in one of the formerly plush theatre seats—now somewhat threadbare and showing the effects of many packets of crisps, fish suppers and various drinks, soft or otherwise—it was impossible to tell.

I was with my Dad and Lil, and I wanted to make an audio reference of Donald's playing and his pipe. I made no attempt to conceal my cassette recorder, and it would have been impossible anyway—these things were seven to eight inches long, two inches thick and four inches wide. They had a series of push-down levers that made a fairly audible "clack" when you pushed them to record. When Donald finished tuning, I pressed "record" and captured his entire piobaireachd on tape.

When the break for morning coffee came, I made ready to leave. A woman seated next to me challenged me with something like, "Don't you think that's a dirty underhand thing to do?" I had no idea what she was talking about and told her so. Her reply was, "Did you have Donald's permission to record him?" I admitted that I had not, and would not have thought it was necessary even to ask. Naïve perhaps, but there it is.

It turned out that this lady was Gwen (Mrs. Donald MacPherson, the title Donald gave for a strathspey named for her—or was it him?) and to add to the awkwardness, as we filed out of the cinema, Gwen, Donald and I were fairly crowded together, and I could tell from his demeanor and the way he looked at me, and her giving me the stink-eye, that she had told him about our encounter.

It seems that Donald had some serious concerns, if not paranoia, about being recorded. He was once invited to visit by Jim Thompson, a piper from Lesmahagow, Scotland, and a contemporary of mine in the early days, who at the time owned a farm in rural Ontario. This place, Ceol Mor Farm, was decidedly out of the way, a good two-and-a half-hour drive northeast from Toronto, and the flood of students expected to travel there for lessons from Donald didn't materialize. I actually felt a bit embarrassed for them both, and as it was a good opportunity to get some tuition from Donald, I arranged to travel there after work for a lesson. One of the set tunes was "Queen Anne's Lament," and I had gone over it with John MacFadyen. I played it for Donald and he was highly critical of my rendering of it—at one point declaring, "I don't know what that is, but it's not piobaireachd." I suggested that we go over it, or have him play it on the practice chanter. He didn't want to do that. He preferred to conduct *me*, playing it on the bagpipe. Fine. So I asked him if I could record my playing of it while he conducted me. He gave a long pause, looked thoughtful, and then said, "Well I guess it's all right, it's not me actually playing is it?" Call me gobsmacked at that point.

In 1981 at the Northern Meeting, Donald and I shared a tuning room—actually one of the dressing rooms reserved for the theatrical performers, with bars of lights for the application of make-up and so on. In fact this may have been the same tuning/dressing room at the Eden Court in Inverness, where I turned around while warming up, and confronted my face in a large mirror, now looking for all the world like my father's. It was a bit chilling.

I had been pretty sure since the morning that I would be asked to play the "Lament for the Laird of Annapool"—it had been chosen for one other piper who had broken down in it. With the sustained "piobaireachd high Gs" throughout the ground and the high level of technical difficulty in the tune, it was not likely a favorite submission of the other pipers, so I tried to get myself ready for the test. I repaired to my B&B at lunch, and there studied the score and listened to Donald Macleod's tape-recorded instruction to me about the tune.

So there was Donald MacPherson sharing the same tuning room with me; I began to play, to rehearse the ridiculously challenging piece, and then took a break. Donald, who had been sitting quietly while I played, raised his head and said, "Stick with it Bill, it's coming along fine." I had no idea what he meant—was it that my piobaireachd playing was gradually getting better, or that my pipe was settling in to the fiendishly challenging business of piobaireachd high Gs over and over? I never did find out which of these he meant and his comment unsettled me—was it good wishes or gamesmanship?

No matter—I will never forget that on that day, in that contest, I won the Clasp, with Iain MacFadyen second and Donald MacPherson third. Fred Morrisson has said that winning that prize, that way, that day, against these fabulous pipers, stands as a testament to "truly winning the Clasp"

OZZIE REID

Characters abound in and around piping, and Ozzie is surely one—a true and dyed-in-the-wool Ulsterman, the Northern Ireland accent undiluted after decades in the U.S.A. A major figure in piping and pipe bands in the western U.S., he was instrumental in organizing the Santa Rosa Highland Games and the amazing event staged in Estes Park Colorado. A very capable player, he taught countless pipers in and around his home in Alameda, near Oakland, California on the east side of the Bay, opposite San Francisco. He was opinionated, forceful, a bit over the top and able to inspire love or its opposite. I fell into the former category.

He was a great friend of Dr. Dan Reid, who died, along with his wife, in 1991 in a mountain-climbing accident. Ozzie launched the Dan Reid Memorial Piping Competition (the DRM) to commemorate him and for twenty years it stood as one of the ritziest, glitziest events on the piping calendar. Held in luxurious surroundings in one or other of the most beautiful hotels in San Francisco, it featured a few of the best pipers in the world—usually five or six—in the Master's Recital. The event morphed from a simple competition to a recital format.

The Master's featured a set of tune requirements that became more demanding as the years went on. There were set tunes for all of the sections or disciplines—one set for the Master's and another for the Cameron-Gillies Recital, which featured three pipers from the "up and coming" ranks.

The Masters were required to play a double march, strathspey and reel, a hornpipe and jig, the ground of a piobaireachd and a full piobaireachd, all from set lists—with no breaks other than for water. It was a challenge of brutal proportions, both physically and musically.

The DRM played a significant role in piping, and in my piping life in particular. Pipers survive, and portray their art, principally through competitions. It's a high-pressure business, and many pipers retire from competition earlier, perhaps, than they should. I had just about reached that point when I received an invitation from Ozzie Reid to participate in the 1993 DRM. I looked at the tune lists, and the other players invited, and it was very clear that if I did accept the invitation, some very hard work was in order. I accepted. The result was a devotion to rebuilding my whole approach to playing. I loved the Dan Reid for that, because it reinforced in me the intuitive understanding that a musician must always be a student.

Some of the prizes that I am most proud of came at the Dan Reid. I had ten consecutive appearances there and won the MSR in 1993, the Piobaireachd five times, placed second twice, third once, and won the overall in 1997 and 2002. The field of five or six in the Master's typically included Willie McCallum, Roddy MacLeod, Angus MacColl, Stuart Liddell, Iain Spiers, Gordon Walker, Jack Lee and others. I cherish these prizes as coming in such richly talented company—the best of the best.

Following the recital (Ozzie insisted on calling it a recital, but make no mistake, it really was a competition of the most challenging sort) there was a black tie cocktail reception, followed by a sumptuous gourmet dinner—with wild boar, venison, game birds—in a glittering dining hall, with endlessly flowing bottles of the best of California's wines. And then after all that, the Master's guys each had to play some tunes in this compromised condition. It's sadly finished now, but what a great ride it was.

ROTTENROW ROW

My relationship with Reid Maxwell became more fraught as time wore on. In those days, he was blunt, outspoken and had the diplomatic skills of a testy Rottweiler. It became ever more unpleasant to be around him. The evidence is very strong that he has changed a great deal, and my personal observation is that this is indeed the case—he's a much different guy these days, a pleasure to be around. Still, at the time of the events described here, the situation had become pretty much unsalvageable. For me, the decisive stroke came when at a band practice, he and I were having a discussion, or perhaps an argument, about some musical point, when he said, "Well if you think that, you're just stupid." There was nothing I could do at that stage of the year, but the damage had been done, and it was only a matter of time until our musical collaboration was over.

In 1990, the RSPBA staged a contest on the Sunday following the Worlds to celebrate the sixtieth anniversary of the Association. If memory serves, we had finished out of the prize list the previous day, and there was a lot of disappointment and tension in the ranks. The Jubilee Competition, as they called it, was fairly silly, and featured a separate event wherein all bands had to play a 6/8 march specially composed for, and named in honor of, the event. It was unplayable rubbish.

Donald Shaw Ramsay was one of the judges, and we were playing a fancied-up version of his "Flora MacLeod's Reel." When I saw him at the trigger, clipboard in hand, I feared a right bollocking. I was not to be disappointed. His score sheet opened as follows. "Whew! Boys, boys, where to begin?" The condescending claptrap of a critique went downhill from there.

The RSPBA had struck special Jubilee Medallions for every member of each band in the prize list. We finished a heart-wrenching sixth. As the prizes, first through sixth, were announced, we were stunned to hear that the Black Bottle Pipe Band, an outfit not close to the top echelon, and shortly after this debacle, disbanded, were placed fifth, ahead of the Frasers. In disgust and disarray, most of the band began to leave the field, and J. Reid Maxwell was certainly among the most vocal in his complaints as he was trudging off the park.

The presentation medallions were set out in a box, and no one headed up to collect them. While I wish, in retrospect, I had swallowed my pride and gone to the presentation stand to pick them up, I did not—they were seen as something of an insult. The RSPBA called repeatedly for a band representative to come and collect the box of medals, and Andrew Berthoff, considering the political repercussions of walking off and the further insult of rejecting these medals, went up and collected them. At this point Reid began taunting Andrew for getting the medals, and as always he was pretty merciless in his choice of words. Andrew went back to the band bus, handed out several of the medals, and we all headed back to Strathclyde University, to our digs in Rottenrow.

The band soon mustered in the old Todd Bar, a much cozier and more inviting place than it has been transformed into since those days. The Todd was outfitted with comfy soft chairs arranged pleasantly around some tables, where folk could sit and chat, as opposed to the non-stop screaming that takes place there now. Andrew was moving around the room, amongst the chairs and tables and his friends, doing something that was important and needed, by informally handing out the medals to members of the band who had not yet received one. Reid was sitting with his drummers, and as only he could manage, snapped his fingers like summoning a lazy waiter, demanding one. Understandably, Andrew passed him by. Coffee, as he truly still was then, shouted a vulgar and insulting name at Andrew, at which point Andrew turned, dropped the box and took a run at him. Now if you're not aware, Andrew is more or less the size of an NBA power forward, and Reid is, as Groucho Marx once said, well over four feet.

The impending bloodshed attracted the notice of Doug Kirkwood, six-foot-two and two hundred and twenty pounds, and a prison guard, as well as Iain Donaldson, about the same size as Doug. These three presented a pretty fearsome display of testosterone, matched to very large bodies. Doug and Iain got in Andrew's way, and while Andrew was trying to lay a haymaker on Reid's jaw, he caught his birl finger on Donaldson, dislocating it. While Doug Kirkwood held Reid down, Donaldson and Jim Murdoch, the bass drummer, took Andrew away from the field of combat.

With all that had gone before, I could not let this stand, and told Reid so. Andrew, Mike Grey, Jim McGillivray, Andrew's wife Julie Wilson and my own dear Lily met the next day for lunch at our universally loved favorite, the Café Gandolfi. There's a photo of that group taken with the pastel light coming through the Gandolfi's high windows, and a group of friends looking at ease yet somehow poignant. It's a moment that captures the troubles that can torment pipe bands, which, after all, are supposed to bring fun and pleasure, at the least.

The whole affair turned out to be much more than a pipe band dust-up. Reid left the Frasers and after one year with the Grade 2 Peel Police band under PM Tom Anderson, Reid moved to B.C., joined Simon Fraser University Pipe Band, and changed both their history and the course and history of pipe bands, winning six world championships and three world drumming championships. That's the stuff this man is capable of; with Reid, the Frasers and me, it was never a question of talent and ability. But if he hadn't gone away, it's almost certain that I would have gone. He's a terrific talent, and it's a great thing that he's found his place and clearly changed those troublesome leopard spots. These days it's hard to imagine a more engaging and thoughtful guy on the scene. Still, I regret that all of that stuff happened, for we were a formidable combination with a powerful band, and it was a shame it had to suffer such a fracture.

17

Loyalty and Otherwise in Pipe Bands

This may be an overly dramatic title for anything having to do with pipe bands, because we all should remember what an insignificant place this art form occupies in the world as a whole. Still, there seems to be a point where personal ambition, and opportunity, or perhaps serendipity, cross paths, and can lead people to do things that are somehow disloyal. This may be nothing more than the human condition at work as everyone strives to "get ahead," in whatever fields of endeavor we variously engage in. Still though, the nature of the pipe band, its sense of camaraderie and friendship, should somehow militate against this kind of thing. Apparently not.

THE COPPER CLIFF HIGHLANDERS

When I was a young kid, just on the edge of leaving boyhood, my dad was the Pipe Major of the Copper Cliff Highlanders Pipe Band. This band was associated with the Copper Cliff Highlanders Cadet Corps, whose head man or commanding officer, was a chap named Robin Swain. Robin was quite the dashing figure— a moustache-sporting, Errol Flynn look-alike (youngers, go and Google Flynn, a swashbuckling movie star of the 1940s and 1950s). Swain was yet another fellow who owned and loved a swagger stick. He was enamored of all things military, especially the pomp and circumstance of it all.

He and his wife Bonnie (a bit of a local TV celebrity who hosted a cooking show) became friends with my parents. I don't know if that friendship led to my dad getting the pipe band, or if it was the other way around. Inco, ever the benevolent patriarchal employer, had the band outfitted in complete Douglas tartan uniforms, and a full complement of new Hardie bagpipes. My dad loved this band and poured hours of work into it, teaching the boys and young men who made up the pipe section, and bringing them along as good competent pipers. I was close pals with Robin's son Brian, and our families visited and partied together regularly. Brian went into broadcasting, and is the father of Diana Swain, a talented and well know TV journalist and broadcaster.

There was a fellow who lived in Sudbury, by the name of Sam Laderoute. Originally from the Ottawa Valley, he held some position in Public Relations at Inco. I believe that may have been how he and Robin Swain got together, through the propinquity of working in the fabled Inco "Office." Sam Laderoute was originally a drummer, and he'd played in the Royal Canadian Air Force Pipe Band under my dad who was that band's first Pipe Major in the early to mid- 1940s. He latterly took up the pipes and as with so many adult beginners, never made much of a job of it, which makes the events described below so galling.

Robin was quite the dandy, and he saw a kindred spirit in Sam, who was all about the show—feather bonnet, cross belts, waist belts, sgian dhus, great dirks strapped to the belt, and plaids a-flowing. He was not, however, a patch on my dad (or even some of my dad's pupils) as a piper. All fur coat and nae knickers, as the Scots say.

I suspect that Mr. Swain wanted a showpiece pipe band. He loved to ditch the office and spend a few weeks at the cadet camp at Fairbank Lake, where military tents were set up for the cadets to practice living in something approaching field conditions, a parade ground was cleared, military drills were conducted and rifle range practice taken. He and the other "officers" would walk about the place wearing army gear—boots, puttees, the works.

What Sam gave him was the PR specialist's touch—a large band, a revolving door of kids learning something about pipes and drums, but to my knowledge not one notable pupil ever came out of this program or his teaching.

What I remember of this episode comes from an overheard telephone conversation between Swain and my dad. The phone rang, and I could hear my father's dumbfounded and outraged voice, as he was summarily told that he was no longer the Pipe Major of the band, it would be Laderoute from here-on out, and that was that.

He was shattered, and carried the hurt and insult forever. And so did I. Sam would come around the Highland games in Ontario from time to time, and whenever he did, he tried to engage me in conversation. His approach to me was cloaked in smiles and apparent sincerity, but I could not abide the smarminess, and I'm afraid I was always rude to this man, who I considered an imposter, and who had undeservedly robbed my dad of one of the great achievements and pleasures of his life. It may seem a bit obsessive to still have these resentments sixty years later, but when I recently spoke to a man (my age) from Sudbury, I can see why I'm not able to let it go. This fellow, a very nice guy by the way and a musician himself, told me about how he and Sam met frequently in Sudbury, listened to fiddle music and talked about things musical. Included in those conversations were Sam's recollections of teaching me bagpipes. Oh dear. He never did. Not one note. Nor could he have. By the time I was ten, I could have been teaching him. This vainglorious nonsense from the man really stings. Some hurts don't heal completely. Perhaps it's right that some shouldn't.

THE CHANGING OF THE GUARD

I was the Pipe Major of the 78th Frasers from its creation in 1982, until I stepped down in August 2010. That twenty-eight years of my life was intense, beautiful, infuriating, disappointing, rewarding and filled with people who will be my friends until I check out. The band made such memorable music that it was a joy to play in it—even when the bovine excrement of internal politics would get into the fan from time to time. A look at the roster over the years discloses how many terrific pipers and drummers I played with in the Frasers. It's no exaggeration to say that I consider the band, and piping generally, as my life's work. Yes I was a lawyer—a pretty good one too—and I enjoyed that as well, but I daresay that I never devoted the time, energy and passion to lawyering that I did to piping. The exception would be the last fifteen or so years, when the demands of solo competition lessened, and the siren song of representing people who had been terribly harmed by medical errors grabbed my attention.

My love for the band, and my pride in it, defined nearly thirty years of my life. The 78th Fraser Highlanders' reputation in the pipe band world was a singular one: the band revolutionized the concept of the medley; we innovated the "concert formation," still used today thirty years later; we made music that is still fresh and well loved; we took risks in competition settings, both with material and style; introduced "round reels" and jigs; and fostered a climate of creativity and compositional excellence within our own ranks. There's more but you get the point... and anyway, how long can this guy blow his own horn?

This preamble is all by way of setting the scene, the backstory if you will, to explain the depth of my hurt brought about by the events I'll talk about now. (Incidentally, my version of the facts is preserved in the email thread which anyone can view if they like. I have a suspicion that there will be few if any takers.)

In February 2008, John Cairns, then the Pipe Sergeant of the Frasers, rather cornered me following a band practice at the Lions Hall in Campbellville, about 30 miles west of Toronto. He asked, in a very direct way, whether I had given more thought to his earlier request for my views on whether and/or when I would step down as Pipe Major. He had raised this issue perhaps a year earlier, and I recall mumbling some sort of non-committal, temporizing reply. I was shocked to be so approached, and following a lifelong pattern of not always dealing with problems in an upfront way, I let it be, thinking and hoping as was, and likely still is, my style, that doing nothing often, indeed usually, led to the problem solving itself. That turned out to be a bad mistake this time.

As we stood there facing one another, with band members filing past us on their way to the after-practice pint, in my surprise and frankly shock, I fumbled for some sort of response. Trial lawyers (include me here) call this doing a tap dance—buy time and say little of consequence. I finally managed to blurt out, feeling the pressure from him, that if we were to win the Worlds that year, I would likely step down, and if not, I would want to carry on. The real truth lay in neither one of these scenarios—I didn't want to leave and didn't need to. I could still play—and still can in fact. In any event, John emailed me first thing the next morning to tell me that if that was indeed my position he'd have to leave the band and seek a leadership role elsewhere. It was only later that I learned that he was already engaged in talks with the Peel Police band, who had offered him the job of Pipe Major. Doubtless his thinking was that landing the PM's spot at the famous Frasers was a plum gig, much more desirable than the Peel thing.

I answered him immediately and told him how I truly felt. I said I couldn't promise any timeline for my stepping down, but would let the natural flow of events guide me. The clear message from him was that if I didn't leave after the 2008 Worlds, John would. I expressed to him how much I loved the band after so many years, and never gave a thought to leaving until he started pressing me. I apologized if I had led him to believe that I would leave soon, and explained to him that my answers to him had not been the result of careful thought and consideration, but rather a quick reaction off the cuff brought on by the shock of hearing his wishes (demands?) and frankly feeling so manipulated.

John was furious with me, and responded accordingly—he said I'd betrayed him, misled him and he'd likely quit the band entirely. When I heard that, I asked that if he left, he wouldn't encourage any band members to leave with him. He promised he would not, but he'd brought several of his pupils to the Frasers and in the end they followed him when he did ultimately leave. Now, faced with this mutiny, and the potential for grievous harm to the band if some solution wasn't found, I proposed to John that I would agree *in writing* that no matter what the outcome of the 2008 World Championship, I would resign after the 2009 World Pipe Band Championship—no equivocation. It would feel like a pretty bad wounding for me, but I'd do it. As I told him, leaving the band under this pressure, would be more difficult than breaking up my law partnership, selling my office building, moving to a new location, worrying about staff who had been with me for over thirty years, and having a war with my former partner over money. And I knew all about those things because I was going through them at the same time as this business with John. I was willing to suffer the wrench of leaving what I'd built over thirty years because I thought it would be for the good of the band.

So it looked like we had a deal: we could each walk away without a bloodletting, and the interests of the band would be served. But then the wheels started to come off. John insisted that Bill Baines, the Band Manager, a cop and a good friend of John's, and Drew Duthart, the leading drummer, be told of our arrangement and my decision. Then he began to nitpick over my words. I had said, "I'll announce my resignation and unequivocally endorse you as the right man to be PM." He responded by demanding to know why I wouldn't "select" him to be PM, and whether there were other candidates. It didn't seem right to me that I try to bind the band to my choice after I'd be gone—rather like ruling from the grave. Anyway I caved and agreed to use the term "select," but I would not agree to tell Baines and Duthart. (A redundant precaution really, as Bill Baines and John were at this very time away on a Caribbean cruise together. And as to Drew, I was told after the dust had settled that he and John were overheard at a band pool party previous to these events at Drew's, as they watched the band members frolicking and having fun, and talking along the lines of, "Just think, soon all of this will be ours." In any event I refused to talk to Baines and Duthart about the deal.

I was affronted and deeply insulted by his attempts to further manipulate and manoeuver me. And he soon removed any doubts I had about his motive. He emailed me with this gem: "Without trying to ruffle your feathers, I am worried that the reason you are taking this stand is that you may change your mind down the road..." That put paid to the whole mess and I emailed John on March 6, 2008, in part as follows:

> ....John this is a thinly veiled attempt to box me in, in a public way, so that there is no chance that I'll change my mind and try to weasel out of the agreement. It's insulting and demeaning. I screwed up. I apologized. I offered to make it right. You accepted. I have tried very hard to take the high road and do the right thing. You have it in writing from me. I have given you everything you asked for, but John, I will not be bullied like this. Don't bust my balls.
>
> What I am doing, I'm doing for the band. Not, as you well know, because I want to, but to avoid trouble for the band and for both you and me. What I see coming from you is paranoia (note your microscopic parsing of every word I write) as well as a healthy dose of self-interest. I will not take any step I perceive as compromising my leadership for the remainder of my time with the band. A lame duck P/M is no better off than a lame duck President.
>
> "Ruffle my feathers... this issue?"
>
> You clearly have little idea how this affects me. My feathers? How insulting. This latest demand is a profound insult to my integrity and I am deeply offended by it. It may be "an issue" to you, but it's my life to me. I created and built this thing and I am being forced to go. Fine. I've made my position clear, and I'll stick with it, but I will not bow down to this demand or any further demands from you. You know that I am a man of even temperament and

great patience, more in fact than you would like to see, and certainly more than you yourself could exhibit. But don't mistake that for spinelessness. Your last demands are over the top.

It seems a shame that this has happened. We had reached a reasonable and sensible accord and resolution. But I cannot let what you have said and done go unanswered. We are now going to have to deal with tension and awkwardness that needn't have been.

Bill

Indeed the remainder of that year was horrible, with John unable to look me in the eye, and the tension in the band palpable. It mercifully ended with his leaving in September 2008 to become PM of Peel Regional Police Pipe Band. As this whole sorry affair was unfolding, there was no one in the band I could talk to. I felt I was being bullied and manipulated in the most egregious way, and I kept wondering, would anyone try a stunt like this with Terry Tully, Richard Parkes, Rob Mathieson, Ian Duncan or Terry Lee? The answer of course was no. Admittedly, I sowed the seeds of discontent when I didn't come clean at the outset, but when it became obvious how I felt, I wonder why he just didn't simply leave. He argued that he had sacrificed a lot for the band—likely true, but true also of a great many members of the band.

In any event, he left and took several of his pupils with him. Loss of those was not a body blow, and in any case his leaving was a massive relief. This whole episode was pretty hard to handle, but in the long run it was best for the band. As John's tenure as PS wore on, I had begun to see what were fundamental differences in how we approached the music, the teaching of it, and the leading of a pipe band.

In a related spin-off story, Jake Watson returned to Ontario from the east coast, where he had been working for several years. He came to me at the Kincardine Highland Games in mid-July 2008, gave me a huge hug, and said "Boss, I'm back home and I'm staying here now... and as long as you stay on as PM I'm with you. When you're done, I'm done." I was touched to be sure, and it was quite an emotional moment, given what I had gone through on with John only a few months before. And then, a bombshell. About a month and a bit later, Jake joined Peel Police as John Cairns' Pipe Sergeant. Feeling gutted?

Yep.

But here's the thing. So much of this stuff that happens in life, and that makes us crazy at the time, fades as maturity and reconciliation begin to rear their welcome heads.

When John Cairns' dad Archie died recently, I was mindful of the fact that their personal relationship was a complete disaster, with father and son not having spoken to each other in many years. I contacted John with a message making it clear that I knew that while they were estranged, still, Archie was his dad, and there had to be a torrent of emotions going on inside of John. John got back to me immediately, and I was very glad that I had reached out. We ran into each other at the Virginia Highland Games in May, 2016, and had a wonderful conversation, which felt so normal and healthy.

I now prefer to remember the grand times we had together in the Frasers. I recall with fondness and pride, the show we produced together...Seannchaid...the first, and to my knowledge the only pipe band concert produced with a coherent sustained voiced-over theme throughout. The voice and theme of the story teller (The Seannchaid) linking all of the music and dance together. And so much of that music was John's, and it was so much fun to play. The other stuff I've talked about happened, and I was very unhappy at the time, but he and I have moved on, or more accurately perhaps, moved back to what we were... friends. There's so much in life that is restorative if we can just get our stubborn heads around things.

There was some rumour that Peel was going to help Jake financially with the Penatangore band, of which Jake was the PM. It's a lower-grade outfit. He was listed as musical director of Penatangore for a while. Jake left Peel Police at the end of the 2014 season, and not a happy guy. Ambitions and dreams—they can be bad trouble. I still haven't heard the *real* reasons Jake left us, but it doesn't matter now. What does matter is that we have buried our differences, played together on the stage of the Glasgow Royal Concert Hall in the Live in Ireland in Scotland show on Jan. 30, 2016, and now happily play together again, this time in the Toronto Police Pipe Band. Restoration and friendship again.

Here's what happened in the near-total demise of the 78th Fraser Highlanders Pipe band. On August 25, 2010, I announced to the band that I was stepping down as PM. This was prompted by a couple of things. The first was an email from Drew Duthart on August 20, 2010, indicating that there were "rumblings" that I intended to put the job of Pipe Major to a vote that fall. That was certainly not true. I had definitely not said this to anyone, and it was only after the debacle described below, that I learned that certain members of the pipe corps were soliciting support for their campaigns to become PM. In fact, this had been happening while the band was in Scotland earlier in August for the World Championship. Indeed there may have been rumblings, but they were initiated from members of the band, not as result of anything that I had said. The thick plottens...

Drew followed up his August 20 email with a phone call in which he asked me point-blank, as only someone like Drew could do, what my intentions were about continuing as PM. While I could detect the underlying motive in his asking, I still felt that maybe there was nothing sinister in any of this. I was sixty-eight years of age, and had led the band for twenty-eight years. It may have been nothing more than forward planning.

May have been.

I decided to leave. If there were "rumblings," and the leading drummer thought it was OK to accost me directly on the subject, it wasn't hard to see the future. On August 25, 2010, I sent the band a message advising them of my resignation. And then the nonsense began. On the morning of August 28, 2010, Drew circulated to the entire band an email with an attached spreadsheet purporting to be a poll on the question of the selection of new Pipe Major. It was a badly misguided attempt, and made more offensive as Drew made clear to all concerned that I should have no part to play in the selection process at all.

The "choices" on this spreadsheet included John Cairns, Jake Watson, James MacHattie, Iain Donaldson, Bruce Gandy, Sean McKeown and Doug MacRae. The sheet had columns for things such as "work ethic," "leadership ability," and the like. When I saw this, I saw red. After what I had gone through with John Cairns and with Jake, it was a profound personal insult to have Drew place them on the list, let alone, as he did, as the number one and two choices. Adding further insult to the injury was the stunning refusal to accept my recommendation for Pipe Major, Sean McKeown. I had created the Frasers, with help from some very important assistants, and run it for twenty-eight successful years. To ignore my preference signaled significant disrespect for me and my role in making the band the unique creature that it was... *was*.

Actually worse however, it made the band a laughing stock. Only two of these candidates had an interest in, or ability to become, PM of the Frasers, and they were both already members of the band: Sean McKeown and Doug MacRae. James and Kylie MacHattie were settled into their new lives at the College of Piping in P.E.I., and Iain Donaldson had moved his home, business and family lock, stock and barrel to Florida. Bruce Gandy was ensconced in Dartmouth N.S., happily working at the Citadel, teaching and playing with his sons, Alex and Fraser, in the 78th Highlanders. News of this spreadsheet reached Scotland in a heartbeat and it was the subject of much scornful mirth: "Why don`t they ask Richard Parkes or Terry Lee?"

A white-hot exchange of emails took place as I expressed my displeasure with the whole precipitate process, with our untidy laundry on display, and my own admittedly tender sensitivities being disrespected. Band members chimed in with their disparate and contentious thoughts, and the plain fact was that there were only two possible candidates, Sean and Doug. This should have been glaringly obvious from the start. Sean concluded that he found the whole process uncomfortable, if not downright unseemly. While he was still a leading contender for the job, Drew approached him and said it was not a good idea for me to continue as a piper in the band as I had suggested I would do. Sean advised him in no uncertain terms that if he was PM and I wanted to play, I would be playing. As the tension and discomfort grew, Sean simply withdrew, and the job fell by default to Doug MacRae. Unfortunately the musical heart of the Frasers now seems to be beating with considerably less fervor.

A final word about Drew Duthart. When he was a kid, he had heard the Caber Feidh band at Princes Street Gardens in Edinburgh, sometime in the late '70s, playing "Lagan Love Song," slide note and all. He more than once told me how he fell in love with the whole thing right then and there, and said to himself, that's the stuff I want to play. But the strange thing is that when he was in the Frasers he had no interest whatever in the repertoire for which we had become known. No interest in concert material, repertoire outside of the pure competition stuff, and no patience whatever with rehearsal time devoted to that music. He made it clear that he thought it was a waste of time that would be better devoted to two medleys and two MSRs. An odd thing indeed. That is not what we were. The collateral music made us want to play. He was a very good drummer to be sure—good technically, with strong hands—but I can't understand why he'd join a band that was so committed to stuff he wouldn't or couldn't play. It was a source of great discomfort for me and made our time together problematic.

As always, crap like the stuff I've described passes and life goes on. I got an invitation to play in the Toronto Police Pipe Band, which I accepted, and I'm glad I did. It's a hard thing as a musician to give up playing. As I said to John Cairns during our imbroglio, I've been freakishly lucky, and can see no reason to end this long innings. So, at the age of seventy-three (in seven days from this writing) I have recordings and other projects on the table, and I'm playing with and contributing to a fine pipe band, which is certain to become much better. I think I'll be a part of that improvement in some small way. Whatever happens, I love to play, was born to play—I'm a player to my toes, and as long as I can, I will. At this moment, I'm just relishing a practice during which I played all fifteen minutes of the "Lament for Macleod of Colbeck"—a fabulous tune, six million toarluaths and crunluaths, and only one slightly muffled. I'll keep working on this stuff.

Think of Max Roach—one of the greatest jazz drummers of all time. At age eighty, he spent one hour of every day in the rehearsal studio doing—what?—practicing.

18

Whither the World Pipe Band Championship?

Creativity: The ability to produce something new through imaginative skill, such as a new artistic object or form; richness of ideas and originality of thinking

Innovation: a new idea, device or method

Derivative: made up of parts of something else; banal

Anyone who knows me at all will see the general drift of where this is going from these definitions. First let me say that this is not to be read as a whiny tribute to those "good old days" when everything was new, exciting and fresh. For the most part that was not, in fact, the case. Absent the Vale of Atholl, the Frasers, and to a lesser if not different extent Shotts, there wasn't much going in the areas of creativity or innovation. I would argue that today's pipe bands are still hobbled, in fact even more than their predecessors, by the stultifying need to play ever-so-safe and canny. This is a complex issue with many focal points.

What immediately comes to mind is the fact that the odds are so staggeringly stacked against the vast majority of bands that compete in the Grade 1 contest. The grade has been dominated by a small number of bands for years, and it appears it will continue to be so dominated for the foreseeable future. It's actually amazing that so many bands are willing—no, actually determined—to invest the time, energy and money in a venture that has almost no chance of success. Of the twenty-four bands that ran the gauntlet at the Grade 1 qualifying round in 2013, a generous guess would have said that a total of eight (or nine to stretch it) had any chance of placing in the top six. And of that group, three bands at the outside could contend for first prize.

And yet here I am at this age, fully engaged in the prospect of playing at the Worlds with the Toronto Police. It would appear it's not enough to have won it, and placed in the prize list, many times while leading the Frasers. And it's not as though I, or my fellow band members, have any illusions about a major breakthrough just yet. I would be hard pressed to explain the lure of it—indeed, with Piping Live now a terrific event in its own right, and enhancing the whole week's experience, it's better than ever. But with or without Piping Live, we'd all still go anyway. It's a puzzle.

So the problem with the Worlds is that there's even greater resistance to take any chances with the music—and I mean *any* chances. Take a read of a comment from a PM of one of the cream of the Grade 1 bands: "be careful in putting together medleys... give the judges some familiar stuff that they can feel comfortable with, and use new tunes sparingly". So that's what we hear—played on faultless instruments, with mind boggling-precision, but little or nothing in the way of something to challenge the listener's thirst for that "holy moley" moment. "Did you hear that? That was amazing—breathtaking—how did they come up with that stuff?"

Instead what passes for innovation has devolved for example, into taking a well-known dot and cut hornpipe and playing it in a round style, or constructing a whole medley concocted around a very tired and hackneyed strathspey, or repeated predictable trips to the intended climactic finish, only to be stepped down and back up, and re-trodden again two or three times perhaps—"Are you all getting it out there? This is the BIG FINISH!" I am not saying the quality of the delivery is faulty or uninteresting—it's not the delivery but the actual goods, the stuff, the content.

I recently had an experience with how terrifically proficient the top bands have become. In 2013, a couple of days before the Worlds, a few of us in the Toronto Police band sought out Field Marshall Montgomery practicing in Kelvingrove Park. The band stood in a very patient and well-disciplined circle as Richard Parkes and Alastair Dunn went round the pipe section tuning chanters. Once they had each brought one or two pipers into perfect tune, either Alastair or Richard would strike up their pipes, and the entire pipe corps would do the same, each one playing whatever he wanted—tuning phrases, jigs, slow airs... It should have been cacophonous. Instead it was rather beautiful—a huge warm blanket of perfectly tuned drones overtop of twenty-four chanters playing nonsense in competition with each other, but all the instruments resonating at precisely the same pitch, and with the chanter intervals seeming to have been tuned by computer.

But that's not musical innovation, nor is it something that will open fresh new ways to create music in pipe bands—what that amazing sound represents is a highly developed technical skill, executed by people who are vetted and hand-picked for their ability to do the job. It's a lovely thing to hear to be sure, but imagine that sound and technical skill applied to the presentation of a five- to seven-minute composition for pipes and drums, created from whole cloth, honoring the tonality and traditions of the instrument and breaking new ground musically. If Don Thompson, not even a piper, could do it in 1987, surely we have people around the scene who could tap into their creative reservoirs and give it a real shot today.

But it is almost certainly not going to happen.

Again, the reasons are complex. First is the very simple and natural desire to be declared world champions. It's an incredible achievement, and one every bandsman lusts after. And if that was the only motivation, as indeed it was in the 80s and early 90s, the scene might still be pretty stagnant creatively. But there is a whole new gloss on the business—a word I choose carefully.

What has happened is a conflation of commercial and monetary interests with the need to win the Worlds. As more and more prominent members of bands, in both pipe and drum sections, became increasingly dependent on their careers as instructors, retailers and manufacturers of piping and drumming materials, pipes, drums, sticks, reeds, pipe bags and more, the need to succeed at the World Championship level became ever more critical. If your livelihood depends on maintaining a dominant place in the pipe band world, it's a certainty that the competition game will be played ever more cautiously and carefully: take no risks, give the judges easily understood and readily accessible material, rock no boats and let the technical and tonal precision win you the top prize(s).

Yes, the top guys are very listenable, and I agree that hearing FMM and the others close behind them is a very pleasing experience. But is that it? Really? There shouldn't be adventure? That's not how music progresses.

Consider Igor Stravinsky's "Rite of Spring." It had its first public performance on May 29, 1913 at the Theatre des Champs-Élysées in Paris. The world was in a precarious state. World War 1 was a heartbeat away. It was the time of Picasso, Gertrude Stein and James Joyce. Amidst all of the global turmoil, these people and others were inventing modern art.

The debut of the Rite is a storied event in the history of classical music. It was preceded by a performance of "La Sylphide," a romantic, well-known and loved ballet. Following a brief intermission, "The Rite of Spring" was launched.

The audience, which includes the artistic avant garde of the time, is seated, looking at a stage with the curtain down. The music begins, and Camille Saint-Saëns asks, "What is that instrument?" On being told it's a bassoon, he declares, "That's the ugliest sound I've ever heard" and stamps out of the theatre. The bassoon was playing higher in its range than anyone had heard before. As the curtain rises people are looking around and asking "What is this?" Just before the thumping, discordant chord pattern of E flat played against E major begins, a gentlemen in the audience is heard to say, "In two seconds, the 20th century is about to begin." As the huge syncopated, accented, dissonant chords progress, someone is seen banging his cane on the top hat of his neighbor, and the great Ravel is standing on his chair screaming, "Genius! Genius!" It became a full knock-em- down, call-the-paddy-wagon riot.

Of course it was because it was utterly, shockingly new. Nothing like it had ever been heard before. It was inspired by Stravinsky's dream of dancing oneself to death during pagan sacrifice. There's a great darkness to it. It sounds anarchistic, but all critics agree that there's enormous method in it. And now it stands as a masterpiece of the 20th century, and a staple of the classical repertoire.

Now consider the fate of the Toronto Police Pipe Band in 2010 at the Cowal Highland Games. Before they were even close to the trigger, they were visited by one or more representatives of the RSPBA. The internet had been ablaze with speculation about whether they would play the bagpipe version of Artie Shaw's clarinet full slide up on the pipe chanter, which had become the signature opening of Gershwin's Rhapsody in Blue. The RSPBA people had been buzzing amongst themselves about a peremptory disqualification—they knew of course that the medley the band intended to play was Mike Grey's composition "Variations on a Theme of Good Intentions," that (*gasp!*) started without three-pace rolls, at least as they had performed it in Ontario. At the behest of one of the smarter, cooler heads in the organization, they sent a delegation to speak to the band, and having received assurance that the band would indeed start with two three-pace rolls, allowed them to play. Then came the response from the judges: they were buried behind and beneath bands whose tonal quality was inferior, whose unison and integration weren't close, but who didn't offend. Of course there was the famous and withering remark by one of the piping judges: "This is nothing but mumbo-jumbo." Within the pipe band world there followed an incredible hissy fit, and an outpouring on the internet of vitriol, bordering on hatred.

Reminiscent of Stravinsky, do you think?

"The Rite of Spring" went on to become a major component of the modern repertoire of symphonic music, studied one hundred years later as an inspiration for modern-day composers. It's arguable that

Michael's medley may not achieve that kind of status, but certainly as long as the present timid, not to say frightened, mentality persists, there will be no further adventures of this kind. This is not to say that I liked that medley. I actually did not. But I loved the bold attempt to create a medley out of whole cloth, and to take a courageous shot at something fresh and new.

A very bright young man who played with me in the Frasers, and now plays with me in the Toronto Police, has inadvertently given me some insight into this subject of new music. I know that scientists scoff at anecdotal evidence, but this young guy, Jarrod Purvis, had a conversation with Lily and me over dinner with him and his wife Lisa, that opened my eyes to the appreciation of new music and what is involved neurologically. He told me that he had a peculiar relationship with "Variations on a Theme of Good Intentions." He wasn't sure he loved it. He didn't even know if he really liked it. But he had such appreciation for it that he must have listened to it thirty-five times. He felt that others may have pushed boundaries within pipe bands, but they didn't break any. "Variations on a Theme" did, in his opinion, and took suites to a new and ground-breaking place that is very important for piping. Whew!

At about this time I was rereading Daniel Levitin's book, *This Is Your Brain on Music*. (Every musician should read this incredible work.) Among the many smart and eye-opening things he says is that we listen to music with our schemas, or patterns, in mind. We have expectations about melody, resolution, harmony and so on and the more often these are violated, and the more extremely so, the less we like it; our brain is thinking ahead to what the different possibilities for the next note are, the trajectory of the music, its intended end point. If the music violates too many of the neurological signposts, we lose our sense of security and can actually become afraid of it. He offers this metaphor: imagine you're hitch-hiking to San Francisco, and the driver says, "I'm turning off here to avoid some construction but we'll join the freeway in a couple of miles." You relax. But if the driver takes you out on back roads with no explanation, and you no longer see any landmarks, your sense of safety is sure to be violated. He observes that different people will react differently to such unanticipated journeys, vehicular or musical. Fear may happen. Some react with sheer panic..."that 'Rite of Spring' is going to kill me!" and some with a sense of adventure at the thrill of discovery... "Coltrane is doing something weird here, but what the hell, it won't hurt me to stick around a while longer. I can find my way back to musical reality if I have to".

As I was reading this, and thinking about Jarrod's fascination with "Variations on a Theme," it occurred to me that he had earlier expressed to me a great love of "The Rite of Spring," and even sang the opening melodic motif. Then I connected the dots. Jarrod had a schema he could reference for Mike's piece. When I asked him to explain his fondness for the Rite, he gave credit to his elementary school music teacher—he played it for the class in grade 7, repeated it for them often, told the story of the riots, and planted the seed of understanding in Jarrod's brain. The young Mr. Purvis went on to listen to it many times. He created a schema for himself which he could reference for Mike's piece. "Variations on a Theme" thus was not totally strange to him, and he sat back, relaxed and went for the ride. Others without that same background joined the rioting crowd at the debut of the Rite, as did the crazies on the internet slagging Mike personally as well as his composition.

"Variations on a Theme" was not Mike's first entrance into this kind of composition. Long ago he ventured into this field with "The Immigrant's Suite," a piece capturing the trauma of the Highland Clearances and migrations to North America, expressing the fear of leaving, the longing for home and the ultimate triumph of a new life. Similarly, in "The Megantic Outlaw" Mike, in pipe music, told the story of Donald Morrison. Donald, the son of Gaelic-speaking immigrants from the Isle of Lewis, had a farm overlooking Lake Megantic, the village in the Eastern Townships of Quebec, famous most recently for the 2013 train disaster and explosion which killed so many.

In the late 1800s, Donald hired a lawyer to challenge and set aside a mortgage that his illiterate parents had placed against the farm.

It turned out that the lawyer was in cahoots with the money-lender, one Malcolm Macaulay, and the parents were bilked out of the farm. During the "supposedly" legal takeover the Morrison's farmhouse burned down. Macaulay hired a gunslinger, Lucian "Jack" Warren, to track down and arrest Donald for arson. Warren challenged Morrison and a gunfight took place in the street. Donald was very fast, shooting and killing Macaulay in this genuine Old West gun battle in the dusty street.

For over a year, detectives, police, jail guards and soldiers hunted him. He was eventually captured in an ambush, stood trial for murder, and was sentenced to 18 years of hard labor. Instead he chose starvation, and died four days after he was recommended for release.

Mike knew this story well as he grew up in the Eastern Townships of Quebec, close to Lake Megantic itself. And what a tale it is. Using the story of Donald Morrison as the libretto, the piece starts with the portrayal of a small, peaceful Gaelic-speaking community, and tracks the listener through the main points of the story. Particularly evocative is the section depicting the year-long chase, with the entire community concealing Donald's whereabouts, and the music shifting the same melodic thread between reel and jig time. There was not one previously known melody in the whole piece, but all sections were written in completely familiar bagpipe music idioms. *This* is original stuff, and if played today would knock the socks off of anything else.

And what's to be done? As the monetizing of the art grows apace, and the other factors play their roles and exert their influence, the problem feeds on itself. We *must* stay on top. We must *not* venture far afield. I wonder – what is the point? When you've won the thing many times, we all get it—you're really good. But why does it not occur to at least some top bands to think "Right, we've done that—now let's try to change the culture for the better—here's some new and adventurous stuff." I feel sure that I can promise that if the top six bands from 2016 agreed (conspired?) to do something absolutely new, the RSPBA would be hogtied. Think about various combinations of starting without two three-pace rolls, playing in concert formation, having the pipe section stop and the drummers carry the show for a bit, or vice versa, some or all original music in a medley. There isn't a lot the RSPBA could or would do, for to disqualify the favored and most popular bands would damage the brand very badly, and the Association is too heavily invested in the Worlds, in every sense of the word, to risk that.

Which leads us to consider the central problem here: the RSPBA doesn't lead. If it did we'd see some exciting and forward-looking things happening, such as, to take only one example, something like a rule that the previous year's top six or even more drastically, all bands in Grade 1 must play medleys consisting of not less than, say, three minutes (or four or whatever) of original music—not "arrangements" of well-known or traditional stuff, *new* stuff. Could it happen? Sure. It just takes courage, leadership and imagination—sadly, therefore, we are not likely to see it, or its ilk.

19

The Art and Mystery of Composition for the Bagpipe

With all this ranting about timidity in the music that pipe bands play, it's a fair question for others to ask me, "What have *you* done to change things?" Without re-hashing all that I've said in these pages, the right course is to recognize that this is a judgment that only others can render. Still I feel confident that a review of the music created, made and borrowed will show that it was, and is, unique.

But it's interesting to think about how many people have said to me "The Frasers changed everything". I wonder how much we really changed...is it really the case? We still take the best musicians from our world, wrap them in traditional garb, and ask them to play their best music in Glasgow in a muddy, rain-soaked sort of pasture, with usually three of the four seasons all happening in one day—rain, wind howling, no proper place for an audience to see or hear, with largely the same music and tunes rehashed and regurgitated, and with all the performers' backs turned to whatever audience will tolerate these conditions. Imagine asking the Kronos Quartet or the Toronto Symphony Orchestra, with their woodwinds, violas, cellos and violins, to do the same thing. Ain't never gonna happen.

Because my current band has not qualified recently, I have had the "opportunity" to attend the Grade 1 final on the second day of the Worlds. This surely is the most depressing display of our art that can be imagined. I know I started talking about what I call the stultification of the actual music being played. Likely if we could get that part of the problem sorted, the elimination of the all of the ridiculous limitations on the structure, location and staging of the Worlds would follow.

So, to the subject of musical composition. The ability to compose music, any music, for the bagpipe or otherwise, is a peculiar talent, and very difficult to describe or define. We know what the results of the effort are, but not much is known about the process itself, or more fundamentally the gift or talent. Everyone has heard a tune composed by someone trying their hand but without much natural ability for it. It's not attractive; perhaps not ghastly, but sure to be consigned to the bin the minute the eager neophyte's back is turned.

Then there are the gems—the timeless treasures. Allow me to talk about only a few of these. Who could disagree with the statement that "The Little Cascade" is the work of a compositional genius, or that "Lochanside" is an exquisite melody, or that "The Knightswood Ceilidh" is a wonderful competition march? Each of these is a lovely example of pure inspiration at work, and they each illustrate an interesting aspect of composition for the bagpipe.

"The Little Cascade," composed in the era of Kurt Weill and Bertholt Brecht, seems to capture some of the mysterious dark zeitgeist of those times. If we ignore the way the pipe has rocketed up in pitch, and accept that it was in earlier times pitched at roughly B flat, it's easy to make the mental leap (really not much of a leap, more like a small hop) to see that the "Cascade" is written in F minor. At the time this was a very rare and exciting tonal breakthrough, and it's still relatively unusual to see compositions in this key and mode. "Chole's Passion" by Dr. Angus MacDonald, and Bruce Gandy's grand jig "Coppermill Studio" are two examples of the rare, but in these two cases successful, attempts to do it.

"The Little Cascade" also forces us to recognize and to understand the keys available for the Highland pipe—and there aren't many, but surprisingly more than some of us imagine. The first step is to know that the pipe scale operates in a myxolidian mode, meaning that the seventh, high G, is flattened by a half tone, and so too is low G. In addition, the pipe note C is slightly below the analogous note that sounds in the piano scale. These features are now easily heard with the advent of digital technology. Simply take a tunable keyboard and adjust it to match the bagpipe low A; that is, tune the keyboard's B flat to a bagpipe low A. The pitch of that note varies from piper to piper, and from band to band, but on a correctly tuned instrument the intervals don't change. The "Cascade" demonstrates that we can write in F minor, but not many do, I suspect because G. S. MacLennan mined that territory so beautifully and thoroughly with "The Little Cascade."

"The Knightswood Ceilidh" reminds us that we can compose in what I would call a faux B flat minor mode, or if you prefer, an implied key of B flat minor. Tunes of this type are usually rooted in low A, (though a tune like "The Royal Scottish Piper's Society" has its focus on E) and achieve the effect of a minor key by simply eliminating the third note of the major mode, "C" on the pipe chanter. There are myriad examples of this type of tune: the hornpipes "Duncan Johnstone" and "Donald MacLeod," to name two.

"Knightswood" is a typical march in this implied B flat minor mode but, as ever, Donald MacLeod poked expectations in the eye by dropping what at first sounds like a completely out of place "C" in the sixth bar of the third part. I once heard Seaumas MacNeill grouse that this "C" was horrible. With great respect, as I have been trained in the law to say, that's rubbish. The whole point of this buckshee "C" is to draw the ear to the melodic quirk. It's rather like the high G inserted into the variations of "The Lament for Mary MacLeod."

This mode of implied B flat minor is very typical of blues music in which the player honours the omission of the third, and drives home the importance of the flattened seventh, setting the moody tone row of a real blues groove. Not surprisingly, this also results in a repeated focus on the fifth, low A to E on the pipe scale. This seems also to be a prominent feature of the tonality of much Celtic/Gaelic music.

"Lochanside" is an example of pure and beautiful melody, produced on the bagpipe, in what is analogous to E flat major. It's so accessible that the Scottish entertainer and singer Andy Stewart made it into a lovely song, sung by the way by him, very beautifully. Ignore his horrid "Donald Where's Your Troosers?" and seek this one out instead.

So we can write pipe music in B flat major and implied B flat minor, E flat major, and F minor. But there's more: think of "The Hen's March," or "The Geese in the Bog"—here we're composing in a low G mode, analogous to A flat major on the retuned digital keyboard, with the triad being the bagpipe Low G, B and D. It's a major key, but it sounds and feels dark and growly, like much minor key music. That's because this mode on the bagpipe is in the basement of the tonal structure, with the drones stoutly refusing to go along. Pretty wonderful stuff, and all done on a scale of eight tones, with no half tones to help us. For piobaireachd composition there are even greater strictures arising from the affinity of piobaireachd, and much Gaelic music, for pentatonic scales.

Composers of pipe music also have the ability (as do composers of other music) to alternate between minor and major modes. Again we go to the brilliant Daniel Levitin's book *This is Your Brain on Music*, where he discusses the brain's "game of expectation" when we fasten on rhythm. When we tap our feet we are predicting what is going to happen in the music next. We play the same game of expectations with pitch, whose rules are key and harmony. Musical key is the tonal context for a piece of music, the tonal center to which it returns. But shifting the tonal center from time to time can provide an arresting and pleasing effect. This is a method I have frequently used in composing. For example, both my hornpipe "Aussie Stevie" and the jig "The Irish Cousins" are written with the first part in a minor key, the second in a major key, the third in minor and the fourth in major.

My own experience of composing music started when I was in my teens, creating rock and roll songs in the simple three- or four-chord form of the times. But still, I was doing it, and they gathered some local popularity. Of course there was a reliance on familiar riffs and patterns, but they still seemed to be "mine." Music grows in just this way... it undergoes a natural metamorphosis in the hands of each new musician who visits it. Which is why the decision in favor of the estate of Marvin

Gaye against Pharell Williams and Robin Thicke is a bad one, and destined to chill the expansion of music in any form.

The inspiration for a piece of music, whether a complex suite or only a tune can come from almost anywhere, and sometimes really from nowhere.

I composed my first jig when I was about sixteen, having been inspired by the syncopated bits in the "Braes of Mellenish." My tune, "The Crooked Finger," employed that little riff sparingly, and it was clearly my own work. Capt. John MacLellan wanted to include it in one of his books of music, and John Wilson told me to ensure that my consent included a condition that all copyright and performing rights remained with me. That was not acceptable to his publishers, so it waited many years before I published it in my own first book.

The hornpipe "The Double Gold for J. K. Cairns," came from necessity and was made from whole cloth. The Frasers needed a closing hornpipe to finish off a medley, nothing was working, and I deliberately set about to create what I hoped was a strong melody with catchy rhythmical features. I can't say how it came into my head, but it seems to be akin to Neil Young's comment about creating music that I mention below: I was fishing, dropped a line in the water and caught one.

When Doug Stronach and I were working on my CD "Northern Man" we had nothing that would work as a title track. Doug, my producer, told me he had always wanted to record the bagpipe "huge" in the style of Davey Spillane's brilliant performance on Uilleann pipes of "Caoineadh cu Chulainn" from Riverdance. I said that tune was out of our range completely. He told me to go and make one of my own. "Yeah, right," said I. Sometime after, Lily and I were watching a haunting film called *The Cuckoo*—it's the story of a Finnish and a Soviet soldier who land at the home of a Sami woman in Lapland, a brilliant, funny and heartbreaking movie. The sound track contains a wonderful bit of music, which plays on the theme of the fifth interval. The feel of the piece captured me, and I tried to think of ways to adapt it to the bagpipe. I worked something up using this as the basic inspiration, thinking it might make a nice slow air, but as it played over in my mind it seemed that it could be part of something bigger and better. I wrote another part, and quickly realized that this new bit would be a good precursor to the melody which I had created from the movie soundtrack. The rest was easy. The whole piece stepped up in keys and drama, if that's not too strong a word, and led to an ending that made the whole thing somewhat anthemic.

My piobaireachd "For Ranald" came unbidden into my head while I was parking the car on Brock St. in Whitby. What a pedestrian beginning. The first two phrases appeared pretty much fully formed, and I had to scribble out some lines on a piece of paper to make a rough manuscript sheet and write them down before they got lost in the detritus that accumulates in any musician's mind. The rest of it took a long time and many edits, but without the opening theme of those first couple of bars, it would never have been completed.

The suite "In Celtic Times" happened in the following way: Lily and I were on holiday in Barbados, and we had gone to the supermarket for supplies. Lily was in the store shopping while I, suffering from a nasty cold and avoiding the Arctic air conditioning, stayed outside in the tropical heat, kicking stones and waiting for her. For some reason, a song called "The Battle of New Orleans" started up in my mind on full repeat like an earworm. This is a tune from my boyhood by a country singer by the name of Johnny Horton, which celebrated the victory over the British at that famous battle. It features an old-fashioned military beating on something like a rope tension drum, in 4/4 time at about 72 beats per minute, with a repeating riff that sounded like "prrum pum pum, prrumpa pumpa pum." I couldn't get this out of my head and soon enough I was toying with a martial kind of melody to support this rhythm. It sounds backwards, I, know but that's how it happened..

We went home to the digs, had some white rum and tonic, and the tune got finished. I *mean* that passive voice—it "got" finished. I created the first part using my brain and sense of music, and the rest just seemed to come along. I didn't set out to create a full suite (a term Mike Grey dislikes, preferring instead to use "medley") but I seemed to get locked into a mind-set that sought something more from a broader source—the notion of Celtic music and Celtic times, both historical times and in the sense of time signatures. A detailed exposition of the creation of the rest of "In Celtic Times" would bore readers to the point of looking to open a vein, I'm sure, but its form can be deduced from the score. It may be instructive to know that the ending section, with its frantic jazz-infused rhythms, was written when we came home from vacation. My Barbados cold had now blossomed into a full-blown flu, with a high fever, lots of medication, and to be candid, reasonable dollops of hot whisky and honey. There are reports of bouts of creativity bursting from this combination of factors, whether from drugs, the sweat lodge or plain dissociation from one's normal reality. In my case, all of these influences conspired to put me into a frenzy of ideas. Turning to "Shooglenifty" for inspiration, the last crazy—as in completely non-piping—section fell into place.

I once heard Robbie Robertson, the guitarist and songwriter of The Band and writer of such classics as "Up on Cripple Creek" and "The Weight," being interviewed on the CBC. He was asked if taking drugs helped him creatively, and he answered, "Well, yeah!" Now I wasn't into that scene, but in those fever-driven moments, I likely approached something like it.

As I mentioned earlier, another great Canadian pop star, Neil Young, said that composition was like fishing. You go to the river, drop in a line, and sometimes you catch one and sometimes you don't. Or consider Keith Richards, who said that songs were out there, fully formed, waiting to be snagged. So it's obvious that explaining the whole phenomenon is a challenge. Leonard Cohen was asked where do great songs come from, and he said "I don't know. If I did I'd go there all the time."

Philip Glass is the greatest living composer of opera, classical music, movie scores and more. One of his most important influences was Ravi Shankar, the Indian sitar genius. Glass once asked him, "Where does music come from?" Ravi turned to a picture of an Indian gentleman, did a complete bowing down to the picture, and said, "By the grace of my guru, the music has come through him to me." Glass thought that was as good an answer as you're going to get.

Now though, his view of the question when asked it by one of his students, is that "Music is a place—as real as Chicago or New Delhi." In an interview on CBC's radio program Q, he said composers of music have one foot in this place and one foot in the usual or "real" world.

In the same interview he noted that until he was forty-one, he supported himself through driving taxi, carpentry, self-taught plumbing (there's a thought) and working in a steel plant—all the while composing in a rigorous and highly disciplined routine. The result, he said, was that he owed no one anything. He didn't live on fellowships, university appointments or any other "outside" help. Because he owed no one anything, he was completely free to compose as he wished. I don't want to stretch the analogy beyond what's reasonable, but it's clear to me that pipe-band music choice and composition owes far too much to the competition scene, and in particular to the World Pipe Band Championships.

I lament the discouraging fact that we are tethered to "the one and only way," and I accept responsibility for not being more courageous and challenging in my own career as leader of a band of such bright and gifted players and thinkers. Maybe Lord Bertrand Russell, the English philosopher and mathematician, captured what I am trying to say when he said, "The world is full of magical things just waiting for our wits to grow sharper."

Having referenced Lord Russell, maybe I can be forgiven for referring to my compositional output with the highfalutin' term my "oeuvre." (highfalutin': "pompous, arrogant, pretentious.") I've always wanted to use that word "oeuvre"; it's so much more impressive than my "tunes." Anyway, there are some eighty plus compositions, all registered with SOCAN, the Canadian copyright protection agency, and now to be all gathered on my website, available to anyone who cares to check them out. Have at them if you like and make your own judgments on their merits or otherwise.

20

Half Full or Half Empty?

It's a perpetual question: is the glass half full or half empty? The optimist says the glass is half full, and the pessimist says it is half empty.

The piper says that the concert promoter should be shot for not providing enough alcohol.

The Glaswegian says, "Did you spill my pint?"

The cop says, "I'll ask the questions around here."

The man, who plays the great Highland bagpipe, sits at his writing table (actually the dining room table littered, as it has been for four-plus years, with pages, drafts, redrafts and research) and runs his hands and eyes through and over all that he has written and not written. He feels that he's looking at some sort of anthology, although not really, as it's not a collection of short stories or music or poetry; or perhaps it's a compendium, but again not so because it's not a compact version of a more complex thing; and certainly not some kind of museum with many exhibits, since it's not intended for education (but it *is* intended for entertainment, another function of museums), and so he settles on thinking of it as a kind of history... a telling of the past, not a re-telling, since it has never been told before. His mind turns to the countless clever aphorisms about the past, present and future, but he settles on a few that catch his interest and some of his feelings:

"The past is always tense, the future perfect." *–Zadie Smith*

"Scars have this strange power to remind us that our past is real." *–Cormac McCarthy*

"When it comes to the past everyone writes fiction." *–Stephen King*

The man wants not to be seen as some doddering old fool living in the past, but there seems to be so damned much of the past that interests him. Perhaps, he hopes, others too. All of these past things—his parents, their pasts and histories; his brother with his sad and unfulfilled life and the children he abandoned; the elusive pasts of his grandparents; the memories of, and his own history of, Copper Cliff—the open pit mines with their plunging 90-degree sides, filled with turquoise water in which nothing lived, and from which neither he nor his boyhood friends would ever escape should they fall in; his first love Delores, quite literally the girl next door, painfully and hurtfully abandoned by him after six years.

Then Bobby Scott fills the screen, a Copper Cliff neighbor the same age as he was and bitterly angry at life and his broken family. The man remembers being beaten by Bobby for no reason other than for Bobby's fun, and then carrying a monkey wrench for weeks as an equalizer should the need arise. And then a smile as he travels back to the Lido Hotel in Sudbury, sitting with Sandy Konikoff, a drummer he played with in the clubs in Sudbury (and who played on Joe Cocker's great album *Mad Dogs and Englishmen*) together with a wild man they called Drambuie Louie. Drambuie was a French Canadian who would spend six months in the bush working in logging camps, head to town at the end of his stint, and spend crazy amounts of his earnings on Drambuie, which he bought by the case, and shared with Sandy and the man under discussion here, and assorted other drifters like Drambuie himself.

His mind flips to another room in what he's now coming to see is perhaps a museum after all, of which he is the curator. There's a picture of the daunting presence of Osgoode Hall in downtown Toronto, home of the Supreme Court of Ontario and the Court of Appeal for Ontario as well as the famous law school by the same name. Here's a shot of the somewhat rebellious and perhaps insolent young man being stopped and upbraided by the Dean of the Law School, Alan (Buck) Leal. As the young law student is hanging with a group of classmates, Buck delivers a frosty dressing down to the young man: "This is a professional school and students are expected to dress the part—jacket and tie, not the jeans and the other stuff you're wearing today, young man." Those law school mates, so many of them Jewish, a creature hardly known in Copper Cliff and Sudbury—Ricky Goldman, Cousy Moscowitz, Eddie Greenspan, Jimmy Stefoff, Arnie Handleman, Danny Keyfetz and on. Others too—Bob Midgely (a tragic victim of MS by his 30s), Mike Horan, Marv Menzies, and all of us frequent visitors to the Pretzel Bell bar with its beer and shuffleboard and incredible meat loaf sandwiches.

Random access memory is not just for computers, it seems. He visits another room with a different set of exhibits, these bringing back the exquisite sensations of being ten years old and rolling naked down the summer warmth of the sand dunes built by the tailing lines. Jump cut to a montage of his first criminal jury trial; it was a charge of rape and he watches the film replay the preliminary hearing, the final trial preparation, the cross examination of the *alleged* victim (he wryly notes the mental emphasis) and the incredible sensation of winning a case like that.

And the piping madmen and characters, like Sherriff Sandy MacPherson and Dougie Ferguson (named here because they are now ensconced in that big tuning room in the sky) and their wicked mischief-making on the train ride from Inverness to Glasgow after his Gold Medal win, an all-nighter featuring too much Glenmorangie whisky while perched upon the narrow bunks of a sleeper car, finally getting to Prestwick airport and there learning he was unable to fly home to a celebration prepared for him because Air Canada didn't have a plane to replace the wounded one he was meant to take.

Here's a collage of images about piping: all those prizes, huge stuff to a piper; countless fish suppers at Norrie's Fish and Chips in Oban, meals at Inverness in Chinese restaurants which, in those days, were pretty much the only reliable source of food. The great Hugh McCallum shaking his hand and offering a warm and sincere "Welcome to the club" after he won his first clasp, and the ubiquitous piobaireachd scholars and geeks. A poignant memory of having played "War or Peace" in the clasp at Inverness and standing at the entrance to the Ness Bar and Restaurant in the Eden Court Theatre, when along came two of the judges of the contest for the lunch break. Major David Murray passing by him saying, "Absolutely terrific tune, Bill" followed by Iain MacFadyen with, "Did you know that you played the ground faster on every repeat?"

"Yes, it was intentional."

"Well it was a great tune." Remembering how chuffed he was that notwithstanding that the contest was about half over, these two members of the bench had virtually assured him of first prize and another clasp. Alas he thinks, how crushing it was then to be placed second.

Now the camera pans to scenes of the heady days at the start of the 78th Frasers, the release of the several volumes of the CD series *A Piobaireachd Diary*, the album *Northern Man*, an unbelievable seven albums with the 78th Frasers, two books of music, and playing at the age of seventy-four with the Toronto Police Pipe Band. As the camera zooms in for a closer look, he sees the amazing Luke Allan, unable to read a note of music, and the wonder of his ability to play the bass drum so fluidly, Alex Duthart calling him the best pipe band drummer in the world.

As the camera zooms out, he watches a broader picture, seeing his much younger piping friends, cherishing his ease with them, and feeling his affection for them. He ponders the dubious influence of money in pipe bands, as well as the RSPBA and its almost FIFA-like opacity when dealing with the musicians who actually make up the organization. There's his and his bride's first home on Lupin Dr. in Whitby, and the Schwedler maples he planted there, now in full glory forty years after having planted them. There loom Inverness and Oban, where he now judges his former peers and younger colleagues; the performances he has heard: Jack Lee in the Former Winners March, Strathspey & Reel at Inverness in 1981—a stunner—John D. Burgess in his last piobaireachd performance at Inverness, "Lament for Ronald MacDonald of Morar"—transported by it, with drones sounding as though they were coming from speakers twenty feet above the stage, but wandering off the tune. Now he drifts back to the seedy but fascinating world of the criminal courts, and the unequalled feeling of helping to heal a family with the settlement of a large medical malpractice lawsuit against nearly insurmountable odds, with the money giving them their lives back, and their teary hugs as they leave the office for the last time with "Thank you, you're a great man"—certainly not true, but still this kind of thing cannot be had or bought with any other kind of lawyering, he thinks. (See Appendix)

He thinks a lot... about what kind of ride it's been to this point. The son of a coal miner from Ayrshire with the temerity to pen a memoir, for God's sake—it seems to him to be contrary to nature, against all reason and common sense, absurd.

Preposterous.

Preposterous, indeed. More tales to follow.

EPILOGUE

Live in Ireland—in Scotland

January 30, 2016

The climate of Scotland is described by meteorologists as Oceanic. When I hear that term, I conjure up images of tropical turquoise seas, cream-colored beaches and tranquil breezes whiffling the palm trees. I picture the Riviera, the Cote d'Azur or the famous beaches of Rio and the luxury of the coast of Spain at Barcelona. Scotland is lovely to be sure, but not in those ways. And Glasgow has a less than enviable place in the overall climate and weather metrics of the world. It is particularly unwelcoming in January:

> It is the coldest month of the year for Glasgow
> It ranks second-last in hours of sunshine for Scotland
> It stands third in the Scottish race for highest monthly amount of precipitation: rain, snow and hail
> It is second in the number of actual days of such precipitation for the entire country

When the idea of revisiting the famous concert which led to the recording *Live in Ireland* was first floated, there were some profoundly discouraging comments made: "Glasgow in January—what a great idea!" with tongue planted ironically in cheek. Or from another prominent source: "Who'd want to go that?"

As it turned out, 2500 highly enthusiastic fans of the music memorialized in that recording wanted to go to that. They filled the Glasgow

Royal Concert Hall to capacity, to hear, relive and cheer the music of that moment in pipe band history. Here's how it happened.

Reid Maxwell and Mike Grey were on a pipe-band judging gig together in 2014. Reid had been listening to the album *Hell Freezes Over* by the Eagles, a favorite band of his when he was a kid. The album name is a reference to a quote from Don Henley after the band broke up in 1980; he said that the band would play again "when hell freezes over." But the Eagles did get back together and put down some wonderful music fourteen years after Henley made that remark. It got Reid to thinking back to the glory days of the 78th Frasers, and his regret that he had left the band. At the first rehearsal for the concert, he said that if he'd known then half of what he knew now, he would never have left. He talked to Mike about all of this, and said something like, "Do you think we could do something like the Eagles did with the guys from the Frasers of 1987?"

Mike said, "I'd like to give it a shot, but the first thing we need to find out is whether Bill would be on board." When Mike asked me, I jumped at it. So the beginnings got underway. Initially there were invitations to all the members of the band who were still around. Some declined citing health, others worried about the financial commitment, a couple were worried about trying to get back into playing shape, and some just didn't respond. It may have seemed high-handed or arbitrary to some, but those pipers who had not played in Grade 1 for a long time were asked to submit a tape to establish that their piping was still at the required level. None did. As the process of building the cast went on, more and more of the top pipers and drummers in the world expressed a keen desire to be part of it, and so the ranks swelled with the best of the best. Preliminary rehearsals started in Toronto, some conducted via Skype with members in Scotland and the U.S., music was put up online and we all set to work.

Mike was a bulldog and a workhorse, attending to every conceivable detail from choosing the uniform we'd wear and sourcing the items to outfit us, to working with McCallum Bagpipes, who provided great sponsorship with chanters, bag covers, and drone ribbons, to chasing down Celtic Connections to nail down practice space and hotel accommodation, to arranging the Wednesday evening reception. He pretty much baby-sat the whole massive affair. Finally we were all in Glasgow, ready to roll.

Take a picture of this: Rehearsals in the function room of the Roderick Dhu pub in downtown Glasgow begin. Around the table are the guys from the 1987 show who are still playing at the required level: Ross Brown, Tommy Bowen, Iain Donaldson, Bruce Gandy, Mike Grey, Gord MacRae, Brian Pollock and me. Supplementing this group are Ian K. MacDonald and Sean McKeown, the former and current Pipe Majors of the Toronto Police Pipe Band, enlisted because they're great players- and because we needed to get the numbers up a bit with a solid foundation of Toronto based talent—as we had at the outset no idea where this thing was headed.

Add to all of this Terry and Alen Tully, former and present Pipe Majors of St. Laurence O'Toole, Iain Duncan, long-time leader of Vale of Atholl, Duncan Nicholson, former Pipe Major of Glasgow Police, Ross Walker, leader of Boghall and Bathgate, Stuart Liddell, one of the greatest soloists of the time and PM of the upstart and brilliant Inverary and District Pipe Band, Roddy MacLeod, another solo artist with wizardry in his playing and the head of the National Piping Centre, and long serving PM of Scottish Power, Bernie Ta (Bernard Bouhadana), with years in SFU and FMM, and Jenny Hazzard, Mike Grey's pupil and an alumna of the 78th Fraser Highlanders.

Off in the drummers' room we find the guys from 1987 who are still playing: J. Reid Maxwell, Stuart Liddell ("Stu"), Maggie MacIver (Brown), Scott Brown, Tim Murphy, and Sean Allan on bass, son of the late Luke Allan, who played bass in the 1987 event. To this already strong base add the leading drummer of Inverary, Steven McWhirter, five times World Solo Champion, the illustrious Paul Turner, Stephen Creighton the lead tip of St. Laurence O'Toole, Duncan Millar, Reid's right-hand man at SFU, Gavin MacRae, Gord's son, and Grant Maxwell, Reid's son.

This group of musicians represents much of the cream of pipe band royalty. What a feeling it was for all of us to be in that room together on the first day.

"Music, being the finest of the arts, helps the soul to rise above differences. It unites souls, because even words are not necessary. Music is beyond words." –*Hazrat Inayat Khan*

"Music is at its essence the sound of spirit. When created from the heart and with pure intention, music is a spiritual expression of the most universal nature and the highest order." –*Frank Fitzpatrick*

Bernie Ta whispered at that first gathering that this felt to him, surreal. Indeed it was somewhat marked by the intense irrational reality of a dream.

From my vantage point, all I could conceive of was the weird challenge of leading and playing with people against whom I had competed for some thirty years, both as a soloist and a pipe major. To be truthful it scared the hell out of me, as I pondered scenes such as telling Stuart Liddell, "Can you just stretch that phrase a bit?" or to Richard Parkes, "I'd like a bit more tempo here."

To my relief, however, there was no need for much of any of that. These giants took the essence of the project to heart, which was to celebrate the music of that time as it came to the pipe band world via the recording *Live in Ireland*. They came prepared. Mike Grey had gathered all of the scores and posted them to a dropbox for all the pipers to download and memorize. He put up the album as well. This was only one more of the countless tasks Mike undertook to bring this thing to fruition.

As the first chanter practice unfolded, everyone (I suppose here I mean me) began to relax, as it was obvious that these musicians loved the music, were here to honor it, and had worked very hard to have it down pat.

Some delightful moments happened during this early phase. As I tend to be a democrat as a leader, I welcome and indeed foster discussion about the music. We were having a debate about whether to jump off a low A after a birl, or hold it before going to high A. After some to-ing and fro-ing with no resolution of the issue, Stuart Liddell leaned in and said, "Bill, just say it, and it will be so." In other words, make up your #%@& mind.

Our first practice on pipes was fraught. Brand-new McCallum chanters. Brand-new reeds donated by Stephen Megarity and David Chesney. With hindsight, I see that it should have been expected and entirely understandable that this first attempt would have been less than stellar. But at the time, I was in despair, thinking that we could never go from this racket to building a sound in five days. There began some intense work on finding a pitch, repeated attempts to get the chanters in the same general area, tuning and tuning of drones, and the beginnings of carving the chanters, but progress was minimal. I was thinking of opening a vein.

Yet a subtle process started to emerge, a process characterized by patience. A tuning team of Duncan Nicholson, Ross Walker and Alen Tully began to coalesce sort of organically. And as always happens, there began some disciplined carving of the chanters as needed, and as we approached ever closer to more precise pitch intervals, we were developing a real sense that this was going to work after all. (Here's a clear and cautionary note: no one should infer that because some chanters needed carving (a brutal term) they were inferior. The complete contrary is the case. These chanters were (*are*) bright, balanced and stable. The issue always is the combination of reed and chanter, and in my nearly fifty years of experience, adjustments are inevitable.)

The week, this very short week, went on. Morning practices, pipes and drums in the afternoon (by Tuesday no more practice chanters), lunch and some fun, evening practices to accommodate the locals who had work and other obligations, more fun, bed and repeat. A *sound* now seemed to be well within reach. Richard Parkes arrived on Wednesday, and he formalized the tuning team and system. (I had asked Richard to take charge of tuning the band—really, who better?) Richard organized his team, seemingly without overt discussion, around Duncan, Alen, Terry, Ross and Stuart.

There were clear guidelines:

Don't touch your reed or tape; ask the tuners.
Don't play unless I tell you to play.
Don't moisten your reed.
Leave the chanters in the pipe or cap them as I tell you to.
A drone that won't strike in must go. It's not about your drones, but about the band's drones.
Above all, if you have any issues, bring them to the tuners.

After the initial blow (which got better each time), the tuning team would gather, get their own chanters in perfect sync, and then fan out and tune each piper's chanter. Along came Jonathan Greenlees of Field Marshall, and Colin MacLellan as drone tuners. They were relentless in their continuous refinement of the drones. Soon a fine sound emerged, rooted at about 486 on a Chesney tuning meter, and it was not merely stable, but full and rich and better every day, so that by Friday we were confident, ready and producing stable sound every time we played. In five days, a sound that would qualify for top six at the Worlds.

When this whole venture started, Mike asked me if I was interested. Absolutely, said I.

"OK," said Mike, "you are to do nothing regarding organization, promotion, details of administration or any of the other tasks required. What we need from you are three things: be healthy, be playing well, and be the Pipe Major of the band."

It didn't work out completely that way, but it's dead certain that Mike did all of the heavy lifting. His dedication and uncountable hours of work brought it off. And that *is* Mike—dedicated, passionate and a guy who by force of his enthusiasm and will makes things happen.

These were some of the mechanics that went into the concert, and they were important. What stands out even more, was the feeling, the emotion, the vibe and the electricity. The shared single-minded goal of making a top-class pipe band in five days with the intention of giving this music the honor that everyone felt it deserved, was palpable. Were there egos in this room? Of course there were. How do you get to be the best in the world without an ego? The walls could hardly contain the sense of security and self-confidence that was evident. But the beauty of it was, or so it seemed to me, that everyone channeled that sense of knowing who they were into one shared goal—to make this band as good as it could be.

The warmth, camaraderie, mutual support and encouragement, developing closeness, and breaking down of the barriers of the competitive pipe band world were uplifting. It was all of that, as much as the success of the concert itself, that I carry away from the experience. As Alen Tully said to me, "This is so different. I see Richard Parkes at a competition and I think, he's my enemy, and I have to kill him today. That's not how I'm feeling now."

I've talked to many in the group and everyone seems to agree with that sentiment, and even with some sense of surprise that so much affection was in the air.

That week in Glasgow in January 2016 was a singular experience. The feel, the vibe, was unlike anything in pipe band life. When something like this happens it's magical—there's some special exciting quality that elevates it to be something different or better than any other like it. And how it became that is mystifying—it may have been ephemeral, happening once and once only. But it had elements that every musician strives for—it was emotional, spiritual, cultural and, in a subtle way, political—as it was striking a blow for the notion of freshness in pipe-band music.

What I know for sure is that, for me, this was one of the great highs of my life in piping.

Another preposterous tale.

GLOSSARY

Should there be readers who are not familiar with the bagpipe and some of the terms of art that apply to it, here's a brief glossary of some of them.

Birl: A movement on the chanter which requires the little finger on the bottom hand to make two rapid strokes in succession

Braemar: A village in the northeast of Scotland, home of the gathering of the same name and nearby to the Royal residence at Balmoral.

Ceol Mor: In Gaelic, literally "Big Music," another word for piobaireachd.

Ceol Beag: "light music" marches, reels jigs etc

Ghillie Brogues: Shoes with loops of leather through which laces are passed, and then wrapped around the calf and tied, similar to dancer's shoes but rough.

Leet: The process by which a large number of competitors are eliminated and winnowed down to a small number who then compete for the prizes.

Lochanside: A famous pipe tune composed by John MacLellan, Dunoon.

MSR: Standing for March, Strathspey and Reel, three types of tune of distinctly different character played together as one set of music.

Piobaireachd: (Pronounced peebroch with the ch sound soft as in loch.) The classical music of the bagpipe, consisting of a theme, the urlar, and increasingly complex variations on it. In Gaelic, *piob* means pipe and the suffix means pipe music.

Sporran: The pouch or purse worn in the front of the kilt.

APPENDIX

Some Adventures in Medical Malpractice Litigation

The world of plaintiff's lawsuits in medical malpractice is the most challenging legal work that I have ever done. First of all, when a case comes in, you must learn the anatomy, whether it's the microscopic cellular structure of the colon, the intricacies of the inner ear, or the progression of a deep vein thrombosis from a painful blood clot in the leg to fatal pulmonary embolism. Your case selection is critical, primarily because most people cannot afford the costs of the litigation so the lawyer must be prepared to front those costs himself. These can mount alarmingly, and very quickly. All successful malpractice cases are dependent on strong expert opinions to support the plaintiff's theory of what happened to cause her to sue a doctor or hospital. It is not uncommon for these expenses to run to sixty or seventy thousand dollars. And if the action fails, the lawyer is stuck, having paid them on an ongoing basis during the long process of getting to trial or settlement.

In Canada, there is an organization called the Canadian Medical Protection Association (CMPA). This outfit insures virtually every doctor in the country. Their mandate is to defend doctors against "frivolous lawsuits." Their default position seems to be that any lawsuit against a doctor is frivolous. They have access to the best medical experts in the country, and they use them very well. If the CMPA is having trouble getting an expert to say that there was no negligence in the doctor's treatment of the plaintiff, they will fall back on the "causation" issue. In that case they might concede that there *may* have been substandard care, but in the end the negligence did not cause or contribute to the injuries sustained... that there was a "pre-existing condition," the plaintiff was a "non-compliant patient" and didn't take the prescribed medication, or "failed to follow the doctor's instructions." Their creativity is impressive. If they can't defend a case medically, they'll try to defend it on such legal theories. They have battalions of extremely good lawyers on hand to respond to claims. Their resources are pretty well limitless, and it's a rare case that gets settled without a great deal of time going by. Doctors are about the best-protected professionals in the country. They pay premiums to the CMPA, some of them (obstetricians, for example) in the amount of $75,000 dollars. And those premiums are tax-deductible, which means the Canadian taxpayers pick up the tab.

Here's an example of what can happen. A very young boy had a terrible problem with soiling himself. The medical term is encopresis. It was a hellish childhood for him, as the embarrassment and humiliation of such a condition made him a recluse. He failed to thrive, was thin and pale and had countless examinations, laxatives, enemas, procedures, medical appointments, hospitalizations and the like, until when he was about fourteen, a prominent adult surgeon pronounced that he had Hirschsprung's disease. The family got to this surgeon by referral from a relative. He didn't examine the boy, didn't review the extensive records from the many specialists and hospitals that had been involved in his care, but simply announced his conclusion that the boy had Hirschsprung's. He told the family he would need a biopsy to confirm it and then he'd do a *total procto-colectomy*, "as the bowel was likely now so distended as to be useless." He'd hook the child up afterwards, and his ostomy bag, which "will only be temporary," would be removed. When they were told that a simple surgery would "cure" the child, they were overjoyed to have a solution to his terrible problem.

But here's what I learned. Most kids with this disease are diagnosed in infancy when there is a failure to pass meconium within 48 hours of birth (meconium is the very first passage of feces). The disease is caused by an absence of cells called ganglion cells in a section of the colon. These cells are responsible for the peristaltic contractions of the bowel that propel food through the digestive tract. The absence of them at any point in the colon causes an obstruction, beyond which the products of digestion cannot pass. Kids with Hirschsprung's never soil. *Nothing* can get by the place where there are no ganglion cells. As a result, the child develops megacolon, a hugely distended colon caused by the total blockage. Simple x-rays can usually pinpoint the problem. The gold standard for diagnosing this disease is to take successive biopsies of the colon starting at two centimeters above the "dentate line." This line is an area close to the anus where even *normal* people have no ganglion cells. Thus a biopsy which includes the dentate line cannot possibly help diagnose the disease. Biopsies proceed proximally (towards the mouth, in layman's terms) until ganglion cells are found. With the area of the bowel having no ganglion cells now clearly identified, it is resected (removed), the two ends of the bowel are hooked up, and the condition is cured. In my client's case, a biopsy was performed. The tissue taken included the "dentate line." It was therefore useless. Nonetheless the surgeon did not have it repeated.

The surgeon involved performed a total colectomy on the child, which led to terrible complications that required the boy to be placed on TPN (total parenteral nutrition): liquid feeding into a vein. My client's ostomy bag became permanent. A life that was difficult before, now became a nightmare.

The lawsuit took seven years to conclude. I had initially been consulted when the family finally found their way to a brilliant pediatric surgeon in Toronto, who pronounced that the child had *never* had Hirschsprung's, that the surgery was absolutely unnecessary, and that even if had had the disease, the correct treatment was to locate the area where ganglion cells were absent, surgically remove that section, which often was very short, create an anastomosis (in common parlance, hook the bowel back up)—and the patient would return to normal bowel function. He told me that the most common belly problem in kids is constipation. He saw it all the time. If it's intractable to treatment with fleet enemas and laxatives, the kid goes to "stool school." The child is admitted to hospital, the colon is cleaned out completely, manually if necessary. The child is kept in hospital, eating and having laxatives, until normal bowel function is restored. It's a condition that can develop around toilet training and should never be mistaken for Hirschsprung's disease, as the presentations are totally different. Moreover, an adult surgeon should not have any involvement in a childhood problem. This wonderful guy was very angry that such a disastrous course had been followed.

I spent a day in a pathology lab, got an education from a pathologist on how ganglion cells and their absence were detected, and read several reports from my own team of experts in the disease, all of whom agreed with our pediatric surgeon's opinion that the whole thing was wrong, completely substandard, and worse, unnecessary. From the very beginning, we were stonewalled by the defense (the CMPA), who made clear that they would never pay compensation for the boy's losses, which included future economic damages resulting from the loss of any career possibility, the cost of care he required for the duration of his life, TPN supplies for his lifetime and the losses suffered by his parents and siblings.

Now if your eyes have not yet glazed over, we're coming to the point. In Ontario there are rules regarding the disclosure of expert opinions at Examinations for Discovery, known in the U.S. as depositions. These examinations are pre-trial proceedings where the parties are questioned under oath by the opposing lawyer. One of these rules states that a party to a lawsuit may, on an Examination for Discovery, obtain from the opposite party, disclosure of the findings, opinions and conclusions of an expert. As nearly all of these cases succeed or fail on the merit of the expert opinions, it's important for each side to know the case to be met. But the CMPA and its lawyers are masters at obfuscating what they have, and more importantly what they have and don't want you to know about. So in my case, when I asked the CMPA's very senior lawyer at Discovery if he had any expert opinions, his response was something like, "only of a very preliminary nature, principally for education purposes, and nothing that could be called an opinion." Now it's fair to concede that lawyers have been very inventive in their attempts to avoid complying with this rule about disclosing the opinions, and it may be that the defense could have hunkered down behind some argument in law. So I'm careful to say that while there may have been no outright flouting of their responsibilities, the point is that they knew a top expert had told them their case was a loser, and by serendipity I only learned that fact *years later*. The answer should have been "Yes, I have an opinion." My next question would have been, "Please provide me with the findings, opinions and conclusions." He'd have said, "No." And I'd have said, "Do you undertake not to call him as a witness?" And his honest and correct in law answer would have been, "Yes."

None of that happened. The case dragged on for years. Expenses mounted to some $75,000, all paid for by my firm—expert reports from economists, future income loss specialists, life expectancy gurus, more medical experts. Settlement meetings happened without success. The firm acting for CMPA sent down a senior lawyer accompanied by a junior, to try to persuade me to go away by using a professional Powerpoint and video presentation showing why they were right and I was wrong. I bristled at the cheek of this but held my tongue. As the case was heading to trial, I retained a formidable malpractice lawyer to assist me, a charming, somewhat unhinged guy with an incredible reputation and track record of winning big cases. As we were nearing trial, the original pediatric surgeon from Toronto asked me, "Bill, why don't you get a completely independent pediatric surgeon to review this case and give an opinion? Someone maybe from outside the province." He gave me three names.

I picked one. I'll call him Dr. Jones. He was in a province over a thousand miles away. I contacted him and asked if he'd review a case involving pediatric surgery for me, and he agreed. I sent a complete brief off to him. He called me a week later. He said, "I know this case." I asked him how that was possible.

His response left me gobsmacked, dumbfounded and in a rage. He told me he had been visited in person by a lawyer from the firm acting for the doctor (the lawyers always say that's who they're acting for, but it's really the CMPA they represent).

This lawyer travelled to the city where Dr. Jones practiced and spent two days with him, going over the entire file and case. Dr. Jones told him the case was unwinnable. The surgeon who mutilated my client fell so far below the standard of care that he advised the CMPA to settle as soon as possible. His conduct could never be justified. And here's the thing—*the CMPA had this meeting with Dr. Jones at the very outset of the case*, long before the Examinations for Discovery took place, and therefore putting the CMPA in the position of knowing that a top expert would not support them, and requiring them to seek out *any* doctor who would support their position. They dragged the case on for seven full years, likely in the hope that my client would die from one of many critical bouts of illness, line infections and other major hospital admissions that happened in that time. If that happened, the loss of income claim, the future care costs claim, and the pain and suffering claim would all be compromised to a fraction of their value.

I immediately wrote to the lawyer for the CMPA. I explained in detail everything I had learned from Dr. Jones. I received a call back right smartly. "Bill, unfortunately you can't use Dr. Jones because I consulted him. Did you know that?"

"Yes, I did."

(Here cue the blood-curdling screams of outrage)

"What the hell are you doing? You know he's now out of bounds for your side."

"I don't think so, Jack (not his real name). You never retained him, and he says you never even paid him. He's ours to use, and he'll come to Toronto to give evidence."

"Bill, have you ever done anything like this in your career before? It's outrageous."

"No I haven't. But this is war now. You guys have known from the get-go that you had no case. You've dragged this on for seven years, hoping that my client would die and get you and your Doc off the hook. And what's worse, you guys lied on discovery about this opinion, and I'd like to see how the Law Society might react to that bit of shenanigans."

Shortly thereafter the case settled in the millions. I'm sure they played me like this because I was not a lawyer who was on their radar, this being my first major malpractice case. I'm equally sure my name soon found its way into their data base, because on the next case I had, when I asked whether they had an opinion, they said yes. Will you provide the opinions and conclusions? No. Do you undertake not to call him/her as a witness? Yes. I knew straight away that their opinion did not support them and we settled soon after.

To return to the case of the boy: my client and his family were made, if not whole again, at least able to deal with what they had facing them. Some of the money was placed in a structured settlement, which provides a guaranteed tax-free income for life, and their joy at the result was the most rewarding moment in my life in the law. When they were leaving my office with the settlement completely in place, the mother of the boy, now a young man, hugged me and thanked me for all the work, and said, "You're a great man." It brought me to tears.

Here's another tale.

A healthy, strapping forty-five-year-old man was cycling to work, crashed his bike, and banged up a knee pretty badly. He went to his family doctor, who cleaned the wounds and sent him home with instructions to follow up in a week or so. When the fellow returned to the doctor he was in such pain in his calf that he could not walk. He asked the staff for a wheelchair to get around the hospital. The doctor examined him and said, "Maybe we should protect against a blood clot." The doc wrote two prescriptions. One for an anti-inflammatory and the other an antibiotic. There was no ultrasound performed to determine if there was a clot, no commencement of anticoagulant medication (i.e. blood thinners). Within a week this gentleman was dead as a result of a massive pulmonary embolism.

Now a lower-limb injury which causes reduced mobility and leads to severe calf pain, swelling and redness (all present here) is a recipe for deep vein thrombosis (DVT). (This is why many people, including world-class athletes, wear compression socks on long flights. These things counter the immobility of a long haul, improve circulation, and reduce the risk of DVT.) DVT needs urgent intervention with blood thinners for the precise reason that the clot can, and will, migrate to the lungs, usually with fatal consequences. This is so well known in medicine as to be trite. Still, about two years later (this one was fast), the CMPA wrote a cheque for another million bucks to the widow, who was my client and a very nice lady. It didn't really mean much to her, because all she wanted was to have the man she loved so much, back.

These and other cases have taught me to be deeply involved in my own health care. While doctors can get miffed about patients getting second opinions from "Dr. Google," had this couple looked up "blood clots in the calf" or the two totally incorrect medications that were prescribed, this disaster could have been avoided. I don't know what the doctor was thinking, but I suspect, like so many physicians who see large numbers of people, he just dropped the ball. The result: no ultrasound, two prescriptions which were utterly useless to the patient, and a very sad widow.

And a final peek at this stuff. I was consulted by a woman who had had an endoscopy procedure—a tube and camera down the throat. The hospital then advised her and about another hundred and ten people that unfortunately the tubes used in their procedures had not been properly sterilized. Yes, cleaned, but not sterilized. So they were all asked to come and be tested for HIV and Hepatitis. I started a class action. The "theory"—actually the reality—was that the hospital said, "Sorry, we put these tubes up the colons of a whole lot of people, and then put them down your throat. Oops." I had two of these class actions and settled them both with modest recovery for all members of the class. It was pretty big numbers overall for the hospitals, but not so much for the individuals. I was lucky though. A subsequent case (not mine) was dismissed against a hospital because the court ruled that unless there was actual physical injury, or a diagnosed psychological condition, there could be no recovery in these circumstances. Mere anxiety and worry would not support an award of damages. Wrong, I'd say, but at least that came after my cases were settled.

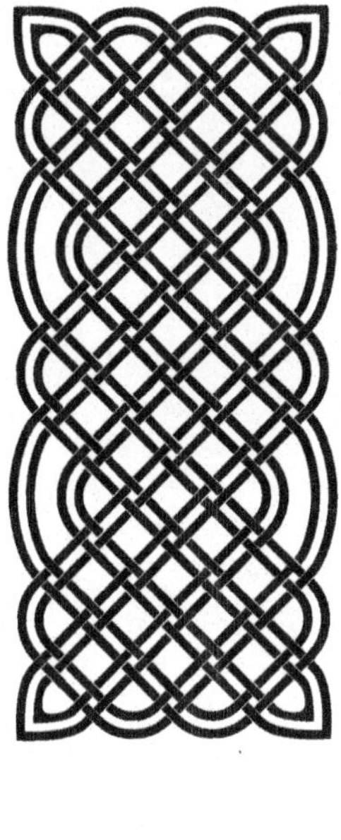